Introduction to JVM Languages

Java, Scala, Clojure, Kotlin, and Groovy

Vincent van der Leun

BIRMINGHAM - MUMBAI

Introduction to JVM Languages

First published: June 2017

Production reference: 1230617

Published by Packt Publishing Ltd.
Livery Place
35 Livery Street
Birmingham
B3 2PB, UK.

ISBN 978-1-78712-794-4

www.packtpub.com

Credits

Author
Vincent van der Leun

Reviewer
Ramasubramanian Sankar

Commissioning Editor
Aaron Lazar

Acquisition Editor
Nitin Dasan

Content Development Editor
Vikas Tiwari

Technical Editor
Subhalaxmi Nadar

Copy Editor
Gladson Monteiro

Project Coordinator
Ulhas Kambali

Proofreader
Safis Editing

Indexer
Rekha Nair

Graphics
Abhinash Sahu

Production Coordinator
Shantanu Zagade

About the Author

Vincent van der Leun is a software engineer living in the city of Utrecht in the Netherlands. Programming since the age of 8, he has worked with many different languages and platforms over the years. Rediscovering Java a few years ago, he loved it so much that he became an Oracle Certified Professional, Java 7 Programmer, and started the JVM Fanboy blog. Currently he works for CloudSuite, a company specializing in modern e-commerce solutions. At CloudSuite he works on various backend systems and web services, writes JavaScript code for frontend applications, supports consultants by providing complex SQL queries, and consumes coffee while having design-related discussions with fellow developers. When not trying out new web frameworks or technologies in his spare time, he is collecting cult movies and obscure action flicks on DVD/Bluray, reading classic science fiction novels, or attending concerts of non-mainstream singers and songwriters.

I am grateful to everyone at Packt, for their hard work in making this book a reality. Thanks to the editors, Nitin, Vikas and Subhalaxmi and to the reviewer, Ramasubramanian. I'd like to thank my parents, Anton and Irene, and my brothers, Alexander and Ruben (and Wendy). Thank you for your awesome support! Thanks to my family and friends. The following persons deserve a special mention: Erik, Guy, Mallory, Job, Jenna, and Nina for their much appreciated support and encouragement during the writing of this book; Natalie and Marco for the good old times. Last but not least, kudos to all my colleagues at CloudSuite; Special thanks to Corné, Rob, Eméli, and Berthold. I dedicate this book to the amazingly funny, kind and always clever Melissa and Esmee Hulstein.

About the Reviewer

Ramasubramanian Sankar is a passionate, polyglot, fullstack developer, and a seasoned technical architect working in the Information Technology industry for over 13 years now. Specializing on JVM-based backend services and distributed systems, he has experience with a diverse set of platforms and languages. After having worked with service companies, banks, antivirus product companies, and product-based start-ups, he is currently working as a consultant for Ajira technologies in Chennai with a group of like-minded technologists. He is passionate about architecting and designing simple, high-performant, and clean solutions for complex business problems. He writes/rants about his learnings on Twitter (@ramsankar83) and on his technology blog (http://technicalitee.blogspot.in/). His current interest is in learning functional programming and putting it to practical use. He loves LISP and is actively looking forward to use it in production some day.

I would like to thank my wife, Gomathi, and kids for giving me the extra time to code outside work and review this book. I am grateful to my parents, Sankar and Geetha, for providing me with an education and buying my first computer. I would also like to thank my employer, Ajira technologies, for giving me the freedom and encouragement to try out cutting-edge tech in customer projects and, thereby, learn a lot.

www.PacktPub.com

For support files and downloads related to your book, please visit www.PacktPub.com.

Did you know that Packt offers eBook versions of every book published, with PDF and ePub files available? You can upgrade to the eBook version at www.PacktPub.com and as a print book customer, you are entitled to a discount on the eBook copy. Get in touch with us at service@packtpub.com for more details.

At www.PacktPub.com, you can also read a collection of free technical articles, sign up for a range of free newsletters and receive exclusive discounts and offers on Packt books and eBooks.

https://www.packtpub.com/mapt

Get the most in-demand software skills with Mapt. Mapt gives you full access to all Packt books and video courses, as well as industry-leading tools to help you plan your personal development and advance your career.

Why subscribe?

- Fully searchable across every book published by Packt
- Copy and paste, print, and bookmark content
- On demand and accessible via a web browser

Customer Feedback

Thanks for purchasing this Packt book. At Packt, quality is at the heart of our editorial process. To help us improve, please leave us an honest review on this book's Amazon page at `https://www.amazon.com/dp/178712794X`.

If you'd like to join our team of regular reviewers, you can e-mail us at `customerreviews@packtpub.com`. We award our regular reviewers with free eBooks and videos in exchange for their valuable feedback. Help us be relentless in improving our products!

Table of Contents

Preface

The Java Virtual Machine is a mature and very versatile platform for running software that takes full advantage of modern hardware features. While it is true that Java-based applications once could be considered slow, bloated, and extremely memory-hungry, things have improved greatly over the years. It's no coincidence that many mainstream cloud-based services and websites, which often have to serve tens of thousands users simultaneously, are powered by a JVM-based backend.

While Java is, without a doubt, the most popular language used to create applications that run on the JVM, other languages are getting more and more popular every year. This book covers five different JVM-based languages: Java, Scala, Clojure, Kotlin, and Groovy. Some of those languages are statically typed while others are dynamically typed. Likewise, this book covers both object-oriented programming languages and functional programming languages. The JVM is versatile enough to make this all possible.

By covering all these languages in a single book, you can easily compare each language with the others and, hopefully, pick your favorite language by building the sample projects.

What this book covers

Chapter 1, *Java Virtual Machine*, provides a high-level overview of the Java platform and the Java Virtual Machine (JVM). It describes popular use cases for applications running on the JVM, namely web applications, big data analysis, and Internet of Things (IoT). Also covered are important JVM concepts, including its just-in-time compiler, type system, and garbage collector.

Chapter 2, *Developing on the Java Virtual Machine*, explains the JVM in more technical detail. Covered are both the installation procedure and organization of the Java Development Kit (JDK) on major operating systems (Windows, macOS, and Linux). Also explained is the organization of the Java Class Library and instructions on how to run JVM-based applications by setting up the ClassPath.

Chapter 3, *Java*, covers the fundamentals of the Java language. It covers creating classes and instantiating objects based on these classes, adding methods and properties to classes, and Java's access modifiers and other modifiers. Some of the other concepts that are discussed include abstract classes, interfaces, arrays, and collections and exceptions. More advanced features such as threading and lambdas are covered as well.

Chapter 4, *Java Programming*, contains a step-by-step guide to creating a simple web service in the Java language. Tools that are used along the way include the Eclipse IDE, the Gradle build tool, and programming libraries such as SparkJava (a micro web service framework) and the JUnit unit testing framework.

Chapter 5, *Scala*, talks about the hybrid functional programming and object-oriented programming language Scala. It describes the installation procedure and the usage of the interactive shell bundled with the language. By using the interactive shell, Scala code can be entered and executed dynamically, without explicitly compiling code. Both object-oriented and functional programming in Scala are discussed.

Chapter 6, *Scala Programming*, contains a step-by-step guide to create a simple console-based application powered by the popular Akka toolkit. Akka is a toolkit specializing in writing scalable applications that take full advantage of modern multicore processors. Many Akka concepts, such as its actor-based system, are discussed thoroughly. To build the project, the Scala Build Tool (SBT) is used, while the ScalaTest library is used for writing unit tests.

Chapter 7, *Clojure*, explains the fundamentals of Clojure, a dynamic functional programming language inspired by Lisp, which is not object-oriented. Like Scala, Clojure comes with an interactive shell that can be used to enter the various examples that are provided. Agents, a technique to handle state in multithreading applications, are discussed as well.

Chapter 8, *Clojure Programming*, provides step-by-step guides for two smaller projects. One project is based on monads, a technique that is commonly used in functional programming languages, especially in Lisp. The second project is a web application that is powered by Luminus, a popular micro web framework for Clojure. The Leiningen build tool is used to build both the projects.

Chapter 9, *Kotlin*, discusses JetBrain's statically typed programming language, Kotlin. Kotlin's type system, which promises null safety, is explained. Other features that are discussed include data classes, lambdas, and inline functions. Procedural programming in Kotlin is covered as well.

Chapter 10, *Kotlin Programming*, contains a step-by-step guide to create a GUI-based desktop application using the JavaFX toolkit. Apache Maven is used to build the project. The Eclipse IDE's debugger is used to find and fix bugs.

`Chapter 11`, *Groovy*, covers the dynamic programming language Groovy, one of the first alternative languages that appeared on the JVM. While Groovy is primarily a dynamic language, it allows compiling statically typed code as well. Both use cases are explained and described in this chapter. Also explored is the Groovy Development Kit, an extensive library of built-in classes, which is distributed as part of the Groovy language distribution.

`Chapter 12`, *Groovy Programming*, provides a step-by-step guide to create a web service in Groovy that pulls data from an embedded database management system using the Java Database Connectivity (JDBC) standard and generates XML using classes from the Groovy Development Kit. The Vert.x framework is used to power the web service.

`Appendix A`, *Other JVM Languages*, covers five other JVM-based languages, often dialects of mainstream languages: Oracle Nashorn (JavaScript), Jython (Python), JRuby (Ruby), Frege (Haskell), and Ceylon, a statically typed language by Red Hat.

`Appendix B`, *Quiz Answers*, gives the solutions to quizes provided at the end of all the chapters.

What you need for this book

To get the most out of this book, a modern laptop or desktop computer is required, running an up-to-date version of either Windows, macOS, or Linux (preferably Ubuntu). About 4 GB of RAM memory is recommended at the minimum; more RAM is always welcome. It is assumed that the reader has a reasonable knowledge of the operating system of their choice and is comfortable with installing programs and adding directories to a path.

Who this book is for

This book is meant for programmers who are interested in the Java Virtual Machine (JVM) and who want to learn more about the most popular programming languages that can be used for JVM development. A basic practical knowledge of a modern programming language that supports object-oriented programming (JavaScript, Python, C#, VB.NET, and C++) is assumed.

Conventions

In this book, you will find a number of text styles that distinguish between different kinds of information. Here are some examples of these styles and an explanation of their meaning.

Code words in text, database table names, folder names, filenames, file extensions, pathnames, dummy URLs, user input, and Twitter handles are shown as follows: "We then call the `setName` method on this object instance."

A block of code is set as follows:

```
Product p = new Product();
p.setName("Box of biscuits");
```

When we wish to draw your attention to a particular part of a code block, the relevant lines or items are set in bold:

```
public String getName() {
  return name;
}
```

Any command-line input or output is written as follows:

```
nano /etc/profile
```

New terms and **important words** are shown in bold. Words that you see on the screen, for example, in menus or dialog boxes, appear in the text like this: "The **System Properties** window appears. Click the **Environment Variables...** button."

Warnings or important notes appear in a box like this.

Tips and tricks appear like this.

Reader feedback

Feedback from our readers is always welcome. Let us know what you think about this book-what you liked or disliked. Reader feedback is important for us as it helps us develop titles that you will really get the most out of.

To send us general feedback, simply e-mail `feedback@packtpub.com`, and mention the book's title in the subject of your message.

If there is a topic that you have expertise in and you are interested in either writing or contributing to a book, see our author guide at www.packtpub.com/authors.

Customer support

Now that you are the proud owner of a Packt book, we have a number of things to help you to get the most from your purchase.

Downloading the example code

You can download the example code files for this book from your account at http://www.packtpub.com. If you purchased this book elsewhere, you can visit http://www.packtpub.com/support and register to have the files e-mailed directly to you.

You can download the code files by following these steps:

1. Log in or register to our website using your e-mail address and password.
2. Hover the mouse pointer on the **SUPPORT** tab at the top.
3. Click on **Code Downloads & Errata**.
4. Enter the name of the book in the **Search** box.
5. Select the book for which you're looking to download the code files.
6. Choose from the drop-down menu where you purchased this book from.
7. Click on **Code Download**.

Once the file is downloaded, please make sure that you unzip or extract the folder using the latest version of:

- WinRAR / 7-Zip for Windows
- Zipeg / iZip / UnRarX for Mac
- 7-Zip / PeaZip for Linux

The code bundle for the book is also hosted on GitHub at https://github.com/PacktPublishing/Introduction-to-JVM-Languages. We also have other code bundles from our rich catalog of books and videos available at https://github.com/PacktPublishing/. Check them out!

Downloading the color images of this book

We also provide you with a PDF file that has color images of the screenshots/diagrams used in this book. The color images will help you better understand the changes in the output. You can download this file from `http://www.packtpub.com/sites/default/files/downloads/IntroductionToJVMLanguages_ColorImages.pdf`.

Errata

Although we have taken every care to ensure the accuracy of our content, mistakes do happen. If you find a mistake in one of our books-maybe a mistake in the text or the code-we would be grateful if you could report this to us. By doing so, you can save other readers from frustration and help us improve subsequent versions of this book. If you find any errata, please report them by visiting `http://www.packtpub.com/submit-errata`, selecting your book, clicking on the **Errata Submission Form** link, and entering the details of your errata. Once your errata are verified, your submission will be accepted and the errata will be uploaded to our website or added to any list of existing errata under the Errata section of that title.

To view the previously submitted errata, go to `https://www.packtpub.com/books/content/support` and enter the name of the book in the search field. The required information will appear under the **Errata** section.

Piracy

Piracy of copyrighted material on the Internet is an ongoing problem across all media. At Packt, we take the protection of our copyright and licenses very seriously. If you come across any illegal copies of our works in any form on the Internet, please provide us with the location address or website name immediately so that we can pursue a remedy.

Please contact us at `copyright@packtpub.com` with a link to the suspected pirated material.

We appreciate your help in protecting our authors and our ability to bring you valuable content.

Questions

If you have a problem with any aspect of this book, you can contact us at `questions@packtpub.com`, and we will do our best to address the problem.

1
Java Virtual Machine

Java Virtual Machine (**JVM**) is a modern platform on which you can develop and deploy software. As the name implies, it was originally created to power applications written in the Java language. However, it didn't take language designers long to realize that they could not only run their languages on JVM, but also take advantage of its features and extensive class library.

Sun Microsystems released Java and the first JVM implementation in 1995. With its focus on Internet applications, Java quickly became popular. It was also designed from the ground up to run anywhere. Its initial goal was to run on set-top boxes, but when Sun Microsystems found out the market was not ready at that time yet, they decided to bring the platform to desktop computers as well. To make all those use cases possible, Sun invented their own binary executable format and called it Java bytecode. To run programs compiled to Java bytecode, a JVM implementation must be installed on the system.

This book will help you get started with five most popular languages that target JVM. By learning the language fundamentals and writing code yourself, you will be able to find the language that best suits you, your team, and your projects.

Before we dive into the **Java Development Kit** (**JDK**) and **Java Class Library** in the next chapter, we will look at some practical points first. With so many competing programming languages and platforms available today, it makes sense to first take a detailed look at what JVM has to offer to developers. Therefore, we will cover the following topics:

- Reasons for developing on JVM
- Popular use cases of JVM
- Introducing JVM concepts
- Java editions
- Other languages on JVM

JVM implementations

It's important to note that this book focuses on JVM implementations compatible with Oracle's Java SE (Standard Edition) 8 (and higher) platform only. This version can be installed on desktop computers, servers, and many single-board computers (including all the models of the popular credit-card-sized Raspberry Pi). We will use Oracle's implementation in this book, but both the open source OpenJDK and IBM's own J9 Java SE implementations of the same version should work equally well.

The Java platform as published by Google on Android phones and tablets is not covered in this book at all. One of the reasons is that the Java version used on Android is based on an older version of Java. While progress has been made to make Android's version of the platform more up to date, it still doesn't have all the features of Oracle's Java SE 8, and it requires different compilers and tools. Another reason is that Google omitted a lot of the Java SE APIs and replaced them with their own unique, incompatible APIs. Some of the languages covered in this book can be used with Android, however. Kotlin, in particular, is a very popular choice for modern Android development. This use case will not be explored in this book, though.

Why develop on JVM?

With so many programming languages and platform options available today, why would you consider developing and deploying your next project on JVM? After all, Java, the language that JVM was originally built for, has been declared obsolete (and, ridiculously, even dead) by fans of different languages more times over the years than anyone cares to remember.

Yet, while many other programming languages have come in and gone out of the spotlight, Java has always managed to return to impressive spots, either near or lately even on top of the list of the most used languages in the world.

Let's look at some of the most important reasons why the JVM platform is so strong:

- It keeps up with the modern times by adapting to market changes
- The Java Class Library, the built-in library of classes, is very strong
- It has an unmatched ecosystem

JVM adapts to market changes

When Java first appeared in the mid-1990s, computers had CPUs with only a single core and didn't have gigabytes of memory, as memory chips used to be prohibitively expensive. Java is one of those languages that kept up with modern developments: when multicore CPUs appeared, Java was soon able to support those additional cores when running code in multiple threads. But it did not stop there. In each newer version, it added new classes that made working with concurrency easier. This trend still continues.

When the functional programming paradigm became popular, Java received built-in support for lambdas and streams in the core language. While Java was quite late to get this support, compared to other popular languages, Java's implementation was better than many others. This was because it offered built-in support for multithreading almost for free.

Adapting to market changes also means that sometimes things have to go. Back when Java was introduced, running Java code directly in the browser was a big thing. These mini applications were called **applets** and required a custom browser plugin for each browser and system. Of course, we now know that the market has chosen the JavaScript language as the standard language to create interactive websites, and Oracle recently deprecated the applet standard.

Java Class Library

For each edition of Java (more on available editions later in this chapter), it has been decided which classes are guaranteed to be available in a JVM implementation of a specific version. The Java Class Library for Java SE 8 is a very large collection of classes, and every JVM runtime installation that adheres to the Java SE 8 platform standard must implement those classes, regardless of the vendor of the JVM implementation.

Classes in this library provide functionalities such as writing or reading from the console window, performing file I/O, and communicating with TCP servers. Also, there are many classes available to start and manage operating system threads. More fundamentally, it contains classes that define data structures, such as lists and maps (called dictionaries in some other languages), among many others. In the next chapter, we will thoroughly look at the classes in the Java Class Library.

The Java Class Library is an important reason why language designers love targeting JVM. Using the data structures defined in the Java Class Library, they are able to focus more on the language design and less on building a full runtime library from scratch. Building a fully tested, multiplatform runtime system library comparable to the Java Class Library is a huge undertaking.

Ecosystem

A built-in class library can obviously not cover all the use cases of a programmer. If something is missing, you can turn to libraries and tools built by other companies, groups, and individuals to save time. Because Java has been so successful for many years, its ecosystem is unmatched. It will be hard to find a platform with proven high-quality tools, libraries, toolkits, and framework choices that are better than the ones available in JVM.

With so many add-on libraries available, Java hardly ever pushes the developer in a certain direction. As an example of how rich the ecosystem is, let's look at the main options JVM developers typically have when creating a web application:

- Build a web application that runs inside a JVM application server
- To quickly have results, a general high-level web framework can be used
- For more control, the application can be built with a microservice framework

Scenario 1 – Using a JVM application server

Developers could take the enterprise route and install a JVM-based application server, either a free open source one or a paid proprietary one, that will run the application along with web applications simultaneously, if desired. The server will handle configuration issues and manage database connections.

There are simple application servers available that just contain enough built-in APIs to run basic web applications. But there are also full blown Oracle-certified application servers that have a magnitude of built-in and standardized APIs, including APIs to access databases, generate or consume XML or JSON documents, communicate with other web services via the SOAP or REST standards, provide web security, send or receive messages from legacy computer systems, and many others.

The two most important frameworks for enterprise development are the following:

- Oracle's Java Enterprise Edition (Java EE) platform, covered later in this book
- The Spring Framework ecosystem (including Spring Boot)

Many applications use both these technologies together.

Some of the popular application servers are the following:

- Apache Tomcat (for basic web applications)
- Apache TomEE
- Red Hat WildFly
- Oracle GlassFish
- Red Hat JBoss Enterprise Application Platform
- Oracle WebLogic

The first four are open source and the last two proprietary.

Scenario 2 – Using a general high-level web application framework

The second possibility would be to use a complete web application framework. These frameworks usually offer higher-level APIs than enterprise frameworks and offer built-in **model-view-controller** (**MVC**) solutions that have the capability to enhance a developer's productivity significantly.

Frameworks such as these usually dictate or steer the developer in a certain direction as they have built-in support for only a few hardcoded libraries/toolkits. Often, plugins are supported to add support to other choices, however. By giving up some freedom, quick development cycles can be achieved. Some frameworks require that the application is run inside a JVM application server, while other frameworks provide their own HTTP server.

Apache Struts used to be very popular in this category, but nowadays, the Play framework is probably the most popular choice.

Scenario 3 – Using a microservice framework

A different choice could be to create the application using the modern microservice framework. Frameworks such as these have a built-in HTTP server to run your application, but they do not provide any other tools or libraries out of the box. In this scenario, it's easier to mix and match other libraries and toolkits that you want to use yourself.

Commonly, the application will be separated into multiple standalone web services to follow the modern microservice architecture, but this is not a strict requirement of these frameworks.

Vert.x and Spark Java (not to be used with the Apache Spark big data platform) are the most commonly used microservice frameworks.

Popular use cases

Now that we've seen some valid points that confirm why JVM is a viable platform for modern software development, let's look at some places where JVM usage is particularly popular:

- Web applications
- Big data analysis
- Internet of Things (IoT)

Web applications

With its focus on performance, JVM is a very popular choice for web applications. When built correctly, applications can scale really well, if needed across many different servers.

JVM is a well-understood platform, meaning that it is predictable. Plus, it provides many tools to debug and profile problematic applications. Because of its open nature, monitoring of JVM internals is also possible. For web applications that have to serve thousands of users concurrently, this is an important advantage.

JVM already plays a huge role in the cloud. Popular examples of companies that use JVM for core parts of their cloud-based services include Twitter (famously using Scala), Amazon, Spotify, and Netflix. The actual list is much larger.

Big data

Big data is a hot topic. When data is regarded too big for traditional databases to be analyzed, one can set up multiple clusters of servers for processing such data. Analyzing data in this context can, for example, refer to searching for something specific, looking for patterns, and calculating statistics.

This data could be obtained from the data collected from web servers (for example, logged visitors' clicks), the output obtained from external sensors at a manufacturer's plant, legacy servers that have been producing log files for many years, and so forth. Data sizes can vary wildly as well, but often, they take up multiple terabytes in total.

Two popular technologies in the big data arena are the following:

- Apache Hadoop (provides storage of data and takes care of data distribution to other servers)
- Apache Spark (uses Hadoop to stream data and makes it possible to analyze incoming data)

Both Hadoop and Spark are for the most part written in Java. While both offer interfaces to a lot of programming languages and platforms, it will not be a surprise that JVM is one among them.

The functional programming paradigm focuses on creating code that would run safely on multiple CPU cores, so languages that are fully specialized in this style, such as Scala or Clojure, are appropriate candidates to be used with either Spark or Hadoop.

IoT

Portable devices that feature Internet connectivity are very common these days. Since Java was created with the idea of running on embedded devices from the beginning, JVM is, yet again, at an advantage here.

For memory-constrained systems, Oracle offers the Java ME Embedded platform. It is meant for commercial IoT devices that do not require a standard graphical or console-based user interface.

For devices that can spare more memory, the Java SE Embedded edition is available. The Java SE Embedded version is very close to the Java SE discussed in this book. When running a full Linux environment, it can be used to provide desktop GUIs for full user interaction.

Both Java ME Embedded and Java SE Embedded platforms can access the **general-purpose input/output** (**GPIO**) pins on the Raspberry Pi, which means that sensors and other peripherals connected to these ports can be accessed by Java code.

JVM concepts

Every aspiring JVM developer should be familiar with its most important concepts:

- JVM is a virtual machine
- Most implementations feature a just-in-time (**JIT**) compiler
- It offers a few built-in primitive datatypes
- Everything else is an object
- Objects are accessed via reference types
- The **garbage collector** (**GC**) process removes obsolete objects from memory
- Build tools are used a lot in the JVM world

Virtual machine

That the Java Virtual Machine is a virtual machine is a rather obvious observation, but it should be kept in mind. One of the consequences is that you are, in theory, writing applications for a type of machine that differs from the machine you are developing or running your applications on.

It generally does not matter whether the code runs on a 32-bit or 64-bit version of the **Java Runtime Environment** (**JRE**). The latter will probably make more memory available to the application than the 32-bit version, but the running program will not care about this difference as long as it doesn't make native operating system calls or require gigabytes of memory.

 Unlike a language, such as C, where datatype sizes are dependent on the native system, Java does not have this issue (or feature, depending on your point of view). An `int` integer on JVM is always signed and is of 32-bit size, no matter on which computer platform or system architecture it is running.

Finally, it should be noted that each application that runs on JVM loads its own instance of JVM on system memory. This means when you run multiple Java applications at the same time, they will all have their own copy of JVM at their disposal; this also means different applications can use different versions of JVM if required for whatever reason. For security reasons, it is not suggested that you have different versions of the JDK or JRE on one system; it's usually better to have only the latest supported versions installed.

The JIT compiler

Although not dictated anywhere, all popular JVM implementations are not just simple interpreters; they feature complex JIT compilers along with their interpreters.

When you launch a Java application, JVM is launched and initialized first. Once this is done, it immediately starts interpreting and running the Java bytecode. If the interpreter believes it makes sense, it will compile sections of the programs and load libraries to native executable code in memory and start executing that version of the code instead of the interpreted Java bytecode version. This often results in code that could be executed much faster.

Whether the code is compiled or interpreted depends on many things. If a routine is called often, it becomes a probable candidate for the JIT compiler to compile it to the native code.

 The advantage of the JIT approach is that the distributed files can be cross-platform and the user does not have to wait for native compiling of the whole application. Applications start executing immediately after JVM is initialized, and the optimization is done under the hood.

Primitive datatypes

JVM has a few so-called built-in primitive datatypes. This is the main reason why Java is not considered a pure OOP language. Variables of these types are not objects and always have a value:

Java name	Description and size	Values (inclusive)
byte	Signed byte (8 bits)	-128 to 127
short	Signed short integer (16 bits)	-32768 to 32767
int	Signed integer (32 bits)	-2^{31} to $2^{31}-1$
long	Signed long integer (64 bits)	-2^{63} to $2^{63}-1$

float	Single-precision floating point (32-bit)	Non-precise floating point values
double	Double-precision floating point (64-bit)	Non-precise floating point values
char	A single Unicode UTF-16 character (16-bit)	Unicode character 0 to 655535
boolean	Boolean	True/False

Note that not all JVM languages support the creation of variables of primitive types and follow this modern assumption: everything takes the object approach. We will see that this is usually not a problem as the Java Class Library has wrapper objects that wrap primitive types, and most languages, including Java, automatically use these wrappers when required. This process is called **auto-boxing**.

Classes

Functions and variables are always declared inside a class. Even the application entry function that is called upon a program launch, called the `main()` function, is a function that is located inside a class.

JVM only supports the single-inheritance model. Classes always inherit from one class at the maximum. This is not a big loss. As we will see in the next chapter, a structure called an interface comes to the rescue. An interface is basically a list of function prototypes (only the definition of functions, without code) and constants. Classes that implement an interface are required by the compiler to have implementations for those functions. Classes can implement as many interfaces as they want, but they must provide implementations for each method of all the implemented interfaces.

 Some languages covered in this book hide these facts completely from the developer. For example, unlike Java, some languages allow functions and variables to be written outside class declarations or even executable code outside function definitions. Other languages support inheritance of multiple classes. Internally, these languages do clever tricks to work around JVM limitations and design decisions.

JVM classes are usually grouped in packages. In the next chapter, we will see how classes are organized.

Reference types

Like most modern programming languages, JVM does not work with direct memory pointers to objects; it uses reference types. A reference type variable either points to a specific instance of a class or it points to nothing.

If a reference type points to an object, it can be used to call the object's methods or access public attributes.

If a reference type points to nothing, it is called a **null reference**. When calling methods or reading attributes using a null reference, an error will be generated at runtime. We will see that some languages covered in this book came up with solutions to this common problem.

References and null references

Let's take a look at the following code:

```
Product p = new Product();
p.setName("Box of biscuits");
```

Assume that Product is a class here that is available to the program. We create a Product instance and the p variable points to it. We then call the setName method on this object instance.

JVM does not give direct access to the memory location where the Product object is stored. It just provides a reference to the created object. When using the variable p, JVM figures out which memory location it has to reach for the object that the variable points to.

We add the following lines to the previous snippet:

```
p = null;
p.setName("This line will produce an error at run-time");
```

A reference can be cleared explicitly by assigning null to it. Note that this is not necessary for variables declared inside a method, as they will be cleared automatically upon exiting the method. However, it is perfectly acceptable to still do it anyway. Now the variable p is a null reference. In the next paragraph, we will see what will happen to object instances that are no longer referenced by any reference type variable.

The preceding code will compile fine. When running the program, the last line will cause a `NullPointerException` error, though. If no error handling capability was implemented in the application, it will crash. Many modern IDEs try to detect these situations and warn the developer about them.

Garbage collector

JVM does not require the programmer to manually allocate and release blocks of memory when creating or disposing of objects. The programmer can generally concentrate on just creating objects when he or she needs them.

A process known as the GC halts the application at certain intervals and scans the memory for objects that are no longer in scope (not reachable by any other object loaded at that point). It will remove those objects that can safely be deleted from the memory and reclaim the freed space.

This process used to cause very serious performance issues in the past, but the algorithm has improved much over the years. Also, if an application needs it, system administrators can configure many parameters of the GC to better control it.

The developer should always keep the high-level concept of the GC algorithm in mind. If you keep creating tons of objects and always keep them in the scope (meaning making it in such a way that all those objects can be reached, for example, by storing them in a list that the application can access), then out of the memory, errors are very likely to occur sooner or later.

Example

Let's assume you have developed an e-commerce application for an online store. Also, let's assume that each logged-in user has their own **ShoppingBasket** instance that holds the products that they add to their basket.

Say, a user has logged in today and is planning to buy a soap bar and a delicious pack of cookies. For this user, the application will create two **Product** instances, one for each chosen product, and add them to the **products** list of **ShoppingBasket**:

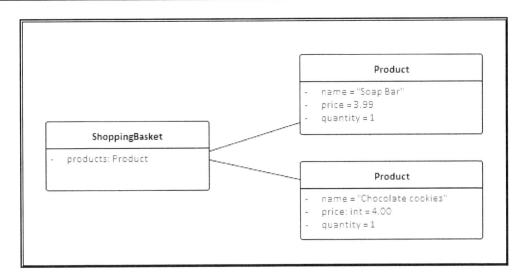

Just before visiting the checkout page, the user sees that Amazon offers the same cookies at a much better price and decides to remove the cookies from the basket. Technically, the application would remove the **Product** instance from the list of products. But from there on, the product instance representing **Chocolate cookies** is an orphan object. As there is no reference to it, it cannot be reached by the application:

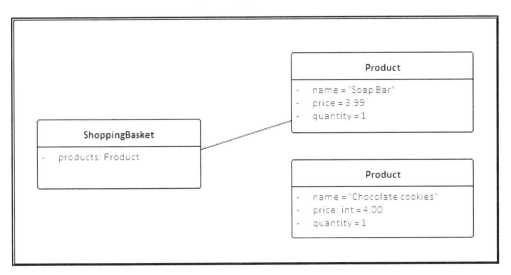

After a while, JVM's GC kicks in and sees the **Chocolate cookies** object instance. It determines that the object cannot be reached in any way by the application anymore and therefore decides to remove it. The memory the object was using up will now be released:

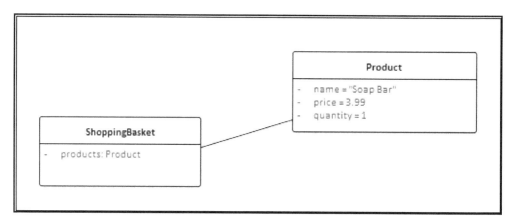

There are several tricks to tame GC. One well-known trick when an application needs to work with lots of similar objects is to put these objects in a pool (list of objects). When an application needs an object, it simply gets one from the pool and modifies the object according to its needs. When it has finished and doesn't need the object anymore, it will put it back in the pool. Since these objects are always in the scope (when not used, in the pool, which the application can access), GC will not try to dispose of these objects.

Backward compatibility

The maintainers of JVM and Java Class Library understand the needs of business developers. The code that is written today should ideally run tomorrow. JVM offers reasonable backward compatibility. Developers familiar with Python 2 and 3 will know that this is not a given in the industry.

Newer JVM versions can run applications that were compiled for older JVM versions, as long as the application's code does not use APIs or technologies that were removed from the JVM version that is running the application. Here's an example: libraries compiled for Java 6 can still be loaded and used in projects that run on a Java 8 JVM instance. But this is not the case the other way around; applications running on a Java 6 JVM instance cannot load classes compiled for later versions.

Of course, like every other platform or language, the JDK and Java Class Library maintainers have to deprecate classes and whole technologies from time to time. While there are issues, backward compatibility on JVM is generally better than many other platforms and languages. Also, APIs are generally only removed if proper and well-documented alternatives exist.

Build tools

Back when projects were simpler, simple batch or operating system shell script files used to automate the compiling and packaging process. As projects became more complex, it became harder to define these scripts. For different operating systems, completely different scripts had to be written.

Soon, the first set of dedicated Java build tools appeared. These worked with XML build files. More or less, cross-platform compatible scripts could be written this way. At first, long and cumbersome scripts had to be written; later, tools worked with the convention over configuration paradigm. When using the conventions suggested by the tool, much less code has to be written; however, if your situation is different from the default behavior, it can take a lot of effort to let the tools do what you want or need. Newer tools ditch XML files and provide script languages to automate the building.

Some of the features that many of those tools offer are as follows:

* Built-in dependency managers that can download add-on libraries from well-known repositories from the Internet
* Automatically run unit tests and conditionally stop packaging if a test fails

The JDK does not offer a build tool itself, but it will be hard to find projects that do not at least use one of the following open source build automation tools:

* Apache Ant (has no built-in dependency manager and works with XML-based build scripts)
* Apache Maven (introduced convention over configuration with XML files and works with plugins)
* Gradle (build scripts written in Groovy or Kotlin)

JVM programmers that use a popular IDE do not have to worry too much about build automation tools. This is because all IDEs can generate build scripts themselves. If you want more control, you can start writing your own scripts manually and let the IDE use that script to compile, test, and run your project.

Java editions

Several editions of Java are available. Each one aims at different use cases. Some of the editions have had numerous name changes over the years; the current names of the editions are as follows:

- **Java Standard Edition (Java SE)**
- **Java Enterprise Edition (Java EE)**
- **Java Micro Edition (Java ME)**

Java SE

This is the most important edition. When people mention the term "Java," they usually refer to this edition. This book concentrates solely on the Java SE platform.

This edition is meant to run on desktop machines and servers, and as we will see later, an embedded version is also available and bundled with Raspberry Pi's Linux distribution. Java SE comes with the complete Java Class Library. It includes the classic **Swing GUI Toolkit**; most versions also contain the modern JavaFX GUI toolkit.

 Note that a recent update of Java SE Embedded removed the JavaFX toolkit. Once you install this JDK update on the Raspberry Pi, the JavaFX component will be gone. Oracle has open sourced their JavaFX port for the Raspberry Pi so that advanced users can still download and compile it.

Java SE is mostly meant to create standalone consoles, desktop GUIs, or headless applications; alternatively, it is used to create external libraries.

Java EE

Java EE builds upon Java SE; therefore, it requires that Java SE is installed. It adds lots of APIs in a lot of categories. Java EE applications usually run inside JVM application servers. This book does not cover Java EE in depth but will mention it from time to time. This is because it is a very important addition to the Java platform, especially for business developers.

It is not possible to download a Java EE standalone edition from the Oracle website; instead, you will have to download a full application server that is compatible with the Java EE platform version you want to use. Some IDEs bundle the Java EE application server as well; we will cover this in the next chapter.

The Java EE standard only describes the APIs that must be available, but it does not dictate the implementation. It's up to the Java EE-compatible application servers to come up with actual implementations that adhere to these standards.

Example – Java Persistence API as implemented by two application servers

Java EE describes the **Java Persistence API (JPA)**. It is an **object relation mapper (ORM)** API, a layer between Java objects and relational databases (often SQL databases, such as Oracle database, Oracle MySQL, PostgreSQL, and so on). With a few lines of code, the content of JVM objects can be written to the database or vice versa: read from the database and put in the object.

Oracle's own reference implementation of Java EE is an open source application server called GlassFish. GlassFish bundles the existing EclipseLink open source project as the implementer of the JPA standard. Meanwhile, Red Hat's WildFly, a different open source Java EE application server, bundles Red Hat's own, more popular, Hibernate ORM open source project, which also implements the JPA standard.

If developers only use the features documented in the JPA standard, then it should not matter to them which implementation is used, but problems arise once features are used that are unique to a specific implementation.

 If you do not agree with the choices made by the vendor of your application server, it is often possible to switch implementations of a particular standard. Yes, JVM developers really love having choices!

Java ME

Before the days of iOS and Android, Java ME happened to be an important platform for feature phones and early smartphones for games and some basic applications. iOS and Android both never supported Java ME applications, so nowadays it does not play a major role anymore.

It featured a subset of the Java Class Library and offered some additional APIs to work with mobile devices. Java ME got a second life as Java ME Embedded, which can be used for commercial IoT devices.

Other languages on JVM

To promote the Java language and platform, Sun published JVM specifications early on. This document was meant for developers who wanted to write a JVM implementation themselves, perhaps for platforms that did not have an official JVM implementation available yet. It described which low-level commands JVM can execute, the required data structures, rules on accessing memory, the Java bytecode's `.class` file format, and much more.

While not originally a goal of the designers, the release of the specifications also made it possible for other language writers to experiment with the Java bytecode, and it didn't take long before other languages could compile to that format. Sun, and later Oracle, liked this development a lot. They liked it so much that Oracle even added new features to JVM, solely to make it easier to support dynamic languages on JVM.

In this chapter, we will cover the following topics related to alternative JVM languages:

- Understanding why should we choose a language other than Java for JVM development
- Discussing the possibility of mixing languages in a single project and the issues that would be expected
- Writing unit tests in a different language than the one used in the main project

Why choose a language other than Java?

Since Java is a language that is originally designed to run on JVM, why would anyone choose another language for JVM development?

There are several reasons why a developer would do this:

- Java is a very verbose language
- Not everyone likes statically typed languages and they are not always the best solution
- Java Class Library misses some classes for common use cases

Java is a very verbose language

Java is notorious for being very verbose. While over the years there have been updates made to the language to improve the situation a bit, many other languages require the writing of less code for the same end result.

Let's look at a simple example.

A standard mutable object often looks like this in Java:

```java
class Person {
  private String name;
  public Person(String name) {
    this.name = name;
  }
  public String getName() {
    return name;
  }
  public void setName(String name) {
    this.name = name;
  }
}
```

In Kotlin, the following line of code does the same (and more):

```kotlin
data class Person(val name: String)
```

No, this is not a joke. Kotlin automatically implements the same methods as shown in the Java example when compiling this code. In fact, it adds even more commonly used methods than shown here in the Java example. In `Chapter 4`, *Java Programming*, we will discuss those additional methods for Java as well.

 While productivity can be seriously enhanced by choosing a different language, the situation for Java is not as bad as it may seem. All modern IDE programming tools can automatically generate boilerplate Java code, such as the one shown in the preceding code, with a simple key press combination.

Java is not ideal for everything or everyone

While Java recently received some serious functional-programming-like features in version 8, at its core, it is still a statically typed imperative language. Not all developers prefer this programming style. Programmers coming from Python or Ruby may cringe when they have to write code for a fully typed language. This can be a valid reason for teams to adopt a different language than Java for JVM development.

Also, some problems can be solved much more elegantly when using a dynamic programming language, while for projects that require complex concurrency situations, a functional programming style is often more suitable. Finally, some libraries and frameworks simply feel more natural when used with certain languages.

Missing classes in Java Class Library

Java Class Library is an extensive library, but sometimes, it simply misses certain classes or it shows that it was introduced more than two decades ago. While missing functionality, in most cases, can be solved by adding free and open source add-on libraries from the JVM ecosystem, it can both be convenient and a time-saving option if you use a language that has built-in solutions for these problems.

A good example of missing functionality in Java SE version 8's Java Class Library is that it currently has no built-in support for the very commonly used JSON standard. Popular add-on libraries that provide JSON support include Jackson and Google's GSON. Also, modern versions of the Java EE platform provide APIs for JSON support classes. Some languages covered in this book have built-in support for JSON.

Another issue is that some popular classes from Java Class Library require a lot of boilerplate code to use them effectively. Languages, such as Groovy, add wrappers to many popular Java Class Library classes that make these APIs much easier to use.

Mixing JVM languages in a project

Many languages offer good interoperability with Java, and therefore, with other JVM languages as well. Languages do this if they use standard Java Class Library classes, where possible, for their data structures and compile methods in a similar way as Java would have done.

It's not uncommon to have certain classes compiled in a different language in a Java project. One should be aware of the various issues, though:

- It can complicate the building process a lot
- Many languages require their own runtime classes that can cause issues

Increasing build process complexity

When combining multiple languages, the build script has to be adapted, and this can lead to complex situations. For example, if a Java project uses a class compiled in Groovy, the order of the compilation is important. First, the Groovy class will have to be compiled, then the Java code. If that Groovy code uses custom classes from the Java project, then it gets even more complex.

 Groovy is a special case, as we will see in the Groovy chapter. The Groovy compiler can compile most Java code, as the Groovy language is largely compatible with the Java language. For projects where this is not possible, or desirable, there's a compiler plugin for the Apache Maven build tool that solves many of these problems.

A solution could be to divide the code into multiple subprojects and list the resulting libraries as a requirement of the main project in the build tool.

Some languages offer another solution: they provide their own custom classes to call the language's source code from Java (or any other JVM language). The source code is then dynamically compiled to the Java bytecode on the fly as these classes load the code. Other languages implement an official standard to embed script languages in Java code. We will take a brief look at this in the appendix when we discuss Oracle's JavaScript interpreter, called Nashorn.

Language runtime libraries

This is somewhat related to building complications. Many alternative JVM languages require their own support libraries to be bundled with the compiled program. These libraries often define data structures that are unique to the language and internal support methods that the language's compiled Java bytecode calls.

This is usually not a problem, but things can get problematic if one of the project's dependencies (or one of the project's dependencies' dependencies...) is compiled in the same language but of a different version. Things can get messy when a different version of the same runtime library is required by multiple libraries of the same project and can result in confusing error messages when compiling or running the project.

This situation is called **dependency hell** and is not really specific to the usage of multiple languages in a single project, but it is something every developer should be aware of. Developers that want to mix languages should also be aware of the fact that sometimes language runtime libraries increase the final size significantly and that some runtime libraries also bundle their own dependencies; this increases the risk of dependency-hell-like problems. Often, dependencies are documented in the language's documentation or website.

 Many language developers, like many framework designers, are aware of these problems and have taken steps to minimize the risks of these problems. For example, they commonly fork the more popular dependencies they use themselves and rename them to prevent class name clashes.

Writing unit tests in a different language

It is quite a common approach to test Java code with unit tests written in a different language. As we have seen earlier in this chapter, the code in other languages can be much more compact than the same code in Java, which is ideal for writing small, concrete, and readable unit tests.

Since the language's runtime library will only be used while running the unit tests, the language's runtime library itself will only be used while executing the tests and it will not have to be bundled with the compiled main project.

 Groovy is especially suited for this use case, as we will see in the `Chapter 11`, *Groovy*. It has some convenient features for writing unit tests, including a built-in `assert` statement that prints very verbose and readable output when the passed value is different than the expected output.

Summary

In this chapter, we described JVM from a fairly higher-level. We started by looking at what JVM offers to developers and also focused on popular use cases and the most important JVM concepts. We also examined the available Java editions. Finally, we covered alternative JVM languages by looking at several possible reasons why a developer would choose another language than Java for JVM development.

In the next chapter, we will install the JDK and take a detailed look at it. We will also cover Java Class Library in detail and install additional developer tools to really get going.

2
Developing on the Java Virtual Machine

In this chapter, we will take an in-depth look at a **Java Virtual Machine (JVM)**. We will focus on concepts that every JVM developer should know, regardless of the chosen programming language. This is what we will cover in this chapter:

- Java Development Kit (JDK)
- Class organization with packages
- Java Class Library
- Running JVM applications on the command line
- Installing the Eclipse Integrated Development Environment (Eclipse IDE)

While this book covers Windows, macOS, and Linux (Ubuntu) operating systems, paths will often be shown in Windows style only. When using macOS and Linux systems, be sure to rewrite the paths using the rules of your operating system.

JDK

Developers who want to develop on a JVM should always install JDK. It bundles the **Java Runtime Environment (JRE)**, the Java compiler, and various development tools, some of which we will explore in this chapter. Even if you are planning to do most of your JVM development in a language other than Java, it is strongly advised that you still install the complete JDK. Many prominent development tools require a fully installed JDK to run. Also, sooner or later, you'll probably want to use some of the tools that are only included in JDK.

The recent version of the Linux distribution of the Raspberry Pi installs the Java SE Embedded 8 JDK automatically when using the default Raspian installation options. Be aware though that, often, the supplied version is not up-to-date. We are not aware of other major operating systems that bundle JDK with their default installation. We will cover the following JDK-related topics:

- Installing JDK (Windows, macOS, and Linux)
- Exploring JDK
- JRE

Installing JDK

We will cover the installation procedure of Oracle's implementation of JDK 8 only. If you have already installed a JDK implementation that is fully compatible with the Java SE 8 platform, including the open source OpenJDK 8 or IBM's J9 JDK 8, then generally, it should work fine and you can skip this section.

 Not all features discussed in this book are available in non-Oracle JDK implementations. When applicable, we will mention exceptions.

On each operating system, an environmental variable, namely `JAVA_HOME`, must be created that points to the installation directory of JDK (or JRE on non-development computers). For the operating systems covered in this book, (Windows, macOS, and Linux) instructions are provided on how to do this. Many important JVM tools require this variable. Applications that require this include build tools and application servers. We will provide instructions for the following topics:

- Downloading JDK
- Installing JDK on Windows
- Installing JDK on macOS
- Installing JDK on Linux
- Downloading the Javadoc API documentation

Downloading JDK

Oracle's implementation of the Windows, macOS, and Linux versions of JDK can be downloaded from Oracle's website. For some platforms, JDK is only available in a 64-bit edition, while other platforms have both a 32-bit and 64-bit edition.

Using your favorite browser, visit Oracle's Java main page (`http://www.oracle.com/java`):

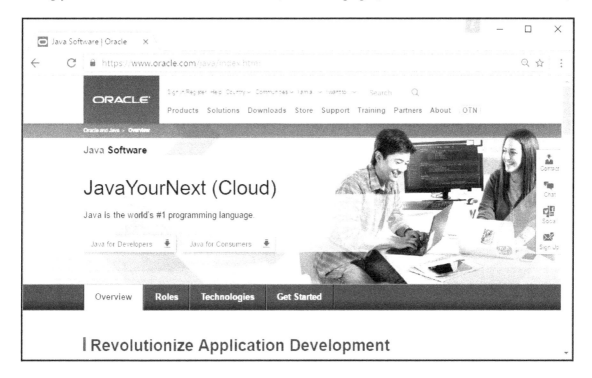

To download JDK, follow this procedure:

1. At the time of writing this book, this page contained a **Java for Developers** button. Once you click on it, you will be redirected to the **Software Downloads** section.
2. Find **Java SE (includes JavaFX)** in the list and click on it (be careful not to click on the **Early Access** link that is placed next to it, if still applicable).
3. You will now have access to the **Java SE Downloads** page. Click on the **Download** button below JDK.
4. Find the version specific to your operating system platform and architecture.
5. If you agree with the license terms, download your copy.

Installing JDK on Windows

For Windows, JDK is available in both 32-bit and 64-bit versions. Simply run the downloaded executable file and follow the prompts. Copy and paste the path where you'll install JDK; you'll need the path after installing it.

Using the default settings, install JRE, which is part of the installation of JDK. It is strongly recommended that you keep the JRE and JDK versions in sync, so it's always best to install JRE directly from the JDK installer. Oracle states that JDK is always installed at the system-wide level; therefore, it will be available to all users.

After the installation, you'll need to add or alter some environment variables. We will show how to do this for Windows 10. For other recent versions of Windows, it should be a familiar procedure:

1. Right-click on your Windows **Start** menu and select **System**. On the left-hand side of the window that appears, click on **Advanced system settings**.
2. The **System Properties** window appears. Click on the **Environment Variables...** button. The **Environment Variables** window appears:

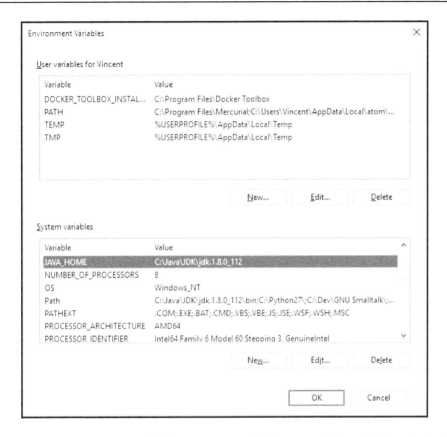

3. Look at the **System variables** section at the bottom of the window. Check whether you see the JAVA_HOME variable. If not, click on the **New...** button; otherwise, edit the existing JAVA_HOME entry.

4. Enter JAVA_HOME as the variable name and the full path to the root of JDK's installation directory as the value. Then click on **OK** to close the window.

5. Now find the existing Path variable and add the full path to the bin subdirectory of the JDK installation directory. Keep in mind that the directories are separated by the ; character.

To verify the installation, do the following:

1. Open a new Command Prompt (for example, by clicking on the **Start** menu, typing `cmd`, and pressing *Enter*)
2. Enter `javac -version` and press *Enter*

You should see the version number that matches the downloaded JDK. If not, double-check whether you altered the environment variables correctly and make sure you opened a new **Command Prompt** window instead of using a previously opened one.

Installing JDK on macOS

Note that JDK requires a recent version of macOS. At the time of writing this, JDK 8 requires at least version 10.8 (Mountain Lion).

The installation of macOS is quite straightforward. Simply double-click on the downloaded image (the `.dmg` file), and in the Finder window that appears, double-click on the package icon. Follow the prompts. Like the Windows version, the macOS version is installed on a system-level basis and is therefore available to all users.

After the installation, you need to ensure the new JDK is the default one. macOS supports the installation of multiple JDK versions at the same time, and you can always switch to any one of them; however, only one version will be active at a time. The easiest way to do this is to open the `.bash_profile` file (note that the filename starts with a dot) in your user's `Home` folder and add the following line to it:

```
export JAVA_HOME="$(/usr/libexec/java_home -v 1.8)"
```

To validate the installation:

- Open a new Terminal window
- Type `javac -version` and press *Enter*

You should see the version number that matches the downloaded JDK version.

Installing JDK on Linux

Both 32-bit and 64-bit versions of the Linux JDK versions are available. They can be downloaded in the following formats:

- As a compressed .tar.gz file for manual installation
- As an **RPM Package Manager** .rpm file for Linux versions supporting this packaging format

Oracle has certified a few Linux distributions for installing JDK. At the time of writing this, various versions of Oracle Linux, Red Hat, and Ubuntu are certified. If your Linux distribution is not one of these, it does not automatically mean that JDK or JVM won't work on your machine - just that it is not officially supported by Oracle.

In this section, we will only cover the installation of JDK on an Ubuntu installation. Ubuntu does not support the RPM format natively, so downloading the .tar.gz file is recommended on Ubuntu. Although not required on Linux, we will install JDK at the system-wide level. If you have a Linux distribution that supports RPM or , does not support some of the commands used below, refer to the **Installation Instructions** link on the **Java SE Downloads** page.

Open a new Terminal window, change to the directory where you placed the .tar.gz file, and type the following commands. A few notes on this:

- The system's root password is required. If not available, substitute su with sudo -s, but sudo -s will only work if your user has root rights
- The VERSION text must be substituted with the version number of the downloaded JDK
- The assumed platform here is the 64-bit (x64) version; if you have downloaded the 32-bit version, replace x64 with i586

Here are the commands you need to type:

```
su
tar xvfz jdk-VERSION-linux-x64.tar.gz
ls
mv jdk1.VERSION /usr/local/
```

Take care that, in the last command, you move the directory extracted from the downloaded file, not the downloaded `.tar.gz` file itself. Also, note that the VERSION format of the directory is different than the downloaded file. Copy the full path to `/usr/local/jdk1.VERSION` to the clipboard or write it down. You will need it in the following step.

Now, set up the `JAVA_HOME` environmental variable. We want the Terminal to load it automatically for each user:

```
nano /etc/profile
```

Scroll to the end and add the following lines to the file. Paste the path you copied to the clipboard after the `JAVA_HOME=` text:

```
JAVA_HOME=/usr/local/jdk1.VERSION
export JAVA_HOME
```

Press *Cltrl* + *X*, say *Y* to save changes, and press *Enter* to confirm the filename.

Lastly, you need to register the JDK and JRE commands with Ubuntu. By entering the following commands in your Terminal window, the proper symbolic links will be created for the two most important commands: `java` (to run JVM applications) and `javac` (the Java compiler):

```
. /etc/profile
update-alternatives --install "/usr/bin/java" "java" $JAVA_HOME/bin/java 1
update-alternatives --install "/usr/bin/javac" "java" $JAVA_HOME/bin/javac 1
```

The first command reloads the modified `/etc/profile` file so that the `JAVA_HOME` variable is available. Note the first dot in the command.

 If you want to use other commands from JDK's `bin` subdirectory in future, you'll have to use the update-alternatives command illustrated in the preceding code in a Terminal with root access, and you'll have to do so for each command that you plan to use.

Type exit twice and close the Terminal window. Now open a new Terminal window (do not request root access) and enter the following command to verify the installation:

```
javac -version
```

If everything goes smoothly, you'll see the version number that would match the downloaded JDK.

Downloading API documentation

Oracle offers a complete online Java Class Library API documentation. For version 8, refer to `https://docs.oracle.com/javase/8/docs/api/`.

It can be beneficial to have a local copy. Oracle recognized this and offers a download:

- Visit the **Java SE Downloads** page (see the **Download JDK** section for instructions on how to get there)
- Find the **Additional Resources** section and click on the **Download** button next to the **Java SE 8 Documentation** entry
- If you agree with the license agreement, you can download the ZIP file

Unzip the file to a convenient location and open the `index.html` file in the `docs` subdirectory in your favorite browser.

 If you plan to create desktop GUI applications with the JavaFX toolkit, you should consider downloading the JavaFX API documentation that is offered on the same download page as well.

Exploring JDK

Arguably, the most important components of JDK are:

- `java` (to run a compiled JVM application, even when it was compiled by a language other than Java)
- `javac` (the Java language compiler)

There's more to JDK than this; in this section, we will take a look at the directory structure and sum up the most important commands in the `bin` directory.

The directory structure

To familiarize yourself with JDK, it can help to take a look at its structure. Here's a graphical overview of the subdirectories directly under the root of JDK's installation directory:

Let's take a more detailed look at those subdirectories:

Directory name	Description
bin	The bin subdirectory contains all the executable commands that are supplied with JDK. The most important commands are discussed in the next paragraph.
db	Everything related to the JavaDB component is stored here. JavaDB is Oracle's supported version of the Apache Derby database project. Derby is an open source file-based relational database system that has strong SQL support. It is fully implemented in Java. This component was removed from JDK version 9, but people interested in it can still download it from the Derby website (https://db.apache.org/derby/).
include	This directory is for advanced programmers. It contains headers for C compilers that can be used to call platform- or operating-system-specific native code from Java code or vice versa.
jre	Here, all the files related to JRE are stored, including Java Class Library. Note that all the commands from the jre/bin directory are also placed in JDK's bin subdirectory.
lib	Libraries used by certain development tools are stored here.

JDK commands

The `bin` directory contains the primary command-line-driven commands that are supplied with JDK. You'll see the most important ones here; not all commands listed below will be discussed further in this book:

Executable command	Description
`java`	Loads a JVM instance and starts the program specified on the command line. This command will be discussed in much more detail in the next paragraph. On Windows systems, this opens a Console text window while the application is running.
`javac`	This is the Java language compiler.
`javadoc`	This extracts documentation from Java source files and generates documentation. We will discuss this briefly in the next chapter.
`javap`	This disassembles the compiled Java code into a readable text format that resembles raw Java bytecode.
`javaw`	This is supplied with the Windows version of JDK and JRE only. It is the same as the `java` command; the only difference is that this version does not open any additional windows itself. If the launched application features a desktop GUI, then the application will still open its own windows.
`jar`	This is the tool to create a new, extract data from, or add files to existing JAR archive files. JAR archive files will be explained in more detail later in this chapter.
`jarsigner`	This protects JAR files by adding a digital signature to them. If the data inside a JAR file is modified without updating the signature, it will no longer be considered valid.
`jdeps`	This outputs dependency information of a JVM-compiled `.class` file or a JAR file.
`jjs`	This launches Oracle Nashorn's interactive interpreter shell. Nashorn is Oracle's JavaScript interpreter and will be discussed in the appendix.

Note that the `bin` directory contains more commands than what's listed in the preceding table. Most of these are applicable only to advanced or specific use cases.

GUI monitoring tools

Three tools that are installed on the `bin` subdirectory but were not listed in the previous table deserve a mention. Unlike the other commands that were specified, these tools offer a full desktop GUI:

- Java VisualVM
- Oracle Mission Control
- JConsole

 Only Oracle's JDK implementation contains all three tools. The open source OpenJDK implementation misses Oracle Mission Control, while none of the mentioned tools are part of IBM J9's JDK.

Java VisualVM

Oracle's JDK and the open source OpenJDK implementations both included the Java VisualVM tool until version 8. VisualVM is an open source tool to monitor JVM instances of each running JVM application. Its built-in features can be further enhanced by installing plugins. The users of Oracle JDK or OpenJDK 9 can download this open source tool from `ht tps://visualvm.github.io/index.html`.

To launch VisualVM with its default settings, type:

```
jvisualvm
```

First, a splash window is displayed, and after a while, VisualVM's main window appears. VisualVM can not only connect to running JVM instances on a network server, but also to locally running JVM instances. In the following screenshot, I was monitoring a locally running NetBeans IDE instance:

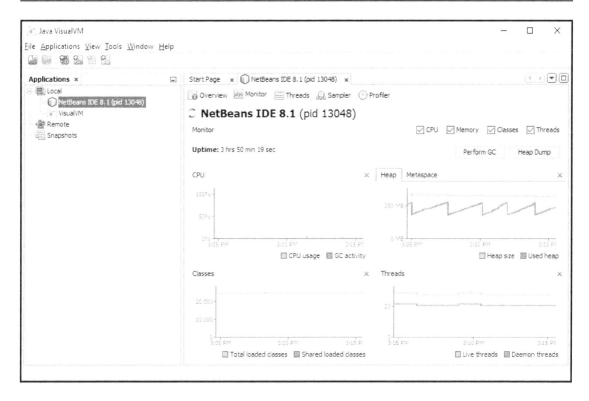

Setting up a JVM instance for remote monitoring takes some effort; it is out of the scope of this book but documented in the VisualVM section of the JDK documentation.

Real-time monitoring always takes up lots of system resources. The monitoring of local processes should only be considered in a development environment. Remote monitoring normally consumes less, but still considerable, server resources.

Oracle Mission Control

Oracle's recent JDK versions come with the **Oracle Mission Control** tool, another tool to monitor JVM instances and running applications. Oracle Mission Control offers an even better user interface than Java VisualVM; otherwise, it has many similar features, including real-time monitoring of running JVM instances and applications.

Oracle Mission Control is proprietary software and has somewhat complicated license terms. Most of its features can be used free of charge, both for development and production use. Its most unique and desirable feature, Java Flight Recorder, can only be freely used in a development environment, though. Using this feature in a production scenario requires a paid license key from Oracle.

To run Oracle Mission Control, execute the following command:

```
jmc
```

With Java Flight Recorder, events from JVM can be recorded for a set time period. After the recording stops, all the recorded data can be analyzed. The advantage of Java Flight Recorder is that it has much less overhead than the real-time monitoring feature of both Oracle Mission Control and VisualVM; therefore, it is much safer to use on production systems (but again, don't forget about its license terms). In the following screenshot, I ran Flight Recorder on the NetBeans IDE process for a minute:

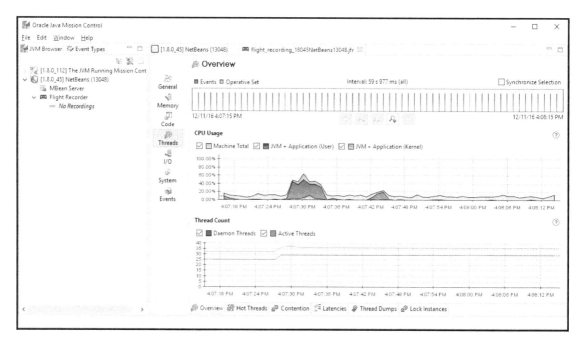

JConsole

JConsole is the oldest monitoring tool that has been bundled with JDK for a long time. Both Java VisualVM and Oracle Mission Control have more features and offer a friendlier GUI. We recommend that you use other tools instead of this one.

If you still want to run JConsole, you can start it with the following command:

```
jconsole
```

JRE

To just run Java programs on a computer, install JRE. It installs the `java` command that launches a JVM instance and the full Java Class Library, and it is used to start applications written in Java or other languages.

JDK installs JRE as part of its installation when using the default installation settings. JRE must only be downloaded separately and installed on computers that will not need development tools.

Mac computers running on older versions of OS X (before Apple rebranded it to macOS) used to come with a Java runtime version preinstalled, but this is not the case anymore since Oracle has taken over the development of macOS's Java SE implementation from Apple.

Two versions of the Java SE 8 JRE are available from the Oracle website:

- JRE
- Server JRE

JRE is supposed to be installed on 32-bit or 64-bit end user desktop machines (note that the 32-bit version is not available for all platforms), while Server JRE is meant to be installed on servers only by advanced system administrators. Server JRE is available to 64-bit systems only and does not include an installer or browser plugins, but it adds the JVM monitoring tools that we discussed earlier.

Class organization with packages

All JVM languages define their own syntaxes for creating classes and instantiating objects, but in the end, they produce class files that would run on the JVM. In order to be able to run on the JVM and be able to offer interoperability with classes written in other languages on the JVM platform, they have to follow JVM's requirements for organizing classes. We'll discuss the following topics:

- Packages
- Choosing a package
- Package examples
- Fully qualified class names

 Knowledge of packages is required to understand the organization of the Java Class Library and how to run JVM applications on the command line. Both these topics are discussed in this chapter.

What are packages?

Most languages covered in this book support grouping classes in packages. Classes that are grouped inside a package form a unique namespace. This is the fundamental feature of a JVM. Some languages cannot group classes in a package themselves, but they still support referencing classes inside a package.

An example is Oracle's Nashorn JavaScript interpreter. The JavaScript language itself does not support packages, but Nashorn can still import existing Java (or compatible) classes that are put in packages.

To demonstrate how classes can be organized in a package, let's look at an implementation of a basket in an e-commerce application again, but this time a little bit more developed example than the previous time.

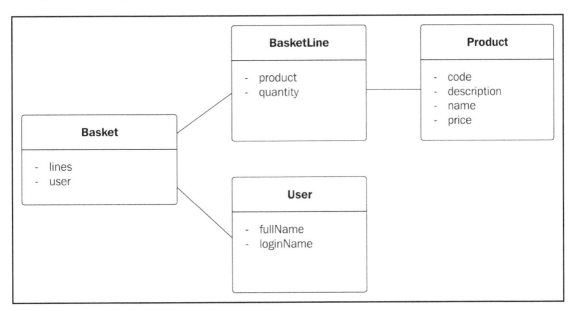

JVM offers a way to organize classes by placing them in packages. By doing this, classes with the same theme can be grouped together. In the example illustrated just now, it would make sense to group classes in the following packages:

Package	Classes in package
basket	Basket BasketLine
product	Product
user	User

I chose this organization because I consider **basket**, **product**, and **user** as the main themes of these classes. Also, I expect that the **Basket**, **Product**, and **User** classes will be used by several other classes in future, and the **BasketLine** class will only be used internally by the **Basket** class.

Packages not only make the structure of larger projects easier to understand, as we will see shortly, but also hide class members from classes in other packages, using access modifiers.

To make efficient usage of packages, you should understand the convention that almost all major JVM projects follow. Although package names, as chosen in the preceding table, are perfectly valid, there's a convention that is recommended when naming packages.

Choosing a package name

There are a few rules that package names must follow:

- A package name can contain dots; in fact, dots are used to separate elements in a name.
- An element in a package name can contain letters, digits, and an underscore.
- Each element in the package name must start with a letter, not a digit. Digits are only allowed after a letter.
- An element in the package name cannot be the same as a keyword reserved by the Java language. This includes the names of primitive types (such as `int`, `short`) and built-in keywords (for example `class`, `for`, or `final`).

There are a few universal naming conventions that most major projects adhere to. It is strongly recommended that you follow these for each package in all your projects:

- The complete package name should be in lowercase.
- Start your package name with the reversed Internet URL of either:
  - Your company's site
  - Your project's site URL
  - Your project's public source code repository URL
  - Your personal home page or blog URL
- You can come up with your own conventions to differentiate classes and prevent naming conflicts between projects. You could add a department name, office region, or project name to your package name.
- If you have an illegal element in your package name, put an underscore before or after the conflicting element to make it legal and/or replace the illegal character with an underscore.

Package name examples

Imagine you are hired to develop an online web programming class for the *JVM University* school and the class would, hypothetically, be accessible via `http://www.example.com/jvm-university`.

Valid package names in this scenario could be:

- `com.example.jvm_university.class_.web_programming`
- `com.example.jvm_university.webprogramming`
- `com.example.jvm.university.web_programming`

Fully qualified class name

In some situations, a fully qualified class name is required. This is the class name prefixed with the full package name. Let's look at an example:

```
package com.example.jvm.university.web_programming;
class Application {
}
```

The fully qualified class name for the preceding class is
`com.example.jvm.university.web_programming.Application`.

Java Class Library

The Java Class Library is also simply known as the Java API. It's a huge collection of prebuilt classes that is distributed with the Java SE platform. Some of the more important themes of the library include:

- Definitions and implementations of common data structures
- Console I/O
- File I/O
- Mathematics
- Networking
- Regular expressions
- XML creation and processing
- Database access
- GUI toolkits
- Reflection

We cannot cover the complete Java Class Library here, but we want to give some examples of the APIs that are available and give you pointers on where to find the classes you need. Before we look at specific classes, we will take a look at the main organization. We'll cover the following topics:

- Java Class Library organization
- Package overview
- Fundamental classes from the java.lang package
- Collections API, namely `java.util.ArrayList` and `java.util.HashMap`

Java Class Library organization

All the classes of the library are put in packages. The most important package names start with either:

- `java`
- `javax`

The distinction between the two is mostly for historical reasons. Modern, reputable Java SE implementations implement classes from both the packages. There are more public classes, though. A few assorted classes are put in packages that start with `org`, such as `org.w3c` and `org.xml`, but we'll ignore these classes in this book.

Vendors have the freedom to add their own classes to their library. In the case of Oracle's implementation, these classes reside in packages that start with the `com.sun`, `sun`, or `com.oracle` prefix. However, it is recommended that you use add-on libraries instead of the classes in these packages.

Package overview

To give you an idea of how the classes are grouped, here's an overview of the most important packages of the library. It's not the complete list, but it's meant as a teaser and to familiarize you with the structure of the Java Class Library.

Package(s)	Description
`java.lang`	This class is considered fundamental. It contains the `String` and `StringBuilder` classes, primitive wrappers, threading, and the mother of all objects: Object.
`java.lang.reflect`	This offers APIs for reflection. Reflection makes it possible to dynamically look at classes to look up method and variable names, invoke methods, and read or write attributes.
`java.uil`	This is one of the most important packages. It contains classes that implement collections, date and time, internationalization, and many others.
`java.util.concurrent`	This contains classes for concurrent programming.

java.io	These are classes for the operating system, file, and networking I/O. It also contains character-set encoding/decoding classes.
java.net	
java.nio	
java.math	This offers the `BigDecimal` class, which is much more precise than the primitive `float` and `double` types and the `BigInteger` class, which can hold much larger integer values than the `int` and `long` primitive types.
java.xml	This refers to the XML processing classes.
java.sql	This contains classes to work with the JDBC database system.
javax.sql	
java.awt	This is Abstract Window Toolkit, the earliest Java GUI toolkit. It offers a layer between the native GUI of the operating system and the JVM.
javax.swing	This refers to the Swing GUI toolkit classes, built on top of the AWT toolkit. A big difference with AWT is that all the GUI controls are implemented in the Java code in them.
javafx	This refers to the JavaFX GUI toolkit classes. This is a very modern offering of 3D accelerated graphics.

Fundamental classes of the java.lang package

Since the classes in the `java.lang` package are considered fundamental to the JVM platform, many classes of this package will be mentioned regularly in the chapters that follow. This section is not meant to replace the Java API docs but to give some insight and background information. The classes that will be discussed here are:

- The Object class (`java.lang.Object`)
- The String class (`java.lang.String`)
- Primitive wrapper classes (Integer, Long, Short, Char, Float, and Double from java.lang)
- Exceptions and errors (`java.lang.Exception` and `java.lang.`)

Here's a class hierarchy diagram of the classes that are discussed here:

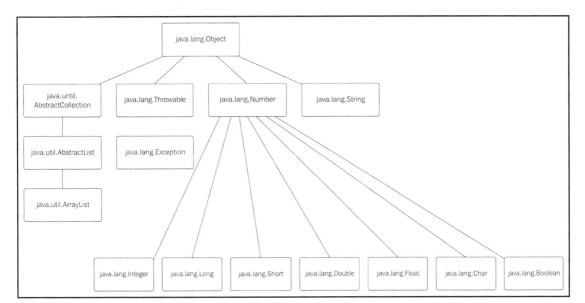

We will look at a lot more classes of the library during the course of this book.

The Object class (java.lang.Object)

The Object class in the `java.lang` package is the mother class of all other classes. It's the only class on a JVM that does not have a parent class itself. In the Java language, any class that does not explicitly inherit another class inherits the `java.lang.Object` class implicitly.

Important object methods

The most commonly used methods of `java.lang.Object` are:

Method name	Return type	Description
`toString()`	String	This returns the textual description of the object.
`equals(Object object)`	boolean	This returns whether the passed object is considered equal to the current object. There are several rules that will be explained later.
`hashCode()`	int	This is called when a hash value of the current class is required. It will be explained in the collections API section.

One of the more important methods that object (and therefore every other JVM object) offers is the `toString()` method that returns a textual description of the current object instance. Oracle's default implementation returns the fully qualified class name plus the object's `hashCode()` result in hexadecimal format, but classes are encouraged to override this method and provide a better readable description of their content.

The `equals()` and `hashCode()` methods are used extensively in the `Collection` API; We'll look at their usage in detail.

Refer to the full API documentation for the list of all the methods of the `java.lang.Object` class.

The String class (java.lang.String)

The `java.lang.String` class represents a JVM's `String` type. It is an immutable object, meaning that changes to the `String` object do not change the original object but produce a new string with the modified content. Strings are always stored internally in UTF-16 encoding.

This class will be covered in more detail in the next chapter. Some languages covered in this book have their own unique string classes that add convenient methods and other unique features to the language's string object. Usually, JVM languages transparently convert between the two string types under the hood.

Primitive wrapper classes (Integer, Long, Short, Char, Float, Double in java.lang)

Not all APIs on the Java platform can work with a JVM's built-in primitive datatypes. When passing a primitive datatype variable, if a primitive wrapper class is required, compilers that support this technique will automatically create an instance of the corresponding wrapper class. The reverse of this situation is also true: when a primitive variable is required and a wrapper object is assigned to it, then the compiler will automatically assign the value of the wrapper class to the primitive variable. This process is called **autoboxing**.

 Not all JVM languages support autoboxing, but most popular ones do, including all the languages covered in this book.

Like the `String` class, all these classes are immutable. When you call methods that modify a value, a new instance is created and returned with the new value.

As mentioned in the previous chapter, some JVM languages follow the "everything is an object" object-orientated programming rule and do not support the creation of primitive datatypes. These languages also use wrapper classes when primitive values are used.

Autoboxing examples

Let's pass a primitive integer to a reference type variable that expects an instance of the `java.lang.Integer` class:

```
int primitiveInt = 42;
Integer wrappedInteger = primitiveInt;
```

A new `Integer` object will be instantiated that could wrap the `42` primitive integer value. This will have the same effect as that of creating a new `Integer` instance yourself:

```
Integer wrappedInteger = new Integer(42);
```

Specifying two Integer instances to an API that requires two primitive int values as parameters also works as expected:

```
System.out.println("Hello world".substring(new Integer(0),
                    new Integer(5)));
```

This will print `Hello`.

Exceptions and errors (java.lang.Exception and java.lang.Error)

Every JVM developer should know how runtime errors are managed on a JVM. Since all languages offer their own mechanisms to handle runtime errors, we will not cover how to handle errors here. We will describe what happens when a runtime error occurs.

When a runtime error occurs inside a method, an exception or Error object is created and thrown. In the Java language, this is done using the `throw` keyword. Let's look at an example when a class throws a generic `Exception` class:

```
throw new Exception("Oops!");
```

Java comes with a lot of built-in classes that inherit either `Exception` or `Error` classes. When you consider creating a new `Exception` subclass, it makes sense to first look for an exception that can be reused. For example, if your method cannot except null references, it should throw a `java.lang.NullPointerException` object instance when null is passed; all good Java APIs do this when null references are provided to a method that cannot support them.

 If you study the class diagram at the beginning of this section carefully, you'll see that both the classes inherit the `Throwable` class. A `Throwable` object can be thrown, but usually, their subclasses are used as they are more convenient to use.

The distinction between the `Exception` and `Error` class is as follows:

- Exceptions are thrown by classes when there's a good chance that the program can handle the error and continue running.
- Errors are thrown when a problem is detected that cannot be really anticipated. Many errors are thrown by the JVM itself.

When an exception or error object is thrown (an exception is assumed from now on), JVMs look at the method that threw the exception. If it contains an error handler that can handle the error, control is transferred to that error handler. If the method does not handle any errors, or not this particular one, then the caller of that method is checked for an error handler. This continues until a method is found that could handle the error without throwing a new one or the first method call is reached. In the latter case, the JVM instance will crash and produce a stack trace such as the following:

```
Exception in thread "main" java.lang.Exception: Oops
  at ExceptionDemo.method3(ExceptionDemo.java:37)
  at ExceptionDemo.method2(ExceptionDemo.java:33)
  at ExceptionDemo.method1(ExceptionDemo.java:29)
  at ExceptionDemo.main(ExceptionDemo.java:25)
```

Many languages compile their source code filenames and line numbers with the generated Java bytecode. This has the advantage that source code line numbers can be returned to the stack trace. This results in readable stack traces.

Java has strict rules for throwing exceptions; not every class can throw all exceptions. Many other JVM languages are much more relaxed in this regard. Java's rules and the important role of the `java.lang.RuntimeException` class in the Java language will be explained in the next chapter.

The Collections API - java.util.ArrayList and java.util.HashMap

The java.util package contains a great assortment of data structures. Only two will be covered here, but we will mention the others from time to time. Some JVM languages use their own variations of these classes that offer additional functionality, but most languages work with the classes discussed here for maximal compatibility with both Java and JVM platforms in general.

Many languages support a technique called **generics**, that limits the types of objects that an object can use. In the case of `Collection` classes, these limit the objects that can be stored inside a collection class. As many languages have different notation rules for generics, this topic will be explained for each language separately and ignored for now. Clojure is one example of a language that is covered in this book that currently does not support generics at all.

It is worth noting that the `Collection` classes only work with objects. When primitive values are used, they are autoboxed into the object and vice versa; this is applicable if the used JVM language could use primitive values. Autoboxing was discussed when we talked about primitive value wrapper classes earlier.

The two Collections classes that we will cover are:

- `java.util.ArrayList` (a list class, backed internally by an array)
- `java.util.HashMap` (a container for key/value combinations)

 Python programmers will recognize these as `list` and `dict` types, respectively, while Ruby programmers will compare them with Ruby's `Array` and `Hash` objects.

ArrayList (java.util.ArrayList)

This is a fairly simple and convenient class to work with. As the name implies, it implements the List structure that can hold other objects.

While the JVM platform and most JVM languages have built-in array support, the `ArrayList` object is easier to work with. A couple of advantages of `ArrayList` over normal arrays are as follows:

- The `ArrayList` object will automatically grow when it is full and more space is needed. Arrays have to be managed manually.
- Arrays only offer one attribute (to get the size of the array), while the `ArrayList` class offers a lot of convenient methods.

 Although the arrays on a JVM do not have built-in methods, Java offers the `java.util.Arrays` class with many methods to make working with arrays easier. Some JVM languages even add methods to arrays.

Let's look at some methods and example code.

Commonly used methods of the ArrayList class

These are some of the most important methods that an `ArrayList` object offers. Note that, when using generics, the `ArrayList` object will not work with objects but the specified type.

Method name	Return type	Description
add(Object o)	boolean	This adds a new object to the internal list (usually backed by an array).
add(int index, Object o)	-	This adds a new object at a specific position in the list.
addAll(Collection c)	boolean	With this function, all the entries of a collection can be added to the current list. Here, Collection is an interface that many classes from the collections API implement.
clear()	-	This clears all the content.
contains(Object o)	Object	This returns whether or not the specified object is in the list.
get(int index)	Object	This retrieves the object at the specified index.
set (int index, Object o)	Object	This replaces the item at the specified index with the passed object.
size()	int	This returns the number of elements in the list.

ArrayList usage example

Here's a simple Java language example that demonstrates some of the ArrayList methods:

```
ArrayList list1 = new ArrayList();
list1.add("this is a test");
list1.add(0, "Hello");

ArrayList list2 = new ArrayList();
list2.addAll(list1);
list1.clear();

System.out.println(list1);
System.out.println(list2);
System.out.println(list2.contains("this is a test"));
```

Its output would be:

```
[]
[Hello, this is a test]
true
```

The first line prints `[]` to indicate `list1` was empty, and `list2` contains two Strings (in this order): `Hello` and `this is a test`. Finally, the word `true` will be printed to the console because `this is a test` is stored inside `list2` of the `ArrayList` object.

HashMap (java.util.HashMap)

HashMap stores key/value combinations. On a JVM, this data structure is called a map. When inserting objects to a map, both the key object and value object are specified. With the key object, the value can be retrieved. This version of the structure does not keep the original order of the keys.

Technically, HashMap works by hashing the key object and storing it in such a way that the key can be quickly searched. Then a value is stored that is associated with the key. We will take a more detailed look at the working of this class after looking at some common methods and example code.

Commonly used methods of the HashMap class

The `HashMap` class offers a lot of methods. The most commonly used ones are printed in the following table, but be sure to check out the full API documentation once you seriously start using the `HashMap` class:

Method name	Return type	Description
`put (Object key, Object value)`	Object	This is to add a new key and value pair. If the key already exists, then the corresponding value is overwritten with the passed value. It returns null if the key is already added; otherwise, it returns the existing value.
`putAll (Map map)`	-	This adds all the key/value pairs from the specified map, again overwriting values when the keys already exist.

putIfAbsent (Object key, Object value)	Object	This adds a key and value only if the key does not exist. If the key already exists, then it does nothing. It returns null when keys/values are added or it returns the value object if the key already exists.
remove (Object key)	Object	This removes the specified key and value pairs if the key can be found. Otherwise, it does nothing.
containsKey (Object key)	boolean	This returns whether the key is currently in the map.
get (Object key)	Object	This returns the value associated with the key, or it returns null when the key is not found.
getOrDefault (Object key, Object defaultValue)	Object	This returns the associated value if the key can be found; otherwise, it returns the passed defaultValue.
clear()	-	This empties the collection; all the key/value pairs will be removed.
size()	int	This returns the number of key/value pairs that the Map currently stores.

HashMap usage example

Here's the Java code that demonstrates some basic HashMap usage:

```
HashMap map = new HashMap();

map.put("key1", "value1");
map.put("key1", "value2");
map.putIfAbsent("key1", "value3");

System.out.println(map.get("key1"));
System.out.println(map.containsKey("value2"));
System.out.println(map.size());
```

This would print:

```
value2
false
1
```

The first printed line is `value2` because the second `map.put` call overwrote the first `value1` value with `value2` and the `map.putIfAbsent` method call did nothing. It printed `false` as its second line because the `map.containsKey` method only looks for keys. The final printed line is `1` because only one key/value pair was stored.

Preparing your classes for the Collections API

As we saw earlier, two important methods of the mother class `java.lang.Object` are:

- `hashCode()`
- `equals(Object other)`

These methods are used extensively by all the collections APIs. For performance reasons, and to ensure that the APIs work as expected, it is important that classes that are put inside a `Collection` object override these methods and provide a good implementation for both. Java programmers who define their own classes must write implementations for both methods themselves; all the other languages covered in this book generally generate implementations for both methods automatically when defining a class.

 If you don't like the `hashCode()` and `equals()` versions that your JVM language generated for you, then most languages allow you to override the methods manually so that you can still provide your own implementations.

Because Java programmers are the most likely candidates to provide their own implementations, the exact rules that both the methods need to follow are explained in the Java chapter. However, we will still take a quick look at these methods so that we can see how hashing mechanisms are used by many `Collection` classes.

About hashCode()

As the name suggests, this method is called when a hash of the object in question is needed.

The `hashCode()` method is supposed to return an integer value that changes when the content of the object changes. Also, if possible, it should return a value that, ideally, is distinct from other similar objects.

It's not an error to return a value that does not identify the object, but this will negatively impact the performance of most `Collection` classes. This is explained in more detail below.

About equals ()

The `equals()` method returns `true` when the passed object is considered the same as the object that the caller of the method used, otherwise it returns `false`. A simple example is as follows:

```
Integer i = 25;
Object o = new Object();
System.out.println(i.equals(o));
```

The example above will print `false` to the console.

The `equals()` method is expected to match both objects and return whether the objects are similar. There are many rules that this method has to adhere to. Again, these are explained in the Java chapter, as typically Java developers will have to write these methods themselves.

 If a class does not provide an implementation that would follow all the rules (also called **contract**) of the `equals()` method, then the correct working of the `Collection` classes cannot be guaranteed.

The hashing mechanism

To demonstrate why both the `hashCode()` and `equals()` methods are so important, let's check out an example.

Consider the following Java code that creates a `HashMap` instance and adds a key/value pair:

```
map = HashMap();
map.put("key1", "value1");
```

The `hashCode()` method will be called on the passed key object, in this case, the String instance `key1`. This will result in an arbitrary number that can be used for hashing, in this example, **123**. Internally, the `HashMap` instance stores the hash of the key in such a way that it will be able to quickly look it up, and it will link both the key and value objects to it.

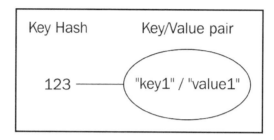

A new key/value pair `key2` and `value2` are added to the map now. Assume that the `hashCode()` method of the `key2` object would return **234**. This hash code was not used earlier, so a new hash code key value is added and the specified key and value objects are associated with it.

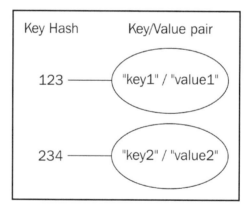

Now, when you add the new `key3` and `value3` pairs, something unexpected happens. The `hashCode()` method of the `key3` String instance returns 234. This hash code points to both the key2/value2 and key3/value3 pairs. This is called a **collision**.

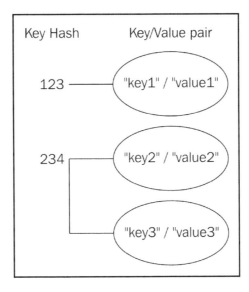

The program requests the value object that corresponds to the key3 key object:

```
Object o = map.get("key3");
```

The HashMap object will call the hashCode() method of the passed key, "key3", which will return 234 again. The HashMap object sees that this hash code is associated with two Key/Value pairs and will, therefore, call the equals() method of both the "key2" and "key3" String objects to determine which of the passed keys match with the "key3" String. In this case, "key3" matches and the "value3" object is returned.

What you learned from this example is that the hashCode() and equals() methods are really important. The fewer the number of collisions that occur when adding key/value pairs, the quicker the keys will be found. If the equals() method implementation is buggy, then the key lookup process will fail as well.

Running JVM applications on the command line

Running applications on a JVM is often considered a fairly complex topic. As mentioned in the previous chapter, compilers that target a JVM compile their source code to binary files with a `.class` file extension. There are a few rules that must be followed before you can have a JVM instance run the code inside the `.class` files:

- At least one class must have a static `main()` method
- All the class files should be stored in specific directories
- The ClassPath has to be specified
- Class files can optionally be placed inside a JAR archive container
- To run the program, the `java` command is used

We will take a quick look at each rule. Then, to demonstrate these concepts as clearly as possible, we will be doing a hands-on demonstration project in Java.

At least one class must have a static main() method

When running a JVM application manually with the `java` command, you'll need to specify the class that has the following static method:

```java
public static void main(String[] args) {
}
```

This is the method that will be called by the `java` command after the JVM instance has finished initializing. It is comparable to C's and C++'s well-known `main()` entry point function. The string array `args` will contain the command-line parameters as passed by the operating system.

The preceding snippet illustrates Java code. Some JVM languages do not require the programmer to write this method manually; they automatically generate one when compiling the class. Also, some JVM frameworks automatically generate or provide this method.

There can be slight variations of the `main()` method, though:

- The name of the method's parameter is not important. The `args` is the convention. Sometimes `argv` is used, but something similar to arguments would also be fine.
- There can be variations of the argument type. A string array (in Java, `String[]`) is usually used, but a var args parameter (`String...`, covered in the next chapter) would work as well.

Here's an example of a valid `main()` function in Java with the string's var args parameter type and a different argument name:

```
public static void main(String... commandLineArguments) { }
```

There can be more than one class with a static `main()` method in your project. But only one can run at a time. The fully qualified class name must be specified on the command-line when running the application with the `java` command.

Required directory structure for class files

Class files will have to be stored in a directory structure that matches their package name. Each dot in the package name means a new subdirectory. Classes that are not put in a package are placed in the root directory that contains the initial package subdirectories.

Let's assume a project with the following fully qualified class names:

- `Main`
- `com.example.app.model.MyModel`
- `com.example.app.view.MyView`
- `com.example.app.controller.MyController`

When compiled, the directory structure should look like this:

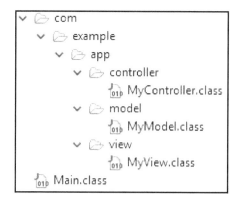

Avoid having classes in your project that are not inside a package. In the preceding example, the `Main` class should ideally have been put in a package.

It must be noted that the compiler usually creates the correct directory structure in order to better understand the ClassPath topic. It is important to be familiar with the requirements described here. Also, note that some compilers, including Java, require that the source code is organized in the same way.

Setting ClassPath for a JVM instance

ClassPath is a list of directories and/or individual JAR archive files that a JVM uses to find the classes referenced in the project. It is required by the `java` command, compilers (Java and most other JVM languages), and many other JDK- and JVM-related tools.

When you don't set a ClassPath explicitly, it defaults to the current directory. If all the class files that are used by the project are stored in the directory that is used to launch the program and the class file's package name matches the directory structure, then it's not necessary to set a ClassPath explicitly.

In the real world, you will use add-on libraries often. As mentioned in the previous chapter, many JVM languages require a runtime library to be loaded; without it, the application will not be able to run. It is a convention to put such add-on library files (often called **dependencies**) in a separate subdirectory. When a library is placed inside a JAR file, as is often the case, you have no other choice than to specify it on the ClassPath, as JVM never attempts to load JAR files automatically.

Let's look at a real-world example. This is the ClassPath that the open source Apache TomCat application server on my Windows machine requires in order to start:

```
C:\apache-tomcat-8.0.44\bin\bootstrap.jar;C:\apache-
tomcat-8.0.44\bin\tomcat-juli.jar
```

The classes that Apache TomCat requires to start are apparently placed inside two JAR files: `bootstrap.jar` and `tomcat-juli.jar`. They are stored in the `bin` directory of Apache Tomcat's . As will be discussed in more detail later, a JAR file contains a collection of class files inside a single file.

Both the absolute and relative paths can be specified for a directory or JAR file. The start point of relative paths is the directory from where the command (for example, `java` or `javac`) is launched. All entries on a ClassPath are read from left to right until the class is found. The order of entries is therefore very important.

Setting a ClassPath can be done on multiple levels. JVM determines a used ClassPath in the following order:

- If the value of the `CLASSPATH` environmental variable is set, it is taken.
- If the `-cp` or `-classpath` command-line option is specified on the `java` (or other JDK tools, such as the `javac` Java compiler) command, then that one is taken. Other tools may require different command-line options.

 Setting the `CLASSPATH` environmental variable is not really recommended, as it becomes difficult to manage when you want to run multiple JVM applications simultaneously.

Most major JVM applications include simple operating system shell scripts (for Linux/macOS) and batch files (for Windows) that set the ClassPath automatically, so that the end-user can start the program simply by launching a script. Some applications even include a native executable file that sets the correct ClassPath and launches the JVM invisibly under the hood; it also hides the fact that the application uses a JVM.

To make it easier for developers to launch their JVM application while testing or developing their applications, most build tools often offer a task (or a plugin that implements this task) that sets the ClassPath automatically and launches the application with a single command. We will investigate this handy feature of the popular Gradle build tool in `Chapter 4`, *Java Programming*.

Placing class files inside a JAR archive

For convenience, a collection of class files can be archived into a single JAR file. A JAR file is a standard ZIP file with a different file extension, but unlike ZIP files, JAR files have strict rules regulating their content. When a JAR file is put on the ClassPath, all the classes that are placed inside the JAR file will be loaded and made available to the JVM instance.

We won't be discussing the creation of JAR archives in this chapter, but we will look at this topic in `Chapter 4`, *Java Programming*, when we build a hands-on Java language example.

 A JAR file may require its own external dependencies. If this is the case, then those dependencies must also be put on the ClassPath. This is usually mentioned in the documentation of the library or tool that provides the JAR file.

Runnable JAR file

A JAR file can be set up in such a way that it could be started using the `java` command. This is only possible if the JAR file was configured correctly to allow this. In this case, the JAR file specifies which class contains the `main()` method that will be run by the `java` command.

This is a convenient feature for end users, as a single JAR file is completely self-contained:

- A JAR file contains all the required dependencies
- Manually setting the ClassPath is not necessary (or even possible) at all
- A user does not have to manually tell the JVM which class contains the `main()` method

 There are limitations: a runnable JAR file cannot find classes that are not placed inside the JAR file. The usual ClassPath cannot be used by classes inside those JAR files.

Running a program with the java command

The `java` command is used to launch a JVM instance and start the application. There are basically two situations:

- Run a project consisting of separate class files
- Run a project that is stored inside a runnable JAR file

We will also take a look at some important parameters of the `java` command.

Run a project consisting of separate class files

When the project is stored in directories that contain class files (even when the project uses JAR files for its dependencies), the `java` command is normally invoked with a command like this:

```
java -cp "CLASSPATH" MAINCLASS ARGUMENTS
```

Substitute `CLASSPATH` with the used class path and `MAINCLASS` with the fully qualified class name that contains the static `main()` method. If the class supports arguments, they can be specified by substituting `ARGUMENTS` with the required arguments.

Let's have a look at a real-world example. This is a slightly simplified example, taken from a Windows batch script that is supplied with Oracle JDK's JavaDB component. It starts the Apache Derby Network Server when launched from the `db` subdirectory of the JDK's installation directory:

```
java -cp
"lib\derby.jar;lib\derbynet.jar;lib\derbyclient.jar;lib\derbytools.jar;lib\
derbyoptionaltools.jar" org.apache.derby.drda.NetworkServerControl start
```

It clearly demonstrates that all the required JAR files are specified one by one on the class path, as the JVM instance will never try to load a JAR file that was not put on the class path explicitly. The fully qualified class name that has the `static void main()` function is `org.apache.derby.drda.NetworkServerControl` and the passed command-line argument to the main function is `start`. Since each class path entry specified a specific JAR file and not just a directory, the mentioned class must have been placed inside one of the specified JAR files.

In modern versions of the JRE, it is possible to specify wildcards. This will also load JAR files that can be matched. Preceding example can be simplified to the following:

```
java -cp "lib\*" org.apache.derby.drda.NetworkServerControl start
```

The wildcard * is required to load JAR files. When only specifying a directory name, without a wildcard, JAR files in that directory will not be added to the ClassPath, only .class files will be added.

Running a project that is placed inside a runnable JAR file

For JAR files that are properly configured to run automatically (as discussed earlier, not every JAR file is), you can use this form of the java command:

```
java -jar PATH
```

Substitute PATH with the path, either absolute or relative to the corresponding JAR file. If the JAR file is configured correctly, the program will now run.

Note that setting a class path is not possible on this form. A JAR archive file is required to include all the required dependencies. The CLASSPATH environmental variable and the -cp and -classpath parameters of the java command will be ignored.

Other useful parameters of the java command

Simply start java without any options to see the full list of available options.

Some noteworthy ones are:

- *-D* to pass properties and values
- *-ea* to enable assertions

Some options have both a short and long form; only the short form is shown here. Also note that parameters are case-sensitive.

-D to pass properties and values

-D is used to set properties. Properties are strings that can be read inside code and can be specified to the JVM in multiple ways, including this parameter. This parameter can be specified multiple times: one for each parameter/value combination that you want to pass to the program.

Here's an example of this:

```
java -cp CLASSPATH -DProperty1=Value1 -DProperty2=Value2 MAINCLASS
```

Properties can be read in the code with the getProperty method of the java.lang.System class, which is also used in the following example to read predefined system properties.

-ea to enable assertions

With this option, assertions can be enabled (by default, they are turned off).

In a language that supports assertions, the programmer can add runtime conditional checks. In Java, this is done by adding an assert statement, followed by a condition. When assertions are disabled, these statements are ignored completely, but when enabled, the JVM throws an error if the condition turns out to be false. This can be used to check whether the program works as expected. An example of an assert statement in Java:

```
int i = 25;

assert i < 24;
```

When assertions are enabled with the -ea option, the preceding code will result in a java.lang.Error instance thrown by the JVM once the assert statement runs. When not explicitly specified on the command line, the preceding code will run fine.

Assertions can be enabled globally and also per package with the -ea:PACKAGE form, where PACKAGE must be substituted with the full package name. You can add the -ea:PACKAGE option to each package that you want assertions enabled for.

Writing unit tests is considered a better mechanism to thoroughly test code, but asserts can still come in handy in some situations.

A hands-on example project to run on JVM

Let's create a slightly over-engineered program that prints some JVM information to the console and consists of three classes. We will not use an IDE but a normal text editor and the Command Prompt (Windows) or Terminal screen (macOS/Linux) to compile the code. Finally, we will run the application on the command line as well. The classes in the project are put in the following packages:

- com.example.app
- com.example.app.model
- com.example.app.view

Create a root directory where you will store both the source files and the compiled files. In this directory, create both src and bin subdirectories.

In the src directory, create the following subdirectories:

- com
- com\example
- com\example\app
- com\example\app\model
- com\example\app\view

Launch your favorite text editor, and in the model subdirectory, create a ModelFoo.java file with the following content:

```
package com.example.app.model;

public class ModelFoo {
  public String getJVMInfo() {
    return "JVM version " + System.getProperty("java.version") +
    " by " + System.getProperty("java.vendor");
  }
}
```

The ModelFoo class contains one public method that returns String with some information about the used JVM. In case you're wondering, the System class is always available in Java, as will be explained in the Java chapter. Its static getProperty() method returns the values of properties - the two used here are both built-in properties that return the JRE version and vendor, respectively.

In the `view` subdirectory, create the `ViewBar.java` file:

```
package com.example.app.view;
import com.example.app.model.ModelFoo;

public class ViewBar {
  public void showJVMInfo(ModelFoo model) {
    System.out.println("This program is running on " +
                       model.getJVMInfo());
  }
}
```

This class simply prints the version information supplied by the model object to the console.

Finally, create the `Controller.java` file in the `app` subdirectory:

```
package com.example.app;
import com.example.app.model.ModelFoo;
import com.example.app.view.ViewBar;

public class Controller {
  public static void main(String[] args) {
    ViewBar view = new ViewBar();
    view.showJVMInfo(new ModelFoo());
  }
}
```

The `Controller` class glues the two other classes together and contains the `main()` method. This is not a very good example of a Model-View-Controller design pattern implementation; I cut some corners to save space.

Note that the `src` subdirectory structure follows the package names. This is a convention of Java; some other languages do not follow this convention for source files. JVMs always require this structure for the language's compiled files, though.

Open your operating system's Command Prompt (Windows) or Terminal Window (macOS/Linux) and change the active directory to your project's root directory (that holds the `src` and `bin` subdirectories). Compile the code by running the following command. Use your operating system's convention to specify the path to `Controller.java`; here, Windows' convention is used:

```
javac -sourcepath src -d bin src\com\example\app\Controller.java
```

Quite a few things are happening here:

- The `-sourcpath src` option tells the compiler that all of the source code resides in the `src` subdirectory.
- The `-d bin` option tells `javac` to put the compiled files in the `bin` subdirectory. This directory must exist; `javac` will create its needed subdirectories automatically, though.
- Finally, the path to the main program's source file is passed.

Because the `Controller.java` source file imports the other two classes and the `src` directory structure matches all the package names, the Java compiler will be able to find all the classes and compile them.

This results in the following output directory, `bin`:

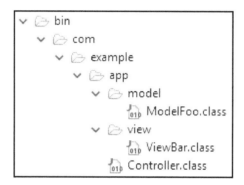

Let's run the application with the `java` command. In your command-line window, change the active directory to the `bin` subdirectory and run the following command:

```
java com.example.app.Controller
```

On my machine, this produces the following line:

```
This is running on JVM version 1.8.0_112 by Oracle Corporation
```

A ClassPath example

To demonstrate how the ClassPath concept works, let's move one of the class files to a different directory. Conceptually, this is the same as using an external dependency, which by convention, is also stored in a different directory than the project's classes. Follow this procedure:

- In your project directory, which contains the src and bin directories, create a new lib directory
- Inside the new lib directory, create the com\example\app\model subdirectories
- Move the ModelFoo.class file to the model subdirectory you created earlier
- For clarity, remove the empty bin\com\example\app\model directory

The directory structure should now look like:

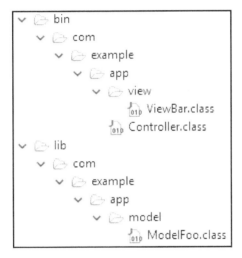

In your Command Prompt or Terminal Window, change the directory to the project's bin subdirectory and try to run the program again:

```
java com.example.app.Controller
```

You should now see a Java stack trace. Get used to this; you'll be seeing errors such as these a lot in your JVM development career. On my machine, it looked like this (cut for brevity):

```
Error: A JNI error has occurred, please check your installation and try
again
Exception in thread "main" java.lang.NoClassDefFoundError:
com/example/app/model/ModelFoo
  at java.lang.Class.getDeclaredMethods0(Native Method)
  at java.lang.Class.privateGetDeclaredMethods(Unknown Source)
  at java.lang.Class.privateGetMethodRecursive(Unknown Source)
  at java.lang.Class.getMethod0(Unknown Source)
. . .
```

Now tell the `java` command that it must look for the classes referenced in the code, both in the current directory and the `lib` directory (which is one level above the current `bin` directory), by passing the `-cp` option to set the ClassPath:

```
java -cp ".;..\lib" com.example.app.Controller
```

When looking for a class, the JVM first looks in the current directory and, if it is unable to find the class there, it tries to find the class in the `..lib` subdirectory. Note that the `-cp` option and value must be specified before the class name; otherwise, they will be passed to the main function argument's String array parameter instead of the `java` command.

Eclipse IDE

As we have seen in the previous section, using a simple text editor to create JVM programs can be a quite cumbersome process. In some languages, including Java, you'll have to make sure that the package name structure matches the directory structure of the source code. As we will soon see, there are more rules that some languages impose on the developer. Java requires that the source code filename should match the corresponding class name. Also, you have to manually specify the ClassPath when running programs. The list goes on.

In the JVM world, most programmers use the sophisticated IDE to develop their projects. Both commercial and open source IDEs that support the JVM concept are available on the market. Java support is extremely strong on all popular IDEs. Java programmers can expect the following features in a modern IDE:

- First is the autocompletion feature. When a class name is recognized, it offers a list of its members while typing (called **IntelliSense** in the Microsoft world).

- Then, it provides sophisticated refactoring tools. When renaming variables or methods, the code of the whole project can be automatically modified to reflect the changes.
- There are fully featured GUI debuggers with breakpoints, variable inspection, and profilers.
- There is an option to automatically rewrite existing code to use new Java features.
- It warns about problems that the Java compiler does not catch, such as accessing members on null references.
- It runs the project itself or runs the project's unit tests with a press of a button.
- It provides automatic deployment of Java EE projects to JVM applications servers.
- Also available are additional tools, such as dialog builders, visual database tools (SQL), and so forth.
- There is plugin support to add other features.

IDE support for JVM languages other than Java sometimes leaves something to be desired, as we will see in the following chapters. However, the situation has improved a lot over the years.

The most well-known IDEs for JVM developers are:

- IntelliJ IDEA (modern IDE available in both a fully featured commercial and simpler, free community edition)
- Apache NetBeans IDE (previously Oracle NetBeans; it is well known for its build tools support and enormous number of built-in features, while also supporting plugins)
- Eclipse IDE (A very good offering from the Eclipse Foundation that includes IBM and many other big companies and, like NetBeans IDE, can be extended with plugins)

Both NetBeans IDE and Eclipse IDE are open source projects, while IntelliJ is proprietary. For this book, I've chosen Eclipse IDE. It was not an easy choice as all the IDEs listed are very good and all have their advantages and disadvantages. Eclipse IDE seemed to have the best support for all the languages covered in this book, although it requires installing some external plugins.

Downloading Eclipse IDE

To download your copy of Eclipse IDE, visit `http://www.eclipse.org`.

Click on the Download button. Eclipse IDE uses a user-friendly installer for all platforms nowadays:

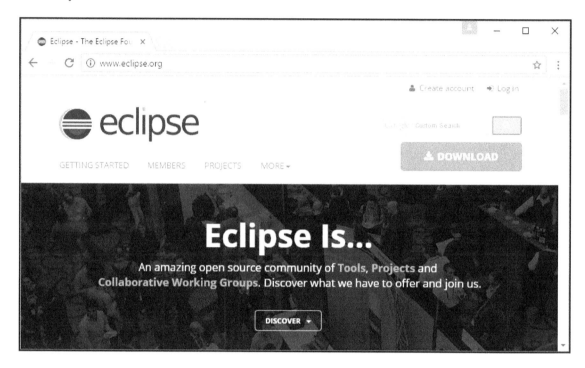

Installing Eclipse IDE

The installation of the Eclipse IDE is really straightforward. Modern versions can be installed with a GUI installation program:

- Launch the downloaded installation program
- When prompted, choose the **Eclipse IDE for Java Developers** edition
- Choose the installation folder and click on Install

After the installation, check whether the program is installed correctly by running it. A splash screen will be displayed, and after a small pause, you should see a window that asks for the workspace directory. This is the directory where your projects will be stored:

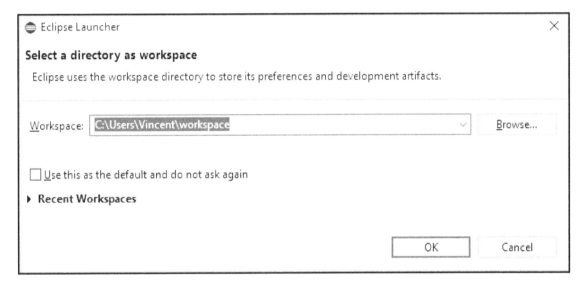

Accept the directory and click on **OK**. A welcome screen should now appear:

We will provide instructions on how to install plugins that are needed in some of the upcoming chapters.

Summary

You learned a lot in this chapter. Let's look back at all the topics that we covered.

You downloaded and installed a JDK on your system. Then, you explored it thoroughly by examining its directory structure and looking at its most important commands. You studied how classes are organized in packages. This knowledge proved to be useful when you looked at the Java Class Library. You looked at some fundamental classes from the `java.lang` package and also studied the important `ArrayList` and `HashMap` classes from the java.util package. You wrote, compiled, and ran a simple program on a JVM instance and learned how to modify the ClassPath. Finally, in order to boost your productivity, you downloaded and installed Eclipse IDE.

Congratulations! Now that you have a good grasp of the JVM concepts, you are ready to dive into the world of JVM programming languages. Let's start with the language that started it all: Java.

3
Java

While exploring the JVM and JDK concepts in the previous chapters, we looked at quite a bit of Java code. Source code written in Java is generally easy to read and comprehend. It started out as a relatively simple language to learn. As more and more features were added to the language over the years, its complexity increased somewhat. However, good news is that beginners don't have to worry about the more advanced topics too much until they are ready to learn them.

Programmers that want to choose a JVM language other than Java can still benefit from this chapter, especially once they start using libraries or frameworks that provide Javadocs as API documentation. As we will see soon, Javadoc is a tool provided with the JDK that generates HTML documentation based on some special comments in the source code. Many libraries and frameworks provide the HTML documents generated by Javadocs as part of their documentation.

These are the topics we will discuss in this chapter:

- Object-oriented programming (OOP) in Java
- Programming in Java

OOP in Java

As discussed in the previous chapters, while Java has primitive types, everything else is an object. While Java is not considered a pure OOP language because of its support for primitive types, it is still a serious OOP language.

To use Java effectively, you should know OOP. Don't worry if your OOP knowledge is rusty. While this chapter does not teach it, we will try to refresh your memory along the way. This chapter concentrates on all OOP-related subjects:

- Defining classes
- Defining packages
- Adding class members: variables and methods
- Constructors and deconstructors
- Inheritance
- Interfaces
- Abstract classes
- Upcasting and downcasting

Defining classes

As we have seen in the examples from previous chapters, a class can simply be defined with Java's `class` keyword, followed by the class name and brackets { }. The brackets visually show the programmer what code is part of the class:

```
class ClassName {
}
```

The preceding code will compile. It complies with all Java's syntax rules. Removing any part will result in compile errors.

The naming convention for JVM classes is CamelCase. The class name starts with a capital letter. If the class name consists of multiple words, then each word is directly added to the previous one (no spaces or underscores are used) and each word starts with a capital letter. There are several rules for choosing a class name:

- The name must start with a non-digit character.
- The name cannot include dashes or spaces. An underscore is valid but not used by convention.
- Digits are allowed after the first character.
- Class names may not be keywords reserved for the Java language itself. At least one character must be added or changed so that the name does not violate this rule.

Class access modifiers

The visibility of classes can be adjusted. When not explicitly specified (as in the example earlier), the visibility is called **package private**. This means that the class can only be referenced to and instantiated by classes in the same package. See the previous chapter for an extensive explanation of how packages work on a JVM.

In most cases, you want to create classes that can be referenced and instantiated anywhere else. When adding the access modifier `public` before the `class` keyword, classes in any package can see this class and, usually, create instances from this class:

```
public class ClassName {
}
```

 Public classes can still have private constructors . When that's the case, the class can still be seen and referenced by classes in other packages, but they cannot be instantiated by code that cannot access the constructor.

An unusual requirement of the Java programming language is that a source code file can only define one public class and that the filename must match the class name exactly. Other JVM languages usually do not have this limitation.

Final class modifier - locking a class

A class can be prefixed with the `final` non-access modifier to prevent the class from being inherited by another class:

```
public final class ThisClassCanNotBeOverriden {
}
```

The `final` keyword can be added before or after a class's access modifier, if present. By convention the access modifier is specified first, followed by non-access modifiers. If another class tries to inherit a `final` class, the compiler will refuse to compile the code.

Defining packages

To put a class inside a package, the `package` keyword is used. If specified, it has to be the first non-commented line in the code. Like all statements in Java, it has to end with a semicolon (`;`). Let's look an example:

```
package com.example.package_name;
```

We discussed packages thoroughly in the previous chapter, including naming conventions and requirements. When no `package` line is present, the class is put in what is called the `default` package.

By convention, the directory structure of the Java source code files should match the package names. All popular IDEs understand the package structure and will not show individual subdirectories but the full package names instead. As an example, here's a screenshot of the Eclipse IDE's project explorer:

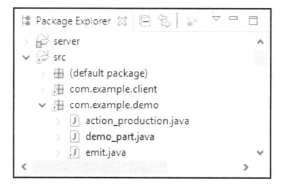

Importing classes

Classes can be referenced in code by using the fully qualified class name. For instance, when using `ArrayList` in a method, code can be written like this:

```
java.util.ArrayList list = new java.util.ArrayList();
```

This requires a lot of keystrokes, even for a language that is known for its verbosity. Of course, Java has a solution. Using the import keyword, classes can be referenced by the class name only. The most basic form looks like this:

```
import java.util.ArrayList;
class Demo {
    ArrayList list = new ArrayList();
}
```

The code of the method can now simply use the ArrayList class name and does not have to provide the fully qualified class name any longer. Import statements must appear after the package keyword, if present, but before the first class definition. It is not possible to specify multiple packages on a single import statement.

When name clashes occur (which happens when the same class name is used in two or more packages), you can import only one of them. Plus, you have to use the fully qualified class name in the code for others.

It's also possible to import all the classes from a package with a single line:

```
import java.util.*;
```

This form is not really recommended in source code intended for larger systems, though. It can increase the chances for unexpected class name clashes. Note that only the classes from the specified packages are imported. Subpackages remain unaffected and have to be imported separately. For example, java.util.concurrent is a package that contains utility classes for concurrent programming. To load classes from both the packages, import statements for both the packages are required.

All the classes of the java.lang package are always imported implicitly and are available at any time.

Adding class members - variables and methods

Without variables and methods, classes would be boring and rather pointless. Variables hold data that methods usually act upon. Like classes, the visibility of both variables and methods can be changed by prefixing them with access modifiers, but both support additional modifiers. We'll describe the syntax to define variables and methods first, then continue with modifiers. This leads us to the following topics:

- Instance variables
- Instance methods
- Access modifiers
- Static modifier
- Final modifier
- Method overloading

Instance variables

Normally, each object instance has its own unique variables; they are called **instance variables**. In Java, instance variables are defined like this:

```
TYPE variableName;
```

`TYPE` can be any one of the primitive types (int, double, and so forth) or a reference type. If the class you want to use is imported using the `import` statement, you only have to specify the class name; otherwise, the fully qualified class name has to be used. It is possible to initialize the variable at the same time as declaring it:

```
public class Test {
  int i = 25;
  Object o = new Object();
}
```

Values that are not initialized explicitly at the class level are implicitly initialized with 0 (`int`, `long`, and `short`), 0.0 (`float` and `double`), `false` for boolean, and null for reference types. Variable names have the same requirements as class names, but the naming convention is different. By convention, they start with a lowercase characters. Like classes, special characters like $ and underscores are supported, but their usage is not recommended.

Methods

A function in Java can either return an object or null. Methods that return nothing use the `void` keyword, as inspired by the C language. A method in a normal class must have a body that's between brackets `{ }`:

```
public class ClassWithTwoMethods {
  boolean b;
  void methodReturnsNothingAndNoParameters() {
  }

  Object methodReturnsAnObject(boolean b, int i) {
    this.b = b;
    return null;
  }
}
```

A method that has a return type must explicitly return either the corresponding object or null in its body; otherwise, the code won't compile. A method that uses the `void` keyword is not allowed to return anything.

Variables declared inside a method must be initialized before they can be used. Unlike class variables or class instance variables, variables inside methods are not initialized automatically.

Note in the example earlier that, inside a method, the `this` keyword can be used to access class members.

Modifiers

Both variables and methods can be prefixed with modifiers. There are two kinds of modifiers:

- Access modifiers
- Non-access modifiers

Many access modifiers and non-access modifiers can be used together. As we will see, when mixing modifiers, the order is not important. It's a convention to start with access modifiers and then the non-access modifiers, but this is not a hard and fast rule.

Protecting class members with access modifiers

The programmer of a class decides which members (variables and methods) can be accessed by other classes by prefixing them with an access modifier. For class members, there are more access modifiers available than for the class itself. Let's take a look at all the access modifiers:

Name	Access modifier	Description
Public	`public`	Public members can be accessed by all parts of the code that have access to the class.
Protected	`protected`	Protected members can be seen and accessed by the class itself, other classes in the same package, and classes that inherit the class. It is hidden from all other classes.
Package-private	When you don't specify an access modifier, the class member can only be seen and accessed by the class itself and other classes in the same package. It will be hidden from classes in other packages, even when such a class could inherit the class.	
Private	`private`	Private members can only be seen and accessed by the class that defines the member. All other classes will not be able to see or access these members.

When a class inherits a class, it can override all the methods that it can access according to the preceding table, except, as we will soon see, methods that are defined with the `final` modifier. Private methods can never be overridden; the class that overrides them can't see or access them.

 This will be an unfamiliar territory to Python developers. In Python, everything inside a class is public and the code can read and alter any class variable and call methods at any time, even those intended for internal use only.

Access modifier example

Let's look at the Java source code comprising two classes.

The first class contains four variables, each one with a different or nil access modifier:

```
package chapter02.access_modifiers.demonstration;
public class DemoVariables {
  public String publicVariable = "This is a public variable";
  protected String protectedVariable = "This is a protected variable";
  String packagePrivateVariable = "This is a package-private variable";
  private String privateVariable = "This is a private variable";
}
```

Note that the preceding class is placed inside the
chapter02.access_modifiers.demonstration package.

The second class is in the chapter02.access_modifiers package and creates an instance of the preceding class:

```
package chapter02.access_modifiers;
import chapter02.access_modifiers.demonstration.DemoVariables;
public class AccessModifiersMain {
  public static void main(String[] args) {
    DemoVariables demo = new DemoVariables();
    System.out.println(demo.publicVariable);
  }
}
```

Even though both the packages start with chapter02.access_modifiers, the JVM regards them as completely unrelated.

 If the full package names do not match, they are considered completely different packages by the JVM.

Also, note that the `AccessModifiersMain` class (which I will refer to using the `main` class name from now on) creates an instance of the `DemoVariables` class (which I will refer to using the `demo` class name); the main class does not inherit the demo class. This leads us to the following observations:

- The main class can freely access the demo class's `publicVariable` variable. In fact, this is the only member of the demo class that the main class can see and therefore access.
- The main class cannot access the demo class's `protectedVariable` variable because both the classes are in different packages and the main class does not inherit the demo class. If one of these conditions were different, then it would have full access to it.
- The `packagePrivateVariable` variable from the demo class would be accessible to the main class only if both the classes were in the same package. As they are not, the main class cannot see and access this member here.
- The `privateVariable` variable is only available to the demo class. It cannot be accessed by any other class.

Static modifier - instance variables and class variables

Normally, you'll create variables that are unique to an instance of a class and add methods that use that data. Each instance of the class has its own value, and changing a variable will only impact that specific instance. A call of a method is only possible on class instances, using an initialized reference type variable.

JVM also supports class variables and class methods. These members can be used without any instance of the class, but they can be shared with every created instance of the class. The class member has to be prefixed with the `static` non-access modifier:

```
public class StaticDemo {
    public static String staticVariable = "This is a static variable";
    public String instanceVariable = "This is a class instance variable";
}
```

A static variable, called a class variable, can be accessed even when there's no instance of the class available. A static method, or class method, can be called even when there's no reference type holding a reference to an instance of that class. Let's look at an example. Let's create a class that creates two instances of the preceding class and alters both the values using both the instances:

```
public class StaticDemoMain {
    public static void main(String[] args) {
```

```
StaticDemo demo1 = new StaticDemo();
demo1.staticVariable = "Demo 1 static";
demo1.instanceVariable = "Demo 1 instance";

StaticDemo demo2 = new StaticDemo();
demo2.staticVariable = "Demo 2 static";
demo2.instanceVariable = "Demo 2 Instance";

System.out.println(StaticDemo.staticVariable);
System.out.println(demo1.instanceVariable);
System.out.println(demo2.instanceVariable);
    }
}
```

When you run this program, the following output would be printed:

```
Demo 2 static
Demo 1 instance
Demo 2 instance
```

Note that in the preceding code, when a reference type (demo1 or demo2) is used to access staticVariable, it's impossible to see that this is a static variable. It is fully clear, however, when the variable is referenced in the first System.out.println(StaticDemo.staticVariable) line; here, the static variable is accessed via the StaticDemo class name.

 It is considered bad practice to access static members via a reference type variable. This is because this hides the fact that the code is accessing a static member. When accessing them via the class name, there isn't any room for confusion.

The code inside a static method can only access static class members of its own class; it cannot use any instance variable or call instance methods directly.

Final modifier - locking a class member

Class methods and variables can be locked by prefixing them with the final non-access modifier. Here's an example of both a final static integer and a final method in Java:

```
class FinalDemo1 {
  public final static int THIS_IS_A_CONSTANT_VALUE = 42;
  public final void thisMethodCanNotBeOverridden() { }
}
```

When you use the `final` keyword on a method, it means that the method cannot be overridden by any class, regardless of the access modifier of the method. If a class still tries to override the method, the compiler will refuse to compile that class.

When used on variables, it means that the variable's value will not change. Basically, the variable is then turned into a constant. It's a convention to make final variables static and use names in uppercase only. Note that while a final variable cannot be changed, if it references a mutable object, then the content of the object can still change. Let's demonstrate this with an example:

```
import java.util.ArrayList;

class FinalDemo2 {
  private static final ArrayList<String> finalList = new ArrayList<>();

  public static final void main(String[] args) {
    finalList.add("Both strings can be added, because");
    finalList.add("the ArrayList itself is mutable.");
  }
}
```

Overloading methods

In Java, it's possible to define different versions of a method. When calling the method, the compiler will match each version until a match is made. If it is unable to find an exact match, it will try to check whether one of the overloaded versions is applicable to the given parameter(s). When multiple overloaded versions match the given parameters exactly or if none of the versions match, the compiler will give an error; otherwise, the compiler will ensure the found method is used. Before we take a look at the rules, let's look at a real-world example: the `java.lang.System.out.println()` method.

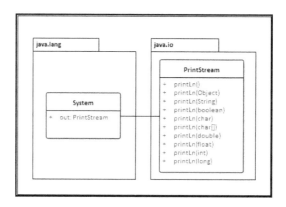

We have used the `System.out.println()` method from the `java.lang.System` class several times in this book. The `System` class is placed in the `java.lang` package, the only package that Java imports implicitly. It has a public `out` static variable (which is final, it is read only) that references a `java.io.PrintStream` object instance. One of the methods of the `java.io.Printstream` class is `println`, which is overloaded several times, as can be seen in the preceding class diagram.

The rules of overloading are as follows:

- The parameter types and/or order must be different for each version. If two versions take a single long parameter, for instance, the compiler would not be able to choose which one to call.
- Ideally, the return type should be the same for each overloaded version of a method. It's a compiler error when only the return type differs while the parameter types and ordering are the same.
- Parameter names are not important at all.
- When no direct match is found, primitive values are widened. Since `int` can always be stored in `long`, a method with the `long` primitive type will be a match. The opposite of this is not true: `long` cannot always be converted into `int` without the loss of data, so that is not tried.
- If there's no direct match and at least one of the parameters is a primitive type, then it is autoboxed to a wrapper class and every method is matched again. This is done for each parameter one at a time until a match is found or all combinations have been tried.
- The same applies to parameters that are primitive wrapper classes; these are autoboxed to their primitive types.
- For each parameter that is an instance of a class, its parent class (or as we will see later, its interface) is looked up. Then, each overloaded version of the method is matched again until all the parameters match and they reach `java.lang.Object class` (remember, this is the mother of all the classes on a JVM).

Constructors and finalizers

Java objects can define custom constructors and a finalizer:

- Constructors are called when an instance of a class is created
- The `finalize()` method is called by the JVM when the object is about to be collected by the garbage collector

Constructors

To define a constructor, the class name has to be repeated along with parentheses ( ) that would include arguments, if any. Here's an example of this:

```java
public class ClassWithConstructor {
  public ClassWithConstructor() {
  }

  public ClassWithConstructor(int a, int b) {
  }
}
```

The constructor has the same access modifiers as that of methods. Like normal methods, constructors can be overloaded. The preceding class can be instantiated with either one of the following constructors:

```java
ClassWithConstructor c1 = new ClassWithConstructor();
ClassWithConstructor c2 = new ClassWithConstructor(1, 2);
```

If a class does not define any constructor, then Java generates one implicitly. It looks like this:

```java
class ClassWithoutConstructor {
  public ClassWithoutConstructor() { }
}
```

As mentioned, the constructor can be prefixed with access modifiers. The access modifiers of constructors have exactly the same meaning as the access modifiers of methods. Like methods, when you don't specify any access modifier at all, the constructor will be considered package-private. A package-private constructor can only be used by classes in the same package as the class.

Finalizers

Unlike C++, Java does not really have real deconstructs. The reason is that all well-known JVM implementations have a garbage collector. It's never guaranteed that an object will be collected by the garbage collector; it depends on whether the program has any references to the remaining objects and some other JVM-implementation-specific factors.

There's a method that the garbage collector is supposed to call when an object is about to be collected by the garbage collector process. The `java.lang.Object` class has a `finalize()` method that can be overridden by any class:

```
@Override
protected void finalize() {
}
```

The `@Override` syntax will be explained soon.

This method can be used to free resources that the class is utilizing, but this must be seen as the last chance to do so. It's recommended that programmers close resources as early as possible. Because it cannot be guaranteed that the `finalize()` method will be called at all, it's much better to close or free resources in other parts of the code .

Some programmers choose to write a log message (or even a simple `System.out.println()` call) when the `finalize()` method has to close resources that are in use, as it usually indicates there's a bug in the program. The resource should have been closed earlier, somewhere else.

Extending a class

As mentioned earlier, JVM is one of those platforms that can only inherit from one class:

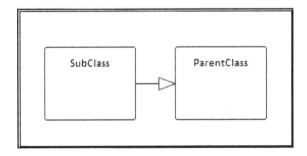

To inherit a class, the following syntax is used:

```
class SubClass extends ParentClass {
}
```

 Remember that a class that is prefixed with the `final` non-access modifier cannot be extended.

The subclass can access members (variables and methods) of its parent class that it can see according to the rules explained in the *Class access modifiers* topic.

Overriding methods

The `super` keyword can be used to access the members of the parent class:

```
class TheParentClass {
  void aMethod() {
  }
}

class TheSubClass extends TheParentClass {
  @Override
  public void aMethod() {
    super.aMethod();
    // More code....
  }
}
```

When overriding a method, the visibility of the method must be considered. Java requires that the visibility of a method that is overridden is not decreased. An overridden method that is protected in the parent class is allowed to be either `protected` or `public` in the subclass, but it cannot be `private` or `package-private` as that would decrease visibility. This concept is demonstrated in the previous code snippet. The `aMethod()` method is package-private in the parent class and public in the subclass.

It is a convention to put the `@Override` annotation above the method that is overridden so that it's easy to see that the method is overriding an existing method. It's a compiler error when it is placed on a method that is not overridden at all.

An annotation is meant as a signal. In this case, it's meant as a reminder for developers that are reading the source code. There are also annotations that are processed by compilers or frameworks.

Calling constructors of a parent class

A constructor of a parent class can be called with the `super` keyword as well:

```
class A {
  public A(int i) { }
}

class B extends A {
  B(int i) {
    super(i);
  }
}
```

Java has some rules regarding constructors:

- Each constructor of the subclass is required by the Java language to call one of the parent's constructors, either explicitly or implicitly.
- If the programmer does not add any constructor to the subclass, then the parent class is required to have a constructor that takes no parameters. Java takes care of calling that constructor implicitly.
- If the parent class does not have a constructor with empty parameters, then each constructor of the subclass must call the parent class's constructor with valid parameters explicitly. This must be the first line in the subclass constructor's body.
- Java calls the parent class's parameterless constructor automatically (if the parent class has one), but the programmer can do this manually as well. It must be the first non-commented line in the constructor body.

Let's look at some examples to clarify the previous rules. First, let's check out a parent class and a subclass, both without explicit constructors:

```
class A { }
class B extends A { }
```

Both classes do not provide any constructors. Java will create a public parameterless constructor for both automatically, called A() and B(), respectively. The generated constructor of B() will automatically call the constructor of A(). The programmer could also manually call the constructor explicitly. It must be the first statement of the constructor; otherwise, the Java compiler will refuse to compile the code. Java will not call the constructor implicitly in that case:

```
class A { }
class B extends A {

  public B() {
    super();
  }
}
```

Here's an example of a class where the parent class has a default public parameterless constructor and the subclass has a public constructor with parameters:

```
class A { }

class B extends A {
  public B(int i) {
  }
}
```

A does not provide a constructor, so the public constructor A() will be created by Java automatically. B specifies a constructor, so it will not get an implicit public parameterless constructor. Although the constructor of the B class does not explicitly call the A() constructor, Java will still call the A() constructor when using the B(int i) constructor.

Here's an example where the parent class has a constructor with parameters:

```
class A {
  public A(String s) {
  }
}

class B extends A {
  public B() {
    super("Hello");
  }
}
```

Things now get interesting. The parent class only has a constructor with a parameter. This means that Java is now not able to implicitly call the constructor in subclasses, as it doesn't want to guess which value to pass to the constructor. It's now a compiler error if the constructor of the subclass does not explicitly call the constructor of the parent class. It must be the first statement in the body of the constructor; otherwise, you'll get a compile error.

Abstract classes

A normal class is called a concrete class. By prefixing the class name with the `abstract` non-access modifier, a class is changed to an abstract class.

An abstract class is a class that can be extended by other classes but cannot be instantiated directly. A difference with concrete classes is that an abstract class has the option of not providing an implementation for its methods:

```
public abstract class AnAbstractClass {
    abstract public void thisIsAnAbstractMethod();
}
```

The `abstract` modifier has to be specified both on the class and on each method that has no implementation. An abstract class can have concrete methods and is not required to have any abstract methods. A concrete class that extends an abstract class must provide implementations for all the abstract methods by overriding these methods.

Like concrete classes, an abstract class can inherit a single other class, which can be either concrete or abstract. Here's an example of this:

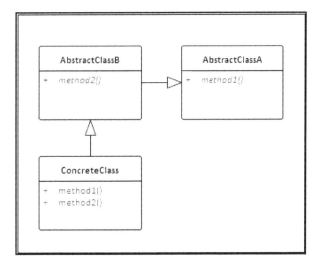

In Java code, preceding example will look like this:

```
abstract class AbstractClassA {
  public abstract void method1();
}

abstract class AbstractClassB extends AbstractClassA {
  public abstract void method2();
}

class ConcreteClass extends AbstractClassB {
  @Override
  public void method1() { } // implementation code...

  @Override
  public void method2() { }  // Implementation code...
}
```

Since the abstract class `AbstractClassB` inherits the abstract class `AbstractClassA`, the concrete class must provide implementations for the abstract methods from both the abstract classes. Abstract classes cannot be instantiated, but reference type variables can reference a class that extended an abstract class either directly or indirectly:

```
AbstractClassA demo = new ConcreteClass();
```

The `demo` can only be used to access members of the `AbstractClassA` class. Any other variables and methods `ConcreteClass` are not available when using the `demo` reference. As we will see later, the `demo` reference can be downcasted to `ConcreteClass`.

Interfaces

Interfaces are somewhat similar to abstract classes. Until Java 8, the biggest difference was that interfaces were unable to provide implementations of any methods. Classes do not extend interfaces; they implement them.

 As we will see shortly, Java 8 introduced the possibility of providing default implementations of methods.

Here's an example of a class that implements two interfaces:

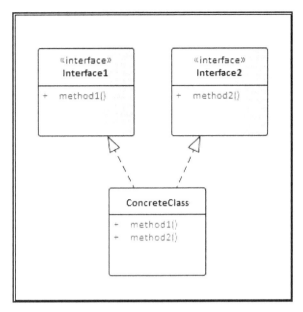

```
interface Interface1 {
  void method1();
}

interface Interface2 {
  public void method2();
}

class ConcreteClass implements Interface1, Interface2 {
  @Override
  public void method1() { } // Implementation code...

  @Override
  public void method2() { } // Implementation code...
}
```

Interfaces have the same rules regarding source code as a class. A public interface must be defined in a source file that matches the interface name exactly; a source file, therefore, can only define one public interface. Furthermore, interfaces support the same access modifiers as classes (public and package-private).

The members of an interface are implicitly abstract and public. You can explicitly add the `abstract` and/or `public` access modifiers. If you omit the `public` modifier, the member is still public, not package-private as you might expect. Only public members can be part of an interface; using any other access modifier will result in compile errors.

Both methods and variables can be part of an interface, but there are some differences:

- The abstract methods in an interface are always public instance methods.
- Variables, on the other hand, always have the `final` and `static` modifiers. Optionally, both the modifiers can be explicitly specified.

Both abstract and concrete classes can implement any number of interfaces they want. Only concrete classes are required to provide implementations of all the methods by overriding them.

`ConcreteClass` implements both `Interface1` and `Interface2` and is, therefore, required to override both the methods. Although `Interface1` does not add the `public` modifier to `method1()`, it is implicitly public anyway. A reference type variable can point to a class that implements a specific interface:

```
Interface2 i = new ConcreteClass();
```

As mentioned, since Java 8, it is possible to provide default implementations of a method. This feature was added because adding new methods to an existing interface always broke its compatibility with the existing classes implemented in that interface. Classes had to be modified before they could be compiled. Now, a default implementation can be provided so that the existing classes can stay compatible with the interfaces that need to be modified. Here's an example of this:

```
interface ExistingInterface {
  public void methodWithoutImplementation();
  default public void methodWithImplementation() {
    // Implementation....
  }
}
```

Also, as of Java 8, it is possible to add static methods to an interface. Interfaces are required to provide implementations for static methods, as they can only be referenced using the interface's name; a reference type variable will not be able to provide access to static methods of an interface.

Upcasting and downcasting

Java is a statically typed OOP language. Objects can be cast to related types. Consider this class diagram:

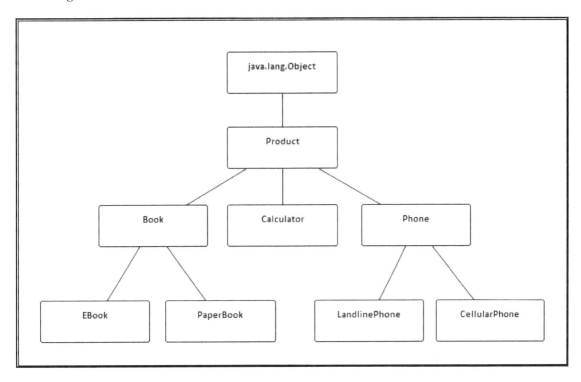

Since the **java.lang.Object** class is the mother of all the classes on the JVM, every object is always **java.lang.Object**, including all the objects in this diagram. Likewise, a **Book** instance is always **Product**, which is also true for **Calculator** and **Phone**. However, **Product** is not necessarily a **Book** instance. It could be **Book**, **Calculator**, **Phone**, or one of their subclasses. We wouldn't know without looking at the code or documentation.

Java has the same dilemmas. When we say that a **PaperBook** instance is an instance of the **Product** class, we are upcasting **PaperBook** to a **Product** instance. In code, casting looks like this:

```
PaperBook paperBook = new PaperBook();
Product product = paperBook;
```

The Java compiler is able to figure out that a `PaperBook` instance can always be upcasted to a `Product` instance. Therefore, the second line is compiled correctly. If the compiler does not agree that this situation is always the case, it will refuse to compile the code. Therefore, the compiler will refuse to compile this code:

```
Product product = new PaperBook();
PaperBook paperBook = product; // This line fails to compile
```

The first line is fine. The `PaperBook` instance can be automatically upcasted to a `Product` instance. The second line, however, fails to compile. The error message of the compiler is `incompatible types: Product cannot be converted to PaperBook`. The compiler only considers that the `product` variable contains a `Product` instance and the compiler cannot guarantee that a `Product` instance can always be successfully downcasted to a `PaperBook` instance. The compiler must now be told that the programmer knows that the casting process can potentially fail. To make the code compile, the following change must be made:

```
Product product = new PaperBook();
PaperBook paperBook = (PaperBook)product;
```

The preceding code will now run fine. At runtime, the `Product` instance is downcasted to a `PaperBook` instance. If, however, we make a mistake, then the code will throw an exception at runtime:

```
Product product = new PaperBook();
Phone phone = (Phone)product;
```

Since the `product` reference type variable references a `PaperBook` instance, the `Product` instance cannot be downcasted to a `Phone` instance in this case. The JVM will throw a `ClassCastException` exception instance at runtime:

```
Exception in thread "main" java.lang.ClassCastException: PaperBook
cannot be cast to Phone
```

If you try to cast to a situation that can never be true, the compiler will still refuse to compile the code. Here's an example of this:

```
LandLinePhone landlinePhone = new LandLinePhone();
CellularPhone cellularPhone = (LandLinePhone)landlinePhone;
// Will not compile
```

The Java compiler is smart enough to understand that a `LandLinePhone` instance can never be a `CellularPhone` instance; therefore, it refuses to compile the code.

Writing Java code

Now that we have discussed all the relevant OOP features of Java, we can start writing classes that actually do something. This part of the chapter will discuss some topics that will guide you in this process:

- Operators
- Plain Old Java Object
- Arrays
- Generics and Collections
- Looping
- Exceptions
- Threads
- Lambdas

Operators

Some of the most important operators of the Java language are summed up in this table. Note that Java knows more operators than the ones listed here. Operators that are very common in all other popular programming languages, such as +, -, >, >=, <, and <=, are not listed here:

Operator	Description
`value++` `value--`	These return the value, then increase or decrease the value
`++value` `--value`	These increase or decrease the value, then return the new value
`!`	This is the logical NOT operator
`%`	This refers to the remainder (integer) of a division
`instanceof`	This returns a Boolean indicating whether the passed object is an instance of the specified class or interface

== !=	These refer to equal to and unequal to signs
&& ||	These are the logical AND and OR operators
=	This refers to an assignment
+= -= *= /= %=	These operators help calculate a new value and directly assign the result to the variable

Here are some examples of the uses of these operators:

```
class OperatorDemo {
  public static void main(String[] args) {
    int i = 0;
    System.out.println(i++);
    System.out.println(++i);
    System.out.println(i += 10);
  }
}
```

When run, this will print the following output to the console:

```
0
2
12
```

Since the `i` integer variable is declared inside a method, it must be explicitly initialized. In this case, it starts with the value 0. The second line in the method prints the current value, which is 0, then increases it silently to value 1. The next line increases the `i` variable with 1, then prints it. Now 2 is printed. Finally, 10 is added and the result is printed, which is 12.

Conditional checks

Two conditional checks are available:

- The `if...else` statement
- The `switch...case` statement

The if...else statement

The `if` and `if...else` statements in Java don't have a lot of surprises. Each condition must return a Boolean result. The `else` parts are optional:

```
if (condition) {
} else if (condition) {
} else {
}
```

Use the logical AND (`&&`) and OR (`||`) operators as follows:

```
if (i > 25 || i == -1) {
}
```

The `==` operator works as expected on primitive variables; however, when used on objects, it checks whether the two object references are the same. The content (properties) of the classes are not compared with each other. The consequence of this is that the content of a `String` variable must always be checked with the `equals()` method overridden from the `java.lang.Object` class, described in the previous chapter, instead of the `==` operator:

```
String foo = "hello";
String bar = "world";
if (!foo.equals(bar))
   System.out.println("Not equal!");
```

 Most IDEs will recognize the possible error of using the `==` operator on Strings and offer to rewrite the code with the String's `equals` method.

The switch...case statement

Like many other programming languages, Java supports the `switch` statement. Here's a simple example of this statement:

```
int value = 3;
String s = "";
switch (value) {
  case 1:
    s = "One";
    break;
  case 2:
  case 3:
    s = "Two or three";
```

```
      break;
    default:
      s = "Something else";
  }
  System.out.println(s);
```

A few remarks about using the `switch` statement:

- The specified expression can either be an integer or String.
- The value specified on the `case` statements must be available at compile time. Therefore, non-final variables cannot be used for specifying the values.
- A `break` statement must be added to transfer control to the end of the switch statement block. Otherwise, control will continue to the next case statement.

POJO

In the beginning, no frameworks were available for the Java language. Developers mostly wrote their own classes. Along the way, many frameworks were introduced and many of them required classes to implement specific interfaces or extend framework classes in order to work with the framework. This coupled classes closely to specific frameworks; code could not be reused anymore unless the projects used the same frameworks. Not everyone was satisfied with this situation and soon a new trend became popular: return to **Plain Old Java Objects (POJO)**. Many popular frameworks support POJO objects nowadays:

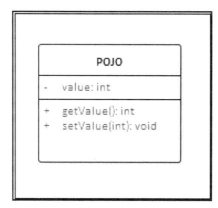

A class is considered a true POJO if:

- It does not extend classes or implement interfaces
- The class is mutable
- It has a public constructor that accepts no parameters
- It uses public methods to store and retrieve the values of private variables

 Even if you require features, such as extending classes and/or implementing interfaces, it can be a good choice to follow the other design choices of a POJO. A POJO is not a hard and fast rule; it's more like a convention.

Here's an example of a POJO class:

```
class POJO {
    private int value = 0;

    public POJO() {
    }

    public int getValue() {
      return value;
    }

    public void setValue(int value) {
        this.value = value;
    }
}
```

In a POJO instance, a value that can be set and retrieved using methods is called a **property**. For each property, the following conventions apply:

- Property values are stored in private variables
- A public getter method is available to return the value
- A public setter method is available to store the value

A getter method's name is prefixed with the get text, usually followed by the variable name. If the variable is a Boolean, the getter name is often prefixed with is instead of get. The setter name usually uses the set prefix for the name, regardless of the variable type.

Commonly, a second overloaded public constructor is added that accepts all the properties of the POJO as parameters. `value` property :

```
public POJO(int value) {
   this.value = value;
}
```

 Most IDEs can generate POJOs or add properties to an existing POJO with the press of a button.

Arrays

Java has built-in support for arrays. An array can be declared by adding `[]` to the type or variable name and using the `new` keyword to create the array and set the size:

```
int[] intArray1 = new int[2];
int intArray2[] = new int[2];
```

In Java, the size of an array must be explicitly set while creating the array. In primitive types, the initial values are 0 (numeric types) or false (Boolean), while reference type array elements are initialized with null.

Like many other popular programming languages, indexes are zero-based. In the previous case, the indexer of `intArray1` and `intArray2` could be 0 and 1, respectively (inclusive). A runtime exception will be thrown if the used index is out of range:

```
intArray1[0] = 10;
intArray1[1] = 20;
```

The size of an array can be read with the `length` read-only variable that the array provides:

```
System.out.println(intArray1.length);
```

This example would print 2 to the console. Arrays miss some convenient features. They do not override the `toString()` method. So, when printing the array variable `intArray1` using the `System.out.println` method, you'll get a default Object output that says nothing about the array content, for example, `[I@659e0bfd`.

There's an `Arrays` utility class in the `java.util` package that has a lot of static, convenient utility methods. It's recommended that you consult the API documentation if you want to convert arrays into a Collection class instance, search an item in an array, sort the array, and so forth. Here's an example of the `java.util.Arrays` class:

```
System.out.println(java.util.Arrays.toString(intArray1));
```

This will print [10, 20].

Arrays can be initialized using accolades while declaring the array:

```
int[] intArray = { 10, 20, 30 };
```

The Java compiler will now automatically declare an array that holds three primitive integer elements and initializes each element with the specified value.

Generics and Collections

We discussed Collections in the previous chapter, as they are so important to the JVM concept. When Collection classes were introduced in Java, they could only hold `java.lang.Object` objects. Since each object on a JVM can be upcast to a `java.lang.Object` instance, this meant that a Collection could store each and every type of object at all times. This flexibility has a drawback: objects had to be downcast in order to access the members of the class. This could result in runtime errors if an object were accidentally added with a different type. Here's an example that will compile fine but will result in an error when you run the program:

```
import java.util.ArrayList;

class ClassCastExceptionExample {
  public static void main(String[] args) {
    ArrayList list = new ArrayList();

    list.add(new Integer(123));
    list.add("This is not an integer");

    Integer i = (Integer)list.get(0);
    i = (Integer)list.get(1); // EXCEPTION AT RUN-TIME!!!!
  }
}
```

A `java.lang.String` instance cannot be cast to a `java.lang.Integer` instance, so a `ClassCastException` exception is thrown when the second item (index 1) is cast to an integer.

Generics were added to the Java language to ensure that certain classes can only be used with a fixed type, that is specified by the developer. For example, it's possible to create an `ArrayList` object that can only store objects that are instances of the `java.lang.Integer` class. The compiler will refuse to compile code that tries to add other objects to that `ArrayList` instance. Generics are a complicated topic and only the basic usage is discussed here. Since we will use `ArrayList` in the examples that follows, first take a look at the following diagram that shows some of the interfaces that `ArrayList` implements:

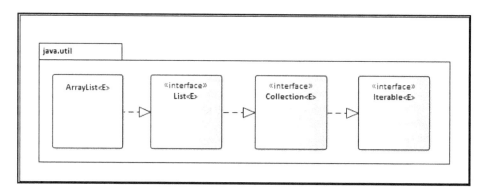

The **<E>** part indicates that this interface (and classes that implement it) support generics. **E** can be considered an alias for the generics type that will be specified when using the `List`. The convention is to use a single letter, in this case **E**, for the element. To declare a `java.util.ArrayList` instance that can only store `java.lang.Integer` instances, use a reference to the List interface:

```
import java.util.ArrayList;
import java.util.List;

class GenericsExample {
  public static void main(String[] args) {
    List<Integer> listWithIntegers = new ArrayList<>();
    listWithIntegers.add(new Integer(1));
  }
}
```

The desired type--in this case, the `Integer` class--is specified by adding the `<Integer>` suffix to the `List` interface type. When creating an instance of `ArrayList`, the `Integer` class does not need to be repeated; instead, `<>` is added. When you now try to add an instance of a class that cannot be upcast to an integer, the compiler will refuse to compile the code. Without generics, the error will only be detected at runtime, so most programmers will consider this an improvement.

Although not required, we let the reference type variable `listWithIntegers` point to the `java.util.List` interface instead of the `ArrayList` class. This is a generic interface that `ArrayList`, along with other data structures in the Collection API, implements. This is a nice convention as the `ArrayList` class can now be replaced with a different data structure that also implements the `java.util.List` interface without changing any other code.

Hiding implementation-specific details is considered a very good design choice in the JVM world. Interfaces and abstract classes make this possible.

Let's look at a `HashMap` example with generics as well. `HashMap` is a class from the `java.util` package. It implements the more generic `java.util.Map` interface. We'll use the `Map` interface again for the reference variable; we'll use it to hide the design information indicating that we are using a `HashMap` class. Let's start by looking at the `Map` interface:

```
public interface Map<K,V>
```

We see that `Map` supports generics and requires two types: `K` and `V`. They stand for key and value. Let's create a `HashMap` instance that maps a `String` key to an `Integer` value:

```
import java.util.HashMap;
import java.util.Map;

class GenericsExample {
  public static void main(String[] args) {
    Map<String, Integer> map = new HashMap<>();
    map.put("one", new Integer(1));
    map.put("ten", new Integer(10));
    System.out.println(map.get("one"));
  }
}
```

This will print the `Integer` value `1` to the console.

Note that generics can only work with objects. Specifying primitive values will result in compiler errors. The compiler will not autobox primitive values to objects or vice versa on generics.

Loops

Arrays and Collections are nice but only if you can loop through them. Here are all the built-in loop constructs in Java:

- The `for` loop
- The `while` loop

The for loop

Java has two forms of `for` loop:

- The normal for loop (using a counter)
- The enhanced for loop (for objects)

The normal for loop

The syntax of a normal `for` loop is:

```
for (int i=0; i < 10; i++) {
   System.out.println(i);
}
```

This will print 0 to 9 on a new line each.

As usual, in other languages, the `for` loop consists of three parts:

- The first part initializes the counter.
- The second part contains the expression, which is checked before starting each iteration. The iteration is stopped when it returns true.
- The last part is the statement that is called after each iteration.

Each part is optional, but the semicolon that separates the three parts must always be present. An unusual construction of an infinite loop can be created by leaving all the parts empty:

```
for (;;) {
}
```

A `for` loop can be stopped with the `break` keyword. The `continue` keyword can be used to stop the current iteration and skip to the next iteration:

```
for (int i=0; i < 4; i++) {
  if (i == 1)
    continue;
  if (i == 3)
    break;
  System.out.println(i);
}
```

The previous `for` loop will skip to the next iteration once `i` is equal to `1` and stop when `i` reaches `3`; therefore, only the values `0` and `2` will be printed to the console.

The enhanced for loop

The enhanced for loop only works with arrays and objects that implement the `java.lang.Iterable<T>` generics-aware interface. Most Collection API classes implement this interface. Here's an example of this with an array:

```
String[] stringArray = { "One", "Two", "Three" };
for (String s: stringArray) {
  System.out.println(s);
}
```

This will print `One`, `Two`, and `Three` on a new line each. It is recommended that you use this version of the for loop whenever you can, as it makes the code more readable.

The while loop

The `while` loop in Java looks like this:

```
int i = 10;
while (i < 10) {
  System.out.println(i);
  i++;
}
```

The expression must return a boolean. This example prints absolutely nothing. Since the integer `i` is equal to `10`, the expression returns `false` and the loop is not entered at all.

Like a `for` loop, the `while` loop can be stopped with the `break` keyword, and it's possible to skip to the next iteration with the `continue` keyword.

The do...while loop

The `do...while` loop is very similar to the `while` loop. The only difference is that it evaluates the expression after the iteration is complete. This loop will always be entered:

```
int i = 10;
do {
  System.out.println(i);
  i++;
} while (i < 10);
```

This will print `10`. The expression is evaluated after the first iteration. Since `11` is bigger than `10`, the expression returns `false` and the iteration stops.

Like `for` and `while` loops, the `do...while` loop can be stopped with the `break` keyword, and it's possible to skip to the next iteration with the `continue` keyword.

Exceptions

Exceptions were discussed in the previous chapter. To handle an exception, the code has to be placed between the try and catch blocks. Multiple exceptions can be defined. A few exceptions are mentioned in the following class diagram:

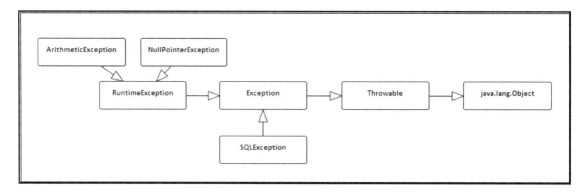

Here's an example code that deliberately causes a division by zero error:

```
try {
  System.out.println(0/0);
  System.out.println("exit");
} catch (NullPointerException e) {
  System.out.println("NULL POINTER EXCEPTION!");
} catch (ArithmeticException e) {
  System.out.println(e.getMessage());
```

```
      e.printStackTrace();
    } catch (Exception e) {
      System.out.println("DIFFERENT ERROR");
    }
```

This will print the following:

```
/ by zero
java.lang.ArithmeticException: / by zero
  at JavaApplication8.main(JavaApplication8.java:4)
```

Note that the `exit` text is not printed because an exception was thrown before that statement was executed. When the `0/0` expression threw `ArithmeticException`, the JVM analyzed all the catch blocks of this error handler. Since `ArithmeticException` was thrown, which is not a subclass of `NullPointerException`, the first catch block was ignored. The second catch block matched the class name exactly, so the second catch block was chosen and the exception's message and stack trace were printed.

If an exception was thrown that was different from `NullPointerException` and `ArithmeticException` and was also not a subclass of one of those exceptions, then the third catch block would have been chosen by the JVM. This is because exceptions are usually subclasses of the `java.lang.Exception` class.

If none of the catch blocks are applicable, the JVM will look at the caller of the method. If it has a `try...catch` block, it will be analyzed. If a match is found, control will be transferred to that catch block. If the caller does not have a `try...catch` block, it will look at the caller of that method until the call stack is exhausted. The program will crash if none of the `try...catch` blocks are able to handle the error.

Catch blocks must be put in the correct order. First, the most concrete `Exception` classes must be listed, then the `Exception` subclasses, and finally the `Exception` itself, if desired. The following example is not allowed:

```
try {
  Integer i = null;
  System.out.println(i.toString());
} catch (Exception e) {
  // ...
} catch (NullPointerException e) {
  // THIS WILL NOT COMPILE!
}
```

Since the `NullPointerException` exception is a subclass of the `Exception` class, the Java compiler understands that the `NullPointerException` catch block can never be reached and will refuse to compile this code.

An optional `finally` block can be added. The statements inside the `finally` block are always executed, even when an exception is thrown:

```
try {
    throw new Exception("oops");
} catch (Exception e) {
    System.out.println("Exception!");
} finally {
    System.out.println("FINALLY!");
}
```

This will print:

```
Exception!
FINALLY!
```

Runtime exceptions

Java has an unusual requirement regarding exceptions that a method can throw. A method can freely throw any exception that is a subclass of `java.lang.RuntimeException`. In the class diagram earlier, you can see that `NullPointerException` and `ArithmeticException` are both subclasses of `RuntimeException`.

If it wants to throw `Exception` instances that are not subclasses of the `java.lang.RuntimeException` class, then the method has to explicitly list all the Exception subclasses that are not a subclass of `RuntimeException`. Let's take a look at the declaration of one of the methods of the `java.sql.ResultSet` interface:

```
public int getInt(String column) throws SQLException
```

This method takes a `String` column name parameter and returns the retrieved integer value from the database. The method signature tells the Java compiler that it can throw `SQLException`, which happens to be a subclass of `java.lang.Exception`, but not `java.lang.RuntimeException`. Now that the Java compiler knows that it can throw this exception, the method .

When overriding a method, either from a concrete class, abstract class, or an interface, the class that overrides the method can either:

- Choose not to throw any of the exceptions by not adding the `throws` keyword at all
- Take over all or only some of the exceptions of the original method using the `throws` keyword
- Replace some or all the classes in the `throws` list of exceptions with classes that are subclasses of the specified exceptions

The overridden method cannot throw any other exceptions unless the exceptions are of `RuntimeException`.

Threads

We will only cover the most simple form of concurrent programming here: launching multiple threads.

The `java.lang.Runnable` interface plays an important role with threads. It's a simple interface with only a single method:

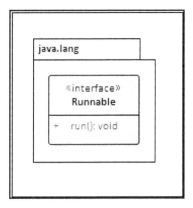

A class that implements this interface and provides an implementation for the `run()` method can be started in a separate thread. Let's look at a simple example.

First, we have a class that implements the `Runnable` interface and can run inside a different thread:

```java
class SleepyClass implements Runnable {
  private int number;

  public SleepyClass(int number) { this.number = number; }

  @Override
  public void run() {
    System.out.println("Thread " + number + " started!");
    try {
      Thread.sleep(3000);
    } catch (InterruptedException e) {
      e.printStackTrace();
    }
    System.out.println("Thread " + number + " ended!");
  }
}
```

Now we have a class that will run two threads with the previous code:

```java
public class ThreadsDemo {
  public static void main(String[] args) {
    Thread thread1 = new Thread(new SleepyClass(1));
    Thread thread2 = new Thread(new SleepyClass(2));
    thread1.start();
    thread2.start();
  }
}
```

When run, the output could be:

```
Thread 1 started!
Thread 2 started!
Thread 2 ended!
Thread 1 ended!
```

The starting sequence of the threads is not guaranteed by the JVM; it's not guaranteed that the thread 1 will start and finish first. If there are enough CPU cores available, it is likely that each separate thread will run on its own CPU core.

The `SleepyClass` class shows an issue regarding exception handling that Java developers encounter frequently. The `sleep` method of the `Thread` class can throw the `InterruptedException` exception instances. This is not a subclass of `RuntimeException`. We cannot add `throws InterruptedException` to the `run()` method declaration because the original `run()` method from the `Runnable` interface does not throw this exception or a subclass of it. Therefore, we chose to handle this exception inside the `run()`.

Concurrent programming is difficult. The programmer has to ensure that multiple threads are not writing to the same variable at the same time, or race conditions can occur, which may result to corrupted values and subtle bugs. These conditions occur because the operations on a variable are most often not atomic operations, and multiple CPU instructions are required to finish an operation. While one operation is running, a different thread will start its own operations on the same variable.

Java has a non-access modifier for methods that ensures that a method can only be called by a single thread at a time. Other threads will wait until that thread has finished, then one by one other threads that are waiting will run the method. This is done with the `synchronized` non-access modifier:

```
public synchronized void synchronizedMethod() {
}
```

The JVM will ensure that the lock is always released when the thread leaves the method, even if an exception is thrown inside the method.

 It is not recommended that you make a lot of use of the synchronized modifier as locking threads is an expensive operation that can possibly hurt the performance of the program a lot.

Take a good look at the classes in the `java.util.concurrent` package if you are interested in concurrent programming.

Lambdas

Lambdas were probably the most welcomed addition to Java 8. They make it possible to pass functions to other methods, just like variables. We will see lambdas in action in a lot of languages covered in this book, as many other languages already have built-in support for lambdas.

To pass a lambda to a function, first a functional interface must be created. A functional interface is a normal interface that contains only one abstract method. Java comes with a lot of interfaces that can be used for lambdas; one of them is the `java.lang.Runnable` interface. As it only has an abstract `run()` method, it's perfectly suited for lambdas. If we only want to run a single thread, we can directly pass an anonymous lambda function to the `Thread` instance:

```java
public class LambdaDemo {
  public static void main(String[] args) {
    Thread thread1 = new Thread( () -> {
      try {
        Thread.sleep(3000);
      } catch (InterruptedException e) {
      }
    });
    thread1.start();
  }
}
```

The syntax may look confusing at first. Consider that the `run()` method of the `java.lang.Runnable` interface does not have any arguments. So, we start by specifying empty parentheses `()`, followed by an arrow sign `->` that signals to the compiler that a lambda is about to begin.

Inside this block, the code of the function that will run using the thread is written as usual.

In the next chapter, we will use more complex lambdas that require parameters.

Style guide

No official up-to-date Java language style guide is available from Oracle until now. The closest to this is a document from 1999 by Sun Microsystems, which is still archived on the Java website at the time of writing this. Some of its most important points, which are still relevant today, are:

- It is recommended that you start each file of a project with the same header comments that at least contain the class name and copyright information.
- The public class, or public interface, must be the first entry in the file. If the file has other classes or interfaces with other access modifiers, they need to be added below the public class or interface.
- This is the order we follow when defining a class or interface:
    1. Javadoc headers of the class or interface (this topic will be discussed in the next chapter).
    2. The `class` or `interface` keyword (including the access modifiers and other modifiers). After the class or interface name, the { character that starts the class block should be on the same line. The corresponding } character to close the class block should be on its own line, however.
    3. If applicable, a comment with implementation information that was not part of the documentation.
    4. Static variables in this order:
        - Public static variables
        - Protected static variables
        - Package-private (no access modifier) static variables
        - Private static variables
    5. Instance variables, using the same order as static variables.
    6. Constructors.
    7. Methods, grouped by functionality, not by access modifiers.
- Do not declare multiple variables on a single line; instead, do one declaration per line.
- If possible, initialize variables at the same time as declaring them.
- Declarations of variables should be put at the beginning of a block, { }. Don't declare variables in the middle of a block.

Quiz

Let's test your knowledge of the Java language with a little quiz. The answers are included in the first appendix. If you earn a great score, congratulations! If not, don't despair and just reread the relevant parts and see if you can do better next time.

1. Will the following code compile? If not, what is wrong with this code?

```
import java.util.ArrayList;
package com.example.quiz1;
public class Question1 {
}
```

    a) The `package` name is wrong; digits are not allowed in package names.

    b) The `ArrayList` is not a class in the `java.util` package.

    c) The `package` statement must be placed before the `import` statement.

    d) None of the other options; the file compiles correctly.

2. Will the following code compile? If not, what's wrong with it?

```
class A {  }

class B {  }

class C extends A, B  {
}
```

    a) Class names with a single letter are not allowed.

    b) In Java, a class cannot inherit (extend) multiple classes.

    c) A single Java source file can never define more than one class.

    d) None of the other options; the file compiles correctly.

3. What is most likely wrong with this code (assume it has been placed in a valid method)?

```
String s1 = "String A";
String s2 = "String B";

if (s1 != s2) {
  // More code is here...
}
```

a) Most likely, the programmer wanted to check the content of the strings and should have used the equals method.

b) Java does not support the != operator.

c) Without seeing more of the code, it is impossible to say whether the snippet has errors in its logic.

d) No surprises here; everything is fine.

4. When overriding a method from a class or interface, is the method completely free to decide which exceptions to throw?

a) Yes

b) No

5. What output will be printed to the console when this method is called (assume it has been placed in the correct class)?

```
void testMethod() {
  try {
    System.out.println("A");
    throw new RuntimeException("Error!");
  } catch (Exception e) {
    System.out.println("C");
    return;
  } finally {
    System.out.println("D");
  }
}
```

a) A, C

b) A, D

c) A, D, C

d) A, C, D

Summary

We have looked at a lot of Java code in this chapter. We started by describing all the OOP features of the Java language, including defining classes, grouping classes in packages, and adding members to the classes by defining new methods and variables. We saw that the object-orientated features of Java did not end there, as abstract classes and interfaces offer a lot of possibilities to make well-structured code. We discussed the most important access modifiers and non-access modifiers, the process of upcasting and downcasting classes, and the POJO convention. We finished the chapter by looking at the various important features of the Java language, including its most important operators: `if...else` conditions, `for` loops, `while` and `do...while` loops. We also looked at arrays, collections, generics, and exceptions. We also tried out some of the more advanced features, such as multithreading and lambdas.

With all this knowledge, we are ready to do our first real project in Java. Let's write some code together!

4
Java Programming

With a lot of theory behind us, let's write a real Java program. We will write a simple standalone web service that will count the frequency of each character that was used in the passed input string and return this in a JSON dictionary. We will use the Gradle build tool to automatically fetch dependencies from the internet and then build and run the project. At the coding stage of the backend class, we will use a test-driven approach and write unit tests along the way. In every step, from the coding stage to running the final web service, we will use Eclipse IDE. In the end, we'll discuss various shortcuts to ensure you are as productive as possible. We'll cover the following topics:

- Configuring Eclipse IDE
- Creating a new Gradle-based project in Eclipse IDE
- Modifying the Gradle build script
- Building the project
- Coding the backend class
- Creating unit tests to test the backend class
- Writing a web service
- Running a web service

Configuring Eclipse IDE

When using the default **Java Project** project type in Eclipse IDE, Eclipse internally generates an XML build script based on Apache's Ant build tool and executes its tasks when the user chooses Eclipse's **Compile** and **Build** options. For small projects, this works fine, but for bigger projects, you normally need more control. In this particular case, we want Eclipse to download add-on dependencies. We have chosen the very popular Gradle build tool for this chapter's project.

As Eclipse IDE has no built-in support for Gradle out-of-the-box, we will need to install a plugin that will add this feature to Eclipse IDE. There are different plugins available that aim to do this. We will use the plugin created by the Gradle team in this case. To install it, follow these instructions:

- From the **Help** menu, choose the **Eclipse Marketplace...** option:

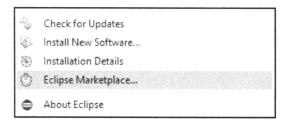

- Enter gradle in the **Find** textbox and press *Enter*. In the list of plugins that are found, scroll down until you see the following entry: **Buildship Gradle Integration 2.0**. Its entry should have the Gradle elephant logo, and it should credit the **Eclipse Buildship Project** team. If not already installed, click on the **Install** button:

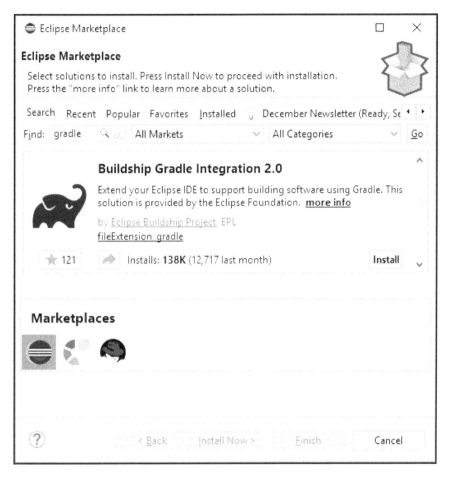

- If you agree with the license terms, accept the terms and click on **Finish**.
- After a short while, the Eclipse IDE will display a dialog stating that the IDE must be restarted. Click on **Yes** to acknowledge the automatic restart.

The plugin is now installed and ready for action.

Creating a web service in Java

We will create a simple web service in Java using the test-driven development approach. The steps that we will follow are:

- Creating the project in Eclipse IDE
- Modifying the Gradle build file
- Coding the backend class
- Coding the web service code

Creating a new Gradle project in Eclipse IDE

We will create a Gradle project and then examine the generated project.

Start Eclipse IDE if it is not already running. If necessary, acknowledge the `workspace` directory. This will be the root directory where Eclipse will create new projects and look for existing ones.

Eclipse IDE's **Welcome** tab will now be displayed. As it does not offer a shortcut for creating a new Gradle-based project, we will ignore it for now. To create a Gradle project, do the following:

- From the **File** menu, move to **New** and choose **Project...** (be sure not to select **Java Project** or Gradle will not be used for building the project):

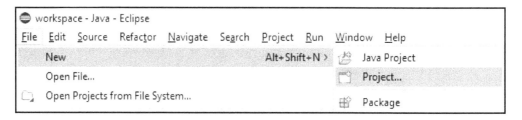

- In the **New Project** wizard window, expand the **Gradle** option and select the **Gradle Project** option. Click on the **Next** button. A welcome window will be displayed; read the text carefully. You have the option to uncheck **Show the welcome page the next time the wizard appears** if you prefer. Click on the **Next** button:

- On the **New Gradle Project** window, specify the project name: `JavaWebservice`. Make sure you agree with the location and click on the **Finish** button. When used for the first time, the plugin may need some time to download and install Gradle. Eventually, the window will close automatically.

Note that the window in the preceding screenshot has been resized; your window will show more options.

Exploring the generated project

A docked window containing the Package Explorer tab should now appear on the left-hand side of the Eclipse IDE window. Expand the `JavaWebservice` project. Let's take a quick look at the generated project.

The Gradle build plugin generates the following project entries:

- The `src/main` entry is a shortcut to the directory that holds the source code of the main program.
- The `src/test` entry is a shortcut to the directory that holds the unit test scripts.
- The `JRE System Library` entry shows the Java platform files that are needed to run the program.

- The `Project and External Dependencies` entry shows the add-on libraries that the program needs. Currently, several libraries are required for the JUnit 4 unit testing framework that Gradle loads by default.
- The `gradle` directory contains the files needed for the Gradle wrapper. This is a script that ensures you can run the project on systems that do not have Gradle installed. It makes sure that the correct version of Gradle is downloaded and used during the process of building such a project.
- The **src** entry shows the full content of the source directory. It currently holds the **main** and **test** subdirectories, as discussed earlier.
- Finally, some Gradle-related files are shown in the project root. Of these, `build.gradle` is the most important file. This is the build file that Gradle will use to compile and build the project and run the unit tests.

Modifying the Gradle build file

For this project, we will use the SparkJava framework. SparkJava, not to be confused with Apache's big data platform, was briefly discussed in the first chapter. It's a framework that makes it easy to create fast, standalone web applications. You can manually download the library from the official site and put the required files in the correct directory, but it's much easier to let the build tool take care of these things.

 Many well-known libraries depend on many other dependencies, which have dependencies of their own. A build tool that can download libraries is essential for modern JVM software development.

Open the `build.gradle` file from Package Explorer by double-clicking on it. The current version of Gradle uses a **domain-specific language** (**DSL**) that is based on Groovy; later versions will support a DSL based on Kotlin. As we will see in the Groovy chapter, Groovy is less strict about syntax than Java; therefore, semicolons and parentheses are often not required in Gradle's build files. Find the line that starts the `dependencies` block:

```
dependencies {
  ....
}
```

If there are lines that start with `compile`, remove them. Be sure to keep the statements that start with `testCompile`, though. Add the following entries to the top of the `dependencies` block:

```
compile 'org.slf4j:slf4j-simple:1.7.21'
compile 'com.sparkjava:spark-core:2.5.4'
compile 'com.fasterxml.jackson.core:jackson-databind:2.8.5'
```

Save the modified file. This tells Gradle that it requires the Simple Logging Facade for Java (SLF4J), SparkJava, and Jackson's JSON handler frameworks to compile this project. It's often a good idea to add the version number to the dependencies since newer versions can introduce breaking changes on existing code. When building the project, Gradle will look at popular repository sites, download the requested versions of each dependency plus their own dependencies, and put everything in the correct directories. The classpath will be set in such a way that you'll be able to run the project without modifying it manually.

 Remember that newer versions of libraries and frameworks can fix important security bugs, which is especially important for production use. It is always advisable to stay up-to-date on the developments of frameworks you depend on.

Building the project

In the lower window of Eclipse IDE, pictured below, find and click on the **Gradle Tasks** tab. Expand the **build** item, then double-click on its **build** task:

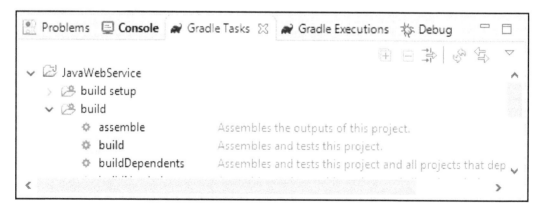

The lower window will now switch to the **Gradle Executions** tab, which displays the progress and status of the tasks that the Gradle plugin ran. If everything went smoothly, you will see green dots next to each task:

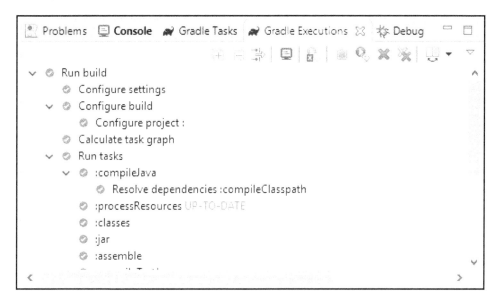

If things don't go well and only the **:compileJava** task shows a red dot, switch to the **Console** tab. This tab contains the output of the Gradle process. Scroll down and check whether you see an error message stating that **tools.jar** was not found. If that's the case, then you probably have to tell the Gradle plugin where your Java installation is located. Follow this procedure if you encounter this issue:

1. Switch back to the **Gradle Tasks** tab.
2. Right-click on the **build** task and choose **Open Gradle Run Configuration....**
3. The **Edit configuration** window should now be displayed. Switch to the **Java Home** tab and click on **Browse**. Navigate to the root of the JDK installation directory and close the window by clicking on the **OK** button. Then, close the **Edit configuration** window by clicking on **OK**.
4. Start the **build** task again by double-clicking on it. The tab should now only show green dots.

An issue with the current version of the Buildship Gradle Integration plugin for Eclipse is that you may have to manually refresh the project when adding, updating, or removing dependencies. If you don't see the `spark-core` JAR file listed when expanding the **Project and External Dependencies** entry in **Package Explorer**, simply right-click on the `JavaWebservice` project and choose **Gradle | Refresh Gradle Project**. Many more JAR files should now be listed as dependencies.

Coding the backend class

We will build a generic, reusable backend class that has no knowledge of the web service technology used. The code we will use to handle the HTTP request will use the backend class to generate a JSON response. We will use the **test-driven development** (**TDD**) approach and cover the following topics:

- Backend class business rules
- Creating a dummy implementation of the method
- Creating the test case class and writing its first unit test
- Implementing the input validation check
- Writing the second unit test
- Implementing the business logic
- Creating the web service

Backend class business rules

Let's create a simple web service that will return the count of each character of a string sent to the web service.

Here are the requirements of the method that will count the usage of each character in the string:

- The class has to be in the `chapter03.backend` package; it must be called **CharacterCounter** and must be public.
- The method must be called `countCharacters`; it should accept `String` as an input value and be public.

- The method has to return an instance of a class that implements the generics-aware `Map<Character, Integer>` interface. This is a map that maps a Character instance to an Integer instance value.
- The returned `Map` object must map each unique UTF-16 character inside the input string to an integer that contains the frequency of that character in `String`.
- The passed string may not be null, or an `IllegalArgumentException` exception must be thrown.

Here's an example of the input and output:

```
"A!Ba?!?!" --> {'A': 1, 'B':1, 'a':1, '?': 2, '!': 3}
```

Creating a dummy implementation of the method

To be able to write a unit test, we need to write a method that follows the method signature requirements (input and output), but we will just let it return null. By doing this, we can write a unit test, see it fail, and then provide the correct implementation and see the test succeed.

If you study the business rules closely, you'll find that you have to write a method that would take an input and generate a response. The method has to be self-contained; it does not seem to require any class instance variables or methods. We, therefore, will choose to write a static class method. During the coding of the unit test, we can determine whether this was a bad choice. If so, we can always change it before the method is added to production code.

 One of the important advantages of TDD is that we can fix wrong design decisions before they make it into production.

Let's create the `chapter03.backend.CharacterCounter` class:

1. In **Package Explorer**, right-click on the `src/main/java` entry and select **New | Class...**.
2. In the **Package** field, type `chapter03.backend`.
3. In the **Name** field, type `CharacterCounter`.

4. Ensure the **public** modifier is selected.
5. Click on **Finish** to generate the class.

The window in the preceding screenshot has been resized; your window will show more options. The following class will be generated by the wizard:

```
package chapter03.backend;
public class CharacterCounter {
}
```

Now we will write a dummy implementation of the method. Move the cursor to the body of the class and do the following:

1. Press *Tab* to indent one level.
2. Type the required access modifier and non-access modifier (`public static`) and add a space.
3. Type the word `Map` and press *Ctrl* + Space bar. A window with a few classes that match the entered name will be displayed. Choose the **Map - java.util** entry and press *Enter*:

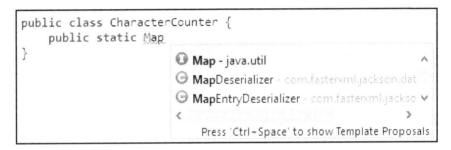

Eclipse will now write both the corresponding package import statement lines and `Map<K, V>` for us; then it will place the cursor on the first `K` type, which represents the map's key.

4. Enter `Char` and press *Ctrl* + Space bar again. Now choose the **Character - java.lang** class and press *Enter*:

```
public class Character K, V ter {
    public static Map<Char, V>|
}
                    ⊖ CharacterCounter - chapter03.backend      ⌃
                    ⊖ Character - java.lang
                    ❶ CharSequence - java.lang                  ⌄
                    ‹                                        ›
                        Press 'Ctrl-Space' to show Template Proposals
```

5. Press *Tab* to move to the V character, enter Int, and press *Ctrl* + Space bar, then choose **Integer - java.lang** and press *Enter*. This represents the used type of the map value.

```
public class Character K, V ter {
    public static Map<Character, Int>
```
```
                                    ⊙ Integer - java.lang              ∧
                                    ⊙ InternalError - java.lang
                                    ⊙ InterruptedException - java.lang  ∨
                                    <                              >
                                    Press 'Ctrl-Space' to show Template Proposals
```

6. Move the cursor to the end of the line, enter countCharacters(String text), and add { to the same line and place } on the next line.

The code should now look like this:

```
package chapter03.backend;
import java.util.Map;
public class CharacterCounter {
    public static Map<Character, Integer> countCharacters(String text) {
    }
}
```

The Eclipse IDE will notify that the class cannot be compiled. Move the mouse to either the red underlined method name or the red **X** icon on the left-hand side. A tooltip will appear that will tell you: **This method must return a result of type Map<Character, Integer>**. It will offer two possible solutions that Eclipse can automatically apply for you, either **Add return statement** or **Change return type to 'void'**:

```
🔲 This method must return a result of type Map<Character,Integer>
2 quick fixes available:
  ↩ Add return statement
  ↩ Change return type to 'void'
                                    Press 'F2' for focus
```

Choose the first solution by selecting **Add return statement**. Eclipse will now automatically write this code:

```
return null;
```

We now have a backend class that can be compiled. Let's write a unit test so that we can check whether our API seems right. If we are satisfied, we can write the valid implementation and check whether it will work as expected.

Creating the test case class and writing its first unit test

The business rules clearly state that the class will throw an `IllegalArgumentException` exception if null is specified instead of a String instance. Let's test whether the class throws this exception when null is passed. For this, first create a class that the JUnit testing framework will use; this class will contain all our tests:

1. In Eclipse IDE, right-click on the `src/test/java` entry and select **JUnit Test Case**.
2. In the **Package** field, type `chapter03.backend`.
3. In the a **Name** field, type `CharacterCounterTests`.
4. Click on **Finish** to generate the class.

The following class is generated (minus some empty lines for brevity):

```java
package chapter03.backend;
import static org.junit.Assert.*;
import org.junit.Test;
public class CharacterCounterTests {
  @Test
  public void test() {
    fail("Not yet implemented");
  }
}
```

The `@Test` annotation signals the JUnit framework that this is the method that will contain the unit test. As we will soon see, it can have optional parameters. A method that contains a unit test is not allowed to return anything; therefore, the `void` keyword is used as the return type. Rename the `test()` method by placing the cursor on the first character of the name, then press *Alt + Shift + R*, change the method name to `testNullInput`, and press *Enter*.

```
@Test
public void testNullInput() {
    fail("Not yet implemented");
}
```
Press **Enter** to refactor. Options... ▾

 It may seem silly to use *Alt+Shift+R* here. If this were a method in a large program, Eclipse would let you apply the change to the whole program, so always try to use it. The more you use a key combination, the easier it will be to remember.

Place the cursor on the line containing the `fail` statement and press *Ctrl + D* to delete the whole line. Rewrite the full method in such a way that it looks exactly like this (remember to press *Ctrl* + Space bar while writing the `expected`, `IllegalArgumentException`, and `CharacterCounter` names to save valuable keystrokes):

```
@Test(expected=IllegalArgumentException.class)
public void testNullInput() {
  CharacterCounter.countCharacters(null);
}
```

This tells JUnit that this particular test is considered successful only if the `IllegalArgumentException` exception is thrown. If the class does not throw this exception, then the test is considered to have failed. This will be a good time to run the test now. Press the *F11* key. Gradle will now build and compile the code and run the test.

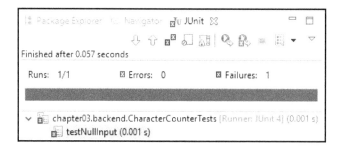

As expected, the test fails. Click on the **Package Explorer** tab and fix the test.

Implementing an input validation check

From `src/main/java`, open the `CharacterCounter` class. Inside the body of its `countCharacters` method, above the `return null` line, enter the following code:

```
if (text == null) {
    throw new IllegalArgumentException("text must not be null");
}
```

This code is largely self-explanatory. Since `IllegalArgumentException` is a subclass of `RuntimeException`, the method is not required to tell the compiler that it will throw this exception.

To verify this claim, double-click on the `IllegalArgumentException` class name and press *F4*, or right-click on it and select the **Open Type hierarchy** option. Click on the **Package Explorer** tab to return to the package explorer.

Press *F11* now to run the test:

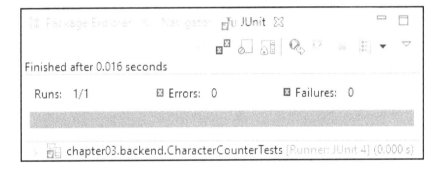

This time it finishes successfully. Congratulations! Don't forget to click on the **Package Explorer** tab again after you have finished celebrating.

Writing the second unit test

Now we create a test that will test the main business logic. To add a new unit test, open the `CharacterCounterTests` class from `src/test/java`, add an empty line after the `testNullInput()` method's body, and add the following method:

```
@Test
public void testStringInput() {
  Map<Character, Integer> map = CharacterCounter
                                .countCharacters("!a!A!");
  assertEquals(map.size(), 3);
  assertEquals(map.get('a').intValue(), 1);
  assertEquals(map.get('!').intValue(), 3);
  assertEquals(map.get('A').intValue(), 1);
}
```

We pass a string and then verify that the returned map does not return more than the expected number of characters; also, test the frequency of each character individually. Here are some notes on this:

- The `Character` class is a primitive wrapper class that wraps a char primitive value. A char (a single UTF-16 Unicode character) in Java uses single quotes for a value, while String values use double quotes. If we pass a String `"A"` instead of a character `'A'`, the map's get method would return `null`.
- The map's `get` method returns the Integer wrapper class that contains the frequency. We convert it into a primitive value so that we can easily use JUnit's overloaded `assertEquals(int, int)` version of the `assertEquals` method. There are a lot of overloaded versions of this method available. We will be required to do some casting to satisfy Java's overloading rules if we don't use the mentioned version.

Press *F11* and see the test fail because of `NullPointerException`. This happens because the returned map is null; therefore, the `map.size()` call fails.

Implementing the business logic

As we're still satisfied with the API, let's implement the business logic and hopefully make the previous test pass. So without wasting time, open the `CharacterCounter` class from `src/main/java` in **Package Explorer**. Add the following code after the null input condition check:

```
Map<Character, Integer> map = new HashMap<>();
for (char c: text.toCharArray()) {
  if (!map.containsKey(c)) {
    map.put(c, 1);
  } else {
    int curValue = map.get(c);
    map.put(c, ++curValue);
  }
}
return map;
```

Here are some notes about the preceding code:

- The `map` variable points to a `HashMap` instance, which maps a `Character` instance (the map's key) to an `Integer` instance (the map's value).
- The `String` datatype does not implement the `Iterable` interface and cannot be used with the enhanced for loop. We have to call its `toCharArray()` method that returns a char array. An array can always be used with the enhanced for loop.
- We use primitive char values in this code. Java will automatically convert these to the `Character` class when using `Map`'s methods, thanks to autoboxing. Remember that generics require the usage of classes.
- If the character is not found in the map, it is added to the map with the character as key and 1 as hardcoded value
- If the character was found in the map, then its current value is retrieved from the map
- Note the `map.put(c, ++curValue);` line. First, the value is incremented, then the key and updated value are stored in the map. As an exercise, try to change `++curValue` into `curValue++` to check whether the test fails.

Press *F11* to run both the tests again. Both should now succeed.

Creating an executable application task

We will not use SparkJava's unit testing functionality. Instead, we will create an executable program that Gradle can run. The easiest way to add a `run` task to this Gradle project is using Gradle's `application` plugin. We will create the class that will start the web service first.

In **Package Explorer**, add a new `Webservice` class to the `chapter03.main` package by right-clicking on the `src/main/java` entry and choosing the **New | Class** option. Add the `main()` method to print a simple String to the console. The class should look like this:

```
package chapter03.main;
public class WebService {
  public static void main(String[] args) {
    System.out.println("The program is running!");
  }
}
```

Using Package Explorer, open the `build.gradle` file. Below the `apply plugin: 'java'` line, add a new entry as specified here:

```
apply plugin: 'java'
apply plugin: 'application'
```

Add an empty line, then add the following entry:

```
mainClassName = "chapter03.main.WebService"
```

This defines the fully qualified class that contains the `main()` method and the class that the plugin will run. Build the project by choosing the **build | build** entry in the **Gradle Tasks** tab. If everything goes smoothly, refresh the **Gradle Tasks** tab by clicking on the fourth small icon on the right-hand side of the tab; it launches the Refresh Tasks for All Projects tooltip. This will add new tasks that the application plugin added to the Gradle project.

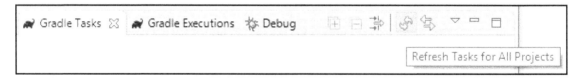

You can now choose the **application | run** task from the **Gradle Tasks** window. The project will be automatically compiled if required. You'll have to switch to the **Console** tab to see the console output. If you don't want Eclipse to automatically switch to the **Gradle Execution** tab, you can disable this feature by following this procedure:

1. Switch to the **Gradle Tasks** tab.
2. Expand the **JavaWebservice** | **application** entry. Right-click on its **run** entry and choose the **Open Gradle Run Configuration...** option.
3. Uncheck the **Show Execution View** option. Close the window by clicking on **OK**.

Now when you choose the **application** | **run** task, the Console tab will be automatically activated instead, and you will be able to see the message that you let the main method print to the console.

Creating a web service

We will transform the main() method into a program that will set up a Spark route to handle your HTTP GET request. Open the chapter03.main.Webservice class. Below the package statement, add the following new import statements:

```
package chapter03.main;
import java.util.Map;
import spark.Spark;
import com.fasterxml.jackson.databind.ObjectMapper;
import chapter03.backend.CharacterCounter;
```

Inside the WebService class, add the private static variable mapper, which is an instance of the ObjectMapper class. This object from the Jackson library will transform the output of the countCharacters method, which is a Map<Character, Integer> instance. In other words, it is a Map object that maps a Character instance key to an Integer instance value, which is mapped to JSON:

```
private static ObjectMapper mapper = new ObjectMapper();
```

Now the main() method can be written. Alter the existing one and don't forget to use the key combinations that were mentioned previously while writing the code:

```
public static void main(String[] args) {
  Spark.get("/main", (req, res) -> {
    res.type("application/json");
    try {
      String value = req.queryMap("value").value();
      value = (value == null ? "" : value);
      Map<Character, Integer> map = CharacterCounter
                              .countCharacters(value);
      return mapper.writeValueAsString(map);
    } catch (Exception e) {
      e.printStackTrace();
      return "{}";
```

```
        }
    });
}
```

Here are some interesting notes:

- By calling the `Spark.get` method, the Spark library sets up a handler function that responds when the specified URL is requested by an HTTP GET request. Once an HTTP handler is defined, Spark will make sure that the HTTP server is automatically launched when the program has finished initializing.
- The second parameter of the `Spark.get()` method is a lambda. In this case, the lambda requires two parameters: request and response. Both the parameters are used by our passed lambda: the request (`req`) to read the HTTP request's query parameters and the response (`res`) to set the web service's output format to JSON. The lambda will be executed when the `/main` URL is requested by an HTTP GET request.
- We use a form of "if" condition that we have not seen before. The part before `?` is the expression. If it evaluates to true, then the first part after `?` is returned (`""` in this case); otherwise, the part after `:` is returned. In this case, when the value retrieved from the query parameters is null, it is changed to an empty String; otherwise, the query parameter's value is returned.
- The static `mapper`, an instance of Jackson's `ObjectMapper`, is responsible for converting the `Map<Character, Integer>` map (the `Map` that maps a `Character` instance key to an `Integer` instance value) into a string that contains a valid JSON representation of the map. If an exception is thrown, the error is printed to the console and an empty JSON object is returned.

Running the web service

To run the web service via the Eclipse IDE's green run icon in the top toolbar's, click on the downward arrow next to the run icon:

All Gradle tasks that can be triggered by this button are listed here, including the **build** and **run** options that will launch the build process and the program, respectively. Select the **run** option so that Eclipse will launch the application when pressing *Ctrl + F11* or the run icon. Eclipse IDE will waste no time and start your application right away.

After a short while, the application will start printing log output to the **Console** window tab. The last message should be **Started** along with the class name of the server that SparkJava is using internally, namely org.eclipse.jetty.server.Server:

With SparkJava's default settings, the HTTP server that SparkJava uses is configured to use port 4567. Launch your browser and visit http://localhost:4567/main?value=Test.

You will have an output that is similar to the following:

The order of the elements in your output could be different from what was printed earlier. The reason is that the HashMap class does not order elements in any meaningful way.

To stop the application, press the red stop button on the **Console** tab.

It may take a short while before the HTTP server is stopped. The button will be grayed out eventually, and the application will then stop. Each Gradle action will open a new console. You can cycle between them by clicking on the button with the Display Selected Console tooltip. Or, you can click on its arrow icon to see a list of all the open consoles:

Click on the button with the Remove All Terminated Gradle Consoles tooltip to close all the inactive windows. This can be handy when you've started a lot of Gradle tasks while developing your project:

As an exercise, in the CharacterCounter class, try to replace the java.util.HashMap instance with a java.util.TreeMap instance. The TreeMap class will order the elements according to the inserted key. Since the TreeMap class implements the Map<K, V> interface, like the HashMap class, your program will keep working correctly. Hiding implementation details by using interfaces is really a very good idea in practice.

Creating Javadoc documentation

Now would be a great time to create some documentation. In the **Gradle Tasks** tab, click on the **Documentation** | **Javadoc** task. You'll have to refresh the project in Package Explorer. After that, open the **Navigator** tab and navigate to the project's build file: **build** | **docs** | **javadocs** | **index.html**. Then right-click on it and select **Open with** | **System editor**; this will launch your default browser.

To add documentation to a class or method, type the following before the class or method definition and press *Enter*:

```
/**
```

Normal multiline comments in Java are between `/*  */` (such as C and C++), and a single-line comment is started with `//`. Javadoc comments start with `/**` and end with `*/` (the same as normal comments). Eclipse will automatically create a block with `/**` and `*/` and add some properties automatically. You'll have to provide the documentation; keep in mind that you'll need to write HTML and can therefore not use some characters without escaping them. An example would be that > is written as `&gt;`.

Summary

I hope that we have debunked the perception that writing a web application in Java always requires much more code than other modern languages. While writing the code, we used various Eclipse IDE features to ease and speed up development. Gradle was used to manage dependencies and build the project. and we added Gradle's application plugin so that we could easily run our application by running a simple Gradle task. By applying TDD, we wrote a backend class. The Jackson library was used to convert this class's output to JSON, and the SparkJava framework was used to create the web service around that.

If you are interested in the SparkJava framework, then be sure to visit `http://sparkjava.com`.

In the next chapter, we will look at Scala. This language has strong support for functional programming, but it is a pure OOP language at the same time.

5
Scala

Scala is a unique language. It has strong support for functional programming and is also a pure **object-oriented programming (OOP)** language at the same time. We will cover both OOP and functional programming in this chapter.

The Scala installation offers two ways of running Scala code. It offers an interactive shell where the code can be directly entered and run right away. This program can also be used to run Scala's source code directly, without manually compiling it first. Also, it offers `scalac`, a traditional compiler that compiles Scala's source code to Java bytecode and generates files with the `.class` extension. This chapter will only focus on the first method; the next chapter will cover the `scalac` compiler.

Scala comes with its own Scala standard library. It complements the Java Class Library that is bundled with the **Java Runtime Environment** (**JRE**) and installed as part of the **Java Development Kit** (**JDK**). Scala's standard library contains classes that are optimized to work with Scala's language features. Among many other things, it implements its own collection classes and still offers compatibility with Java's collections.

These are the topics that we will discuss in this chapter:

- Installing Scala
- Scala's Read-Eval-Print-Loop shell
- Functional versus imperative programming
- Scala language syntax and rules
- OOP in Scala
- Scala's standard library
- Functional programming in Scala

Many concepts used in this chapter are covered in detail in the previous chapters, particularly in Chapter 3, *Java*. We recommend that you read that chapter first before you start with this.

Installing Scala

From the official Scala site, download the latest version:

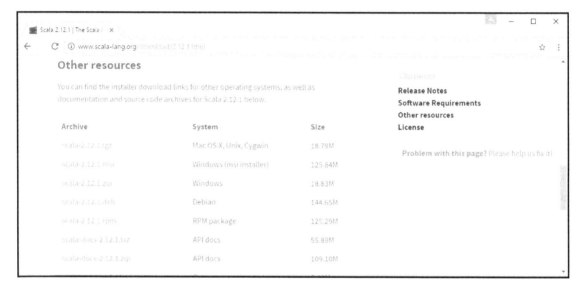

Scala is distributed for many different operating systems. While you can download an archive (ZIP file for Windows or a .tgz file for Linux and macOS) and install everything manually, automatic installation packages for popular operating systems are available as well.

On the **DOWNLOAD** page, scroll down to **Other resources**, find your preferred archive format, and download it. Simply unpack it somewhere and add its bin subdirectory to your path. Consult Chapter 2, *Developing on the Java Virtual Machine*, for instructions on how to add a directory to the path on Windows, macOS, and Linux systems. When you choose to use the installer, just follow its prompts.

To verify the installation, open Command Prompt (Windows) or the Terminal screen (Linux or OS X), type the following command, and press *Enter*:

```
scala
```

If the installation was successful, then something similar to the following will appear on the console:

```
Welcome to Scala 2.12.1 (Java HotSpot(TM) 64-Bit Server VM, Java
1.8.0_112).
Type in expressions for evaluation. Or try :help.

scala>
```

Enter :quit and press *Enter* to quit.

The Scala site offers online documentation. It is recommended that you keep the following URLs nearby for reference:

* http://docs.scala-lang.org
* http://www.scala-lang.org/api/current/

Scala's Read-Eval-Print-Loop shell

The scala command demonstrated in the preceding section starts the Scala interactive shell, also known as Scala's **Read-Eval-Print-Loop** (**REPL**) environment. You enter a line and the REPL program evaluates it and prints a response (if applicable). It does this in an infinite loop until you quit the program.

In the Scala shell, you can write Scala code interactively. Because Scala is a compiled language, not an interpreted language, you can dynamically enter and execute Scala code in this program. Under the hood, Scala compiles your code and runs the compiled version. The Scala interactive shell is meant for trying Scala expressions, not for writing full programs. It is ideal for trying out the snippets in this chapter. The shell has commands of its own. Enter the `:help` command and press *Enter* to see all the shell commands.

In this chapter, we will only use the `scala` command to run Scala code. In the next chapter, we will cover the `scalac` compiler. To run code in this chapter, you can enter it directly in the shell. You can also use a text editor to create a file with the source code. You can directly run the script by passing the path as an argument to the `scala` command. By passing a path, the shell will compile the script and run it right away, without storing the compiled files. It will also exit automatically when the script finishes.

Functional versus imperative programming

At its heart, Java is an imperative language. In an imperative language, it is normal to have mutable variables and classes that keep internal states. In Java, a normal **Plain Old Java Object (POJO)** is an excellent example of the imperative programming paradigm. A standard POJO has variables that can be freely changed by calling the setter methods. Any code that can reach a POJO instance can modify its variables. This can lead to both subtle and hard-to-find bugs, especially when multiple threads try to alter a variable at the same time.

In functional programming, code is written in such a way that existing variables are not modified while the program is running. Values are specified as function parameters and output is generated based on their parameters. Functions are required to return the same output when specifying the same parameters on each call.

Let's look at a very simple, naive example. Do not worry too much about the syntax; the Scala language syntax will be covered in much more detail in the upcoming sections. First, a traditional object-orientated example in Scala:

```scala
class AddDemoOOP {
  var x = 0
  def add(y: Int): Int = {
    x += y
    x
  }
}

val a = new AddDemoOOP()
```

```
print(a.add(1))
print(a.add(1))
```

This will print 1 and 2. While the add method received the same parameter (integer 1) two times in a row, it returned a different value on each call. This is because the state of the class was changed while calling the method. In pure functional programming, this is not allowed. The same class in a more functional style would be as follows:

```
class AddDemoFunctional {
  def add(x: Int, y: Int): Int = {
    x + y
  }
}

val b = new AddDemoFunctional
print(b.add(0, 1))
print(b.add(0, 1))
```

This prints 1 two times. This version of the class does not hold any internal state. To let the add method return different values, different parameters will have to be passed to the add method.

Note that while Scala is a pure OOP language, it is not considered a pure functional programming language. As demonstrated in the first example, it is easy to write code in Scala that does not adhere to functional programming rules.

Functional programming is a popular choice for programs that use multiple threads. Because methods cannot alter the state of data structures that are used in multiple threads, it is often much more safe than using imperative code. It requires a different mindset from the developer, though.

There's much more that can be said about functional programming. We will cover more topics related to this concept in this chapter.

Unlike many other functional languages, Scala allows you to learn functional programming at your own pace, as Scala is a pure object-orientated language.

Scala language syntax and rules

Scala is a less strict and verbose language than Java: semicolons are optional; even parentheses on function calls are not required when not needed (note the `val b = new AddDemoFunctional` line in the last example). We'll cover the following topics:

- Statically typed language
- Mutable and immutable variables
- Common Scala types

Statically typed language

Like Java, Scala is a statically typed language; you'll have to declare variables before you can use them. It is also a strongly typed language. You can always specify the used types, like you would in Java code. Unlike Java, you are not always required to specify the types explicitly, though.

Types must be specified when declaring method input parameters and the method's return value. Types are not required when declaring variables inside a method or function body, because the Scala compiler usually can detect the correct types from the code.

Here's an example of this:

```
var i = 10;
var j = new java.lang.Object();
```

Once a mutable variable has been declared, it can be used to store instances of the same type, or types that can can be upcast to that type. For example, this would be allowed after the preceding code:

```
j = "Hello world"
```

Since a `String` type can be upcast to `java.lang.Object`, the j variable will happily store a reference to the "Hello world" string. Assigning a `String` type to the i variable would be impossible because the i variable has been assigned to Scala's `Int` instance and the `String` cannot be upcast to an `Int` instance.

It is possible to explicitly specify the type of a variable. This information may be required when dealing with a family of classes:

```
val i: Integer = 10
```

Mutable and immutable variables

Scala has support for two types of variables. When declaring method parameters or class instance members, they should be prefixed with one of the following:

- `var` for mutable variables
- `val` for fixed variables

A variable is comparable to normal variables in the Java language; they are fully mutable and can be freely changed. Fixed variables are comparable to `final` variables in Java; they can be assigned to an instance only once. If a fixed variable references a mutable class instance, the content of that class can still be changed, as discussed in `Chapter 2`, *Developing on the Java Virtual Machine*.

 When applying functional programming, you should try to use immutable variables as often as you can. Immutable values are the cornerstone of functional programming.

Scala does not support the creation of static variables (also known as class variables), but as we will cover later, it has support for singleton objects that can be used instead.

Common Scala types

While Scala can use Java's commonly used classes, it offers its own classes that should be used whenever possible. These classes work more in the vein of Scala. We will cover the following types here:

- `Any`
- `AnyRef`
- `AnyVal`
- `Strings`

Any class

Java's mother class is the `Object` class. Scala's parent class is the `Any` class. When not inheriting a class explicitly, this class is inherited implicitly.

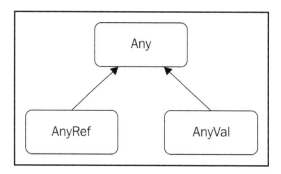

As the preceding diagram shows, the **Any** class has two subclasses:

- **AnyRef**
- **AnyVal**

AnyRef class - reference classes

The `AnyRef` class is used by reference variables. It is similar to Java's `java.lang.Object` class and provides similar methods, such as `equals()`, `hashCode()`, and `finalize()`. This class is inherited either directly or indirectly by most classes provided by the Scala language.

AnyVal class - value classes

Unlike Java, Scala is a pure object-orientated language. As such, it cannot create primitive values. Instead, Scala wraps primitive values in its own wrapper classes:

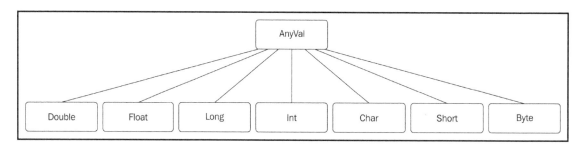

These wrapper classes are subclasses of the `AnyVal` class. These classes are called **value classes** and get special treatment from Scala's compiler.

You may wonder why Scala uses its own wrapper classes instead of using the wrapper classes from the Java class library. One reason is that Scala tries to improve performance by not boxing values when not strictly needed and needs its own internal logic to be able to do this. Another major reason is that Scala, unlike Java, supports operator overloading. As we will soon discuss in more detail, Scala's wrapper subclasses implement all the binary operators that are used for calculations.

Strings

While many languages on the JVM offer their own string classes that offer additional convenient methods and fields above Java's standard `String` class, Scala is not among them. Scala uses the normal `String` class of the `java.lang` package from the Java class library.

Java strings are immutable. If a method is called that modifies the string, a new `String` instance is returned that contains the modification while the original `String` instance remains untouched. This immutability is a perfect fit for Scala's functional programming features.

OOP in Scala

Similar to Java, the Scala compiler requires code to be wrapped inside a class. The interactive Scala REPL shell works around this limitation by automatically wrapping the entered code in an invisible class that is generated under the hood. When using the `scala` command, you can immediately start writing functions or code that must be executed, like you would do in a typical Python or different script language. We will cover the following topics:

- Defining packages and subpackages
- Importing members
- Defining classes
- Instance methods and variables
- Constructors

- Extending a class
- Overloading methods
- Abstract classes
- Traits
- Singleton objects
- Operator overloading
- Case classes

Defining packages and subpackages

Scala has a `package` statement. It can be defined at the top of a file:

```
package PACKAGENAME
```

This form works in the same way as Java. Every class that is defined in the same source file is placed inside the PACKAGENAME package.

Scala offers more control, though. As we will soon see in a more thorough fashion, Scala supports subpackages. In Scala, packages that have the same prefixes are automatically related. It is possible to define a subpackage in the same source file that contains the package statement:

```
package com.example.parent
class A {
}

package subpackage {
  class B { }
  class C { }
}
```

This results in three public classes:

- The `com.example.parent` package comprising:
  - Class A
- The `com.example.parent.subpackage` package comprising:
  - Class B
  - Class C

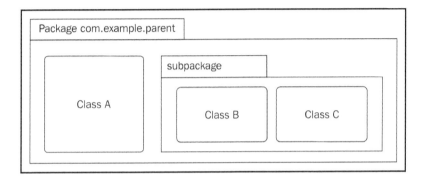

The `package` statement cannot be used inside the REPL shell. This is because the shell generates an invisible class that contains your entered code. You'll always need to compile source code that contains package statements with the `scalac` compiler.

Importing members

Scala's `import` statement is more powerful than that of Java. The basic form is the same:

```
import com.example.parent.A
```

To import all the members of a package, Scala does not use the * wildcard, but _ instead:

```
import com.example.parent._
```

It is possible to import multiple members in one statement:

```
import com.example.parent.subpackage.{B, C}
```

Renaming an imported member is also possible:

```
import com.example.parent.subpackage.{C => D}
```

In the preceding example, the class name D must be used in the source code while it references the com.example.parent.subpackage.C class. This can come in handy when name clashes occur (different members have the same name).

As mentioned earlier, Scala supports subpackages. Subpackages can access private members from its parent packages. In the preceding example, this means that the code in com.example.parent.subpackage can access the private members of com.example.parent, and it does not even need to import those classes.

Another neat feature is that packages can be imported:

```
import com.example.parent
```

When the preceding line is present, you can reference the members of the parent package in the code:

```
var c = new parent.subpackage.C()
```

Defining classes

As we have already seen in some earlier examples, a class is defined in a very similar way as that in Java:

```
class TheClassName {
}
```

In Scala, you can define any number of public classes in a single source file, and the source file is not required to have the same filename as that of any class the source file defines.

Scala supports the following explicit access modifier for classes:

- private

When not specifying an access modifier, the class is implicitly public. This is the big difference with Java. Scala cannot create classes that are package-private and doesn't have an explicit public access modifier. If, for whatever reason, you want to create an empty class, you do not have to specify the { } block.

Instance variables and methods

Classes can contain instance variables and instance methods.

Scala does not support static members (class variables and class methods); there is no `static` or equivalent keyword. Scala has support for singleton classes that fills this void. We will look at singleton classes later in this chapter.

Instance variables

Instance variables can be added by simply defining `def` and `val` variables inside the class body. In most cases, types do not have to be specified explicitly as Scala will detect the type from the initialization. Types can still optionally be specified:

```
var anIntegerVariable: Int
val anIntegerValue = 0
```

When explicitly specifying a type, the instance variable does not have to be initialized explicitly right away; it will automatically be initialized with a null value. When omitting the type, a value must be assigned at the same time you declare the variable or value; otherwise, Scala would not know which type it has to assign to the variable.

Instance methods

A method declaration in Scala is quite similar to that of Java. If a method has input parameters, their types need to be specified, and methods can return either nothing or one object instance. A return type can optionally be specified explicitly:

```
def methodName(parameter1: Int, parameter2: Int): Int = {
  parameter1 + parameter2
}
```

One difference with Java is that the return type does not have to be specified explicitly, except if the Scala compiler believes there can be confusion. In the preceding case, it understands that two `Int` instances are added together, so the return type will always be an `Int` as well. Therefore, the compiler will accept this:

```
def methodName(parameter1: Int, parameter2: Int) = {
  parameter1 + parameter2
}
```

The last expression of any method is the value that is automatically returned. Scala has an explicit return statement, but it is not required and its usage is not recommended at all. In Scala, methods and functions should not return early. When still using the return statement, it is a requirement that the return type of the method is explicitly defined.

If a method does not return anything (`void` in Java), in Scala, this is specified with the `Unit` class name as the return type:

```
def methodWithoutReturnValue(): Unit = {
}
```

When no return type is defined and the method body does not contain a line with only one expression, Scala will implicitly choose the `Unit` return type:

```
def methodWithoutReturnValue() = {
}
```

If a method explicitly declares the `Unit` return type and its body still contains a line with only one expression, it produces a compiler warning and the expression is ignored.

If the implementation of a method requires only one line, then a { } block is not required. So, the following is valid:

```
def helloWorld() = println("Hello world")
```

Access modifiers for class instance members

Like classes, class members are public when no access modifier has been explicitly specified. The other access modifiers that Scala supports are:

- `protected`
- `private`

There are some important differences regarding access modifiers between Scala and Java:

- Scala knows the subpackages concept. Classes in a subpackage can access private members from their parent packages, as discussed earlier while talking about the `import` statement.
- In a Scala class instance, members using the `protected` access modifier are not visible to other classes in the same package. In Java, protected members are visible to other classes in the same package.

Constructors

The main constructor, called the primary constructor, is defined by adding parameters and input types to the class block:

```
class ClassWithParameterizedConstructor(var parm1: Int, parm2: Int)
{
    println("This code is executed as part of the constructor")
}
```

This defines a primary constructor with a variable called `parm1` and a fixed `parm2` value, both of the `Int` type. There are a few things to note here:

- Scala automatically creates fields for the parameters with the same name.
- Public getters, setters in the case of `var` fields, will be generated implicitly; therefore, constructor parameters can freely be accessed by code that can access this class.
- When not specifying the `var` or `val` keywords, `val` is implicitly chosen.
- All of the code inside the class can access these variables and values, even nested classes, methods, and functions.

Statements that are in the body of a class are executed when the main constructor is used. Constructors can be overloaded. In Scala, they are referred to as **auxiliary** constructors. To create an additional constructor, the `this` keyword is used:

```
class ClassWithParameterizedConstructor(var parm1: Int,
                                        val parm2: Int) {
    def this(parm1: Int) = this(parm1, 0)
}
```

Like methods, you can start a block with { } after the = sign if you need a constructor body that is longer than one line:

```
class ClassWithParameterizedConstructor(var parm1: Int,
                                        val parm2: Int) {
    def this(parm1: Int) = {
        this(parm1, 0)
    }
}
```

There is an important rule for auxiliary constructors: The first line of an auxiliary constructor's body must either call the primary constructor or one of the other auxiliary constructors that may have been defined before the current one.

Extending a class

Classes are extended with the familiar extends keyword.

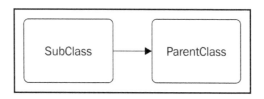

```
class ParentClass {
}

class SubClass extends ParentClass {
}
```

Like Java, Scala only supports the inheritance of a single other class. If a class does not inherit any other class explicitly, it inherits the AnyRef class implicitly (which is a subclass of the Any class).

In Scala, only the primary constructor of a subclass can call the constructor of the parent class. This is done as follows:

```
class ParentClass(param1: Int, param2: Int) {
}

class SubClass(var param1: Int) extends ParentClass(param1, 10) {
}
```

The primary constructor of SubClass (which has one parameter) calls the primary constructor of ParentClass, which has two parameters. It could have called the auxiliary constructors of ParentClass if ParentClass had them.

As we will soon see, the extends keyword is also used to implement traits. It is a requirement that the overridden class is the first entry when extending both a class and implementing traits.

Overriding methods

Methods can be overridden by prefixing them with the `override` keyword in the child class:

```
class ParentClass {
  def test() = print("Hello, from the parent class")
}

class SubClass extends ParentClass {
  override def test() = {
    super.test()
    print(" and from the child class as well")
  }
}
```

As demonstrated earlier, members of the parent class can be accessed using the `super` keyword.

Overloading methods

Scala supports overloading of methods. This works just like Java and the same rules apply. Here's an example of this:

```
class OverloadExample {
  def anOverloadedMethod(i: Int) { }
  def anOverloadedMethod(s: String) { }
}
```

Abstract classes

Abstract classes can be created by prefixing the class keyword with `abstract`:

```
abstract class AbstractClassName {
  def methodWithNoImplementationYet
  def methodWithImplementation() { }
}
```

Unlike Java, abstract methods are not prefixed with the `abstract` keyword; instead, no implementation is specified in this method.

Traits

A trait is very similar to Java interfaces. Like Java 8 interfaces, traits can define both abstract methods and methods with an implementation. Let's look at an example:

```
trait TraitName {
  def methodWithImplementation() {
    // Code here...
  }

  def methodWithoutImplementation()
}
```

Scala uses the `extends` keyword to extend a parent class; it is also used for implementing traits. Just as Java classes can implement any number of interfaces, classes in Scala can extend any number of traits.

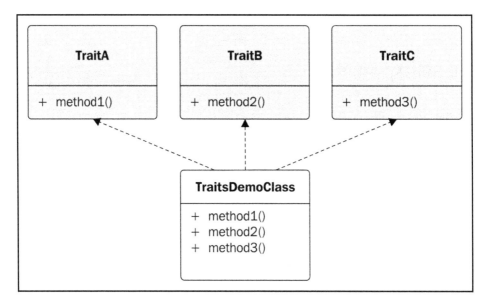

Curiously, entries in the `extends` list have to be separated by using the `with` keyword:

```
trait TraitA { def method1() }
trait TraitB { def method2() }
trait TraitC { def method3() }
```

```
class TraitsDemoClass extends TraitA with TraitB with TraitC {
  def method1() { }
  def method2() { }
  def method3() { }
}
```

 Note that when extending a class and one or more traits, the class has to be specified as the first entry; otherwise, a compiler error will occur.

Abstract classes that extend one or more traits are allowed, but not required, to provide implementations of their abstract methods. Concrete classes must provide implementations of all traits, either directly (as shown already) or indirectly (for example, by extending a different class that provides some of the implementations of a trait).

Singleton objects

Scala has a handy `object` type. It is very similar to a `class` definition, but the difference is that it not only creates a class, but also an object instance that can be referenced with the specified object name. This class is a singleton, meaning it is guaranteed that only one instance would ever be created. Here's an example:

```
object SingletonObjectName {
  var x = 100
  def printX() = println(x)
}
```

This object does not need to be instantiated. Scala will ensure that this happens automatically. The `SingletonObjectName` instance can be reached by simply using its name:

```
SingletonObjectName.x = 250
SingletonObjectName.printX()
```

This will print `250`. Of course, adding mutable variables to a singleton object isn't a very good idea, especially if the class is going to be used in multiple threads. Having mutable global variables is never a good idea.

Since Scala does not support static class members, singleton objects can be used as an alternative. Since there's always only one instance of this class, it has the same effect as storing data in static variables or having static methods.

Operator overloading

As mentioned while discussing the `AnyVal` subclasses, Scala supports operator overloading. In Java, operators such as + and * cannot be overridden. You can only use operators on primitive types (when using operators on wrapper classes, they are internally unboxed to their primitive representations and back to their original state after the calculation).

When executing 1 + 1, in Java, the Java compiler compiles binary Java bytecode that calls a low-level JVM-assembly-like command that knows how to add up two integer values. Java operators can never be used on custom classes. When calling + on instances of your class, the compiler will refuse to compile your code. As an example, this Java code will not compile:

```
class A {
  public static void main(String[] args) {
    // COMPILE ERROR: bad operand types for binary operator '+'
    A result = new A() + new A();
  }
}
```

Scala, on the other hand, implements operators as ordinary methods. Scala's Int class contains the + method. Therefore, in Scala, it's possible to override operators and implement them in custom classes. If you override the + operator in your class, the code can simply use the + operator, and the + method will decide what will happen when two instances of your class (or even instances from different classes) are added together. Let's look at a simple Scala example of a custom class that implements the + operator:

```
class CustomClass(var x: Int) {
  def + (other: CustomClass) = {
    new CustomClass(x + other.x)
  }
}

val result = new CustomClass(400) + new CustomClass(155)
print(result.x)
```

This will print 555.

Case classes

Scala knows a special case of classes (pun intended!), called case classes. As a programmer, you are probably familiar with having to deal with data structures that are similar to each other but with little differences. Often, when handling these structures, the hard-to-maintain switch... case (C, C#, Java, and JavaScript), case...when (Ruby), Select Case (VisualBASIC), or if ...else blocks (other languages) have to be written to retrieve correct data from these structures and handle them accordingly.

Case classes are an elegant way to deal with this problem. Let's look at a simple example:

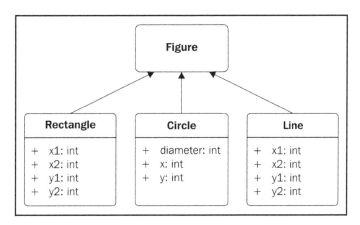

An abstract class Figure is extended by the Rectangle, Circle and Line case classes:

```
abstract class Figure
case class Rectangle(x1: Int, y1: Int, x2: Int, y2: Int) extends
          Figure
case class Circle(x: Int, y: Int, diameter: Int) extends Figure
case class Line(x1: Int, y1: Int, x2: Int, y2: Int) extends Figure
```

First, an empty Figure abstract class is created so that we can group case classes logically. We declare case classes for a family of figures that a drawing program can draw. Each case class provides the fields that the figure needs. It's very easy to create instances of these classes:

```
val rectangle = Rectangle(10, 20, 80, 50)
val circle = Circle(100, 200, 30)
```

It's interesting to note that the `new` keyword is not used to instantiate case classes. To handle these classes, you need to use a technique called **pattern matching**:

```
def drawFigure(figure: Figure): Unit = {
  figure match {
    case Rectangle(x1, y1, _, _) => _draw(x1, y1)
    case Circle(x, y, _) => _draw(x, y)
    case Line(x1, y1, _, _) => _draw(x1, y1)
  }

  def _draw(x: Int, y: Int): Unit = println("Start drawing at "
                                             + x + ", " + y)
}

drawFigure(rectangle)
drawFigure(circle)
```

It's a convention to use the underscore (_) for fields that you won't need at this time.

Scala's standard library

Now that we have discussed OOP thoroughly, let's start writing classes and methods that do something useful. Part of the Scala installation is the Scala standard library, a big library of classes that is unique to Scala. We will discuss the following topics here:

- Generics
- Collections
- XML processing

Generics

Java used the `ClassName<T>` notation for generics-aware classes. As we have seen, some classes, such as the `Map<K, V>` interface, requires more types. For `Map`, types need be specified for both the keys and the corresponding values that the map will hold.

In Scala, the `ClassName[T]` notation is used instead:

```
val aList = List[Int](1, 2, 3, 5)
```

This creates an immutable list with five elements. Since `List[Int]` is specified, adding an instance of any type other than `Int` or an instance of a class that cannot be upcast to `Int` is not allowed.

Similarly, when a class requires two types, it is written as:

```
val m = Map[String, String]("key1" -> "value1", "key2" -> "value2")
```

Here a map is created that maps the `"key1"` key to the `"value1"` string value and the `"key2"` key to the `"value2"` string.

Collections

Scala's standard library offers a lot of collection APIs. They can be divided into two types:

- Immutable collections
- Mutable collections

Immutable collections are generally put in the `scala.collection.immutable` package, while mutable classes are stored in the `scala.collection.mutable` package. The Scala package that is always implicitly imported by the language contains references to several immutable collection classes. So, immutable versions are the default versions that are used when you don't explicitly import an immutable or mutable collection class.

Immutable list

The preceding examples were immutable versions of the List and Map data structures, respectively. These should be populated while being initialized. You can use immutable collections to create new lists. Here's an example that creates a new list that is based on the content of an existing list:

```
val immutableList = List[Int](1, 2, 3, 4, 5)
val newImmutableList1 = 0 :: immutableList
val newImmutableList2 = immutableList ::: List(6, 7)
```

This may look confusing at first. The second line creates a new instance of the list that contains 0 and a copy of the rest of the list, so newInstance1 will be List[Int](0, 1, 2, 3, 4, 5). The left-hand side part of the :: operator has the value that will be added to the newly created instance, while the right-hand side part has the list that will be copied. Since the List class is optimized for **LIFO** (**last in, first out**) usage, it is easier to create a new list instance with new items before the items of the existing list.

Still, it is possible to create a new list instance where new items could be added to the end of the list. The ::: operator can be used for this, but this time, both the specified objects must be lists. In the preceding example, newImmutableList2 contains these elements: 1, 2, 3, 4, 5, 6, 7.

Note that the original list, aList, was not modified while creating the new lists.

Mutable list

There's a mutable version of List, which is called ListBuffer and is inside the scala.collection.mutable package. Quite predictably, this version offers familiar methods, such as append(), remove(), and clear():

```
import scala.collection.mutable
val aMutableList = mutable.ListBuffer[Int](1, 2, 5)
aMutableList.remove(2)
aMutableList.append(3)
println(aMutableList(0))
println(aMutableList)
```

This will print 1 and ListBuffer(1, 2, 3).

In Scala, it's a good practice to use operators where possible. Here's the same example with operators:

```
import scala.collection.mutable

val aMutableList = mutable.ListBuffer[Int](1, 2, 5)
aMutableList -= 5
aMutableList += 3
println(aMutableList)
```

The -= operator removes the specified value from the list, while += adds a new value.

 Note that when using the -= operator, the value has to be specified. Also, note the index of the item that must be removed.

Among the many collection classes that Scala offers, there's also the mutable `ArrayBuffer` class. This one is backed by an internal array and is much more efficient when using indexes to reach specific elements:

```
import scala.collection.mutable

val aMutableArray = mutable.ArrayBuffer[Int](1, 2, 3)
aMutableArray += 4
println(aMutableArray(3))
```

This will print 4. Like the `ListBuffer` class, `ArrayBuffer` implements many operators.

Immutable map

The Scala standard library contains various immutable map classes with different implementations. We will discuss the standard `Map` class here, which is immutable:

```
val immutableMap = Map[Int, String](10 -> "ten", 20 -> "twenty")
println(immutableMap(20))
```

It's easy to create a new instance of a map that is based on an existing map. Here's an example that modifies that map defined earlier:

```
val newImmutableMap = immutableMap + (30 -> "thirty")
```

You can combine two maps with the ++ operator:

```
val combinedMap = newImmutableMap ++ Map[Int, String]
                      (24 -> "twentyfour")
```

Mutable map

One of the mutable map classes in the Scala standard library is `HashMap`, which is quite similar to Java's `java.lang.HashMap` class:

```
import scala.collection.mutable

val mutableMap = mutable.HashMap[Int, String](10->"ten",
                                               50->"fifty")
mutableMap += (100 -> "Hundred", 150 -> "Hundred and fifty")
mutableMap -= 10
println(mutableMap)
```

This will print `mutableMap.type = Map(50 -> fifty, 100 -> Hundred, 150 -> Hundred and fifty)`.

Note that the operators demonstrated in the immutable map examples still work on the `HashMap` instance. Their working will not change; they will still create new instances instead of modifying the current `HashMap` instance.

XML processing

The Scala standard library comes with a powerful XML library that has some helpful features, both for generating and consuming XML documents. We will demonstrate how to generate XML documents using XML literals here. Using this feature, you can enter XML content directly in the Scala source code. Under the hood, the Scala compiler uses its XML library to populate variables and validate the generated XML.

It is recommended that you do not enter the following examples directly in the `scala` REPL shell. With your favorite text editor, create a source file and pass the path to the `scala` command, instead. The interactive parser may fail when mixing code and XML directly in the REPL shell.

Here's a simple example that generates a String containing XML:

```
val productCode = "PC Monitor"
val qty = 2.toString()
val xmlContent =
                <basket>
                <line>
                  <product qty={ qty }>{ productCode }</product>
                </line>
                </basket>
```

```
println(xmlContent)
```

Note that all the variables used in XML elements must be strings. Also, note that the 2 literal value is an object in Scala; therefore, its `toString()` method can be called. The preceding program will produce the following output:

```
<basket>
  <line>
    <product qty="2">PC Monitor</product>
  </line>
</basket>
```

By creating functions that return XML elements, you can easily add collections to the XML output. A function that returns an XML element should return an `xml.Elem` instance:

```
def createXMLProduct(productCode: String): xml.Elem = {
  <product qty="1">{ productCode }</product>
}

val productCodes = List[String]("Keyboard", "Mouse")
def lines =
  <basket>
    <products> {
      productCodes.map(x => createXMLProduct(x))
    }</products>
  </basket>

println(lines.toString())
```

Instead of manually looping through the collection, the `map` method is called. It transforms a list by passing a lambda function that returns new content for each item in the collection. In this case, it transforms the `productCodes` list with Strings into a new list with XML elements. The `map` function is a nice example of functional programming and is therefore discussed in more detail in the next section. The output of the preceding script is:

```
<basket>
  <products>
    <product qty="1">Computer Keyboard</product>
    <product qty="1">Mouse</product></lines>
  </products>
</basket>
```

Note that in a real-life scenario, the quantity (the `qty` attribute) should not be hardcoded to the value 1.

Functional programming in Scala

As said earlier, functional programming requires a different mindset to imperative programming. We will look at several functional-programming-related topics here:

- Iterating through collections using functions
- The map, filter, and reduce design pattern
- Currying

Iterating through collections using functions

In functional programming, it is unusual to use both `for` or `while` loops to iterate through arrays and collections and process each item inside the loop's body. Instead, a method is called on the array or collection instance, which internally iterates through the array or collection. The method takes a lambda function as a parameter and ensures that the function is called for each item:

```
var a = List[Int](5, 10, 15, 20, 25)
a.foreach((x: Int) => println("%03d".format(x)))
```

This will print `005`, `010`, `015`, `020`, and `025`. It uses the `format` method of Java's `java.lang.String` class to ensure that the printed integer has up to three leading zeroes.

The map, filter, and reduce design pattern

A well-known design pattern that is related to functional programming is called map, filter, and reduce. We will cover each pattern separately:

- Map
- Filter
- Reduce

Map - transform data

When each element inside an array or collection needs to be transformed into something else, you can use the `map` method:

```
var a = List[Int](1, 2, 3)
var b = a.map((x: Int) => 2 * x)
println(b)
```

This will display `List(2, 4, 6)`.

The map method requires a lambda function that has one input parameter with the same type as that of the items inside the array or collection. In this case, we create a lambda function that accepts the `x` value of the type `Int` and returns this value: `2 * x`. The `map` function calls the passed function for every item and creates a new list.

Filter - filter items from a collection or array

The `filter` method, which is implemented in arrays and collection classes, can remove items from a collection or array by passing a function that returns a Boolean indicating whether or not the passed item must stay in the filter's resulting list or array:

```
var a = List[Int](100, 150, 200, 300)
var b = a.filter((x: Int) => x > 150)
println(b)
```

The printed result is `List(200, 300)`. Since `100` and `150` are not greater than `150`, the function that was passed to the filter returned false for these items; therefore, they were not added to the result.

Reduce - for performing calculations

The lambda that is passed to the `reduce` method takes two parameters: a start value and the current item. The return value is used as the start value for the next call. To create a simple `sum` function, see the following example:

```
var a = List[Int](10, 20, 30, 40, 50)
var b = a.reduce((x: Int, y: Int) => x + y)
println(b)
```

This will print the result 150. Another example follows, using Scala's max operator:

```
var a = List[Int](100, 2, 30, 60, 555)
var b = a.reduce((x: Int, y: Int) => x max y)
println(b)
```

This will print 555. The max operator returns the largest of the two values. As expected, Scala also has the min operator.

 Like all operators that we have seen in this chapter, both min and max operators are also implemented as methods in the Int class.

Currying

In Scala, it is possible to provide multiple lists of input parameters to a method or function:

```
class CurryingTest {
  def curryingMethod(a: Int, b: Int)(c: Int): Int = {
    a * b * c
  }
}
```

This is called **currying**. The preceding method definition has two sets of input parameters. One set takes the a and b parameters, and the second set takes the single c parameter. Calling this method with all the parameters must be done like this:

```
var c = new CurryingTest()
var result = c.curryingMethod(2, 3)(4)
println(result)
```

As expected, this returns 24. If the method would only be called this way in your program, the whole point of currying would be rather useless. Currying is useful when you want to pass functions to other methods or functions, which is a very common thing to do in functional programming. Here's an example of this:

```
def doCurrying(x: Int, fun: Int => Int): Int = {
  fun(x)
}

var result = doCurrying(30, c.curryingMethod(10, 20))
println(result)
```

This prints `6000`. Let's closely look at what happens in this code:

1. The `doCurrying` method takes two parameters as input:
   - x, which is a normal `Int` instance
   - fun, which is a function that takes one `Int` parameter and returns an `Int` instance as its return value

2. The body of the `doCurrying` function calls the `fun` function, passing x as the input parameter. It returns the return value of `fun`.

3. When calling the `doCurrying` function, Scala created an anonymous (meaning it had no name) temporary function that calls the passed `curryingMethod` method with the first set of parameters: a=10 and b=20. The resulting function needs one additional set of parameters--in this case, it consisted only of the c parameter-- before it can execute `curryingMethod`. Therefore, the generated function requires one Int input parameter.

4. Since the signature of the generated temporary and anonymous function is compatible with the `Int => Int` definition (taking one input `Int` and having an `Int` result), the Scala compiler accepts this generated function as an input parameter for `doCurrying`.

5. The `doCurrying` method executes the passed (in this case, the generated anonymous) function by passing x as an input parameter. Now both the sets of parameters are known and the anonymous function can call the `c.curryingMethod` method with all the three parameters. The compiler knows this will return `Int`, which complies with the integer that is returned with the object declaration of `doCurrying`.

Quiz

1. Can Scala be considered a pure OOP and functional programming language?

   a) Yes, Scala is both a pure OOP and functional programming language

   b) No, Scala is a pure OOP language, but it cannot be considered a pure functional programming language

c) No, Scala is a pure functional programming language, but it cannot be considered a pure OOP language

d) No, Scala is neither pure OOP, nor a pure functional programming language

2. Will this code compile? If not, why?

```
class A { def method1 = {} }
trait B { def method2 }
trait C { def method3 }
abstract class D extends A with B with C { }
```

a) Yes, it will compile and run correctly

b) No, traits need to be implemented using the `implements` keyword

c) No, `class D` does not implement the methods from `class A` and/or `trait B` and `trait C`

d) Answers b and c are correct

3. What's wrong with the following class definition?

```
public class A
```

a) This class will compile fine; nothing is wrong

b) It will not compile because no body (= `{ }`) is specified

c) It will not compile because the `public` access modifier does not exist in Scala

d) Answers b and c are both correct

4. In functional programming, which design pattern is the most likely candidate to calculate the sum of an array containing only Int values?

a) The map design pattern

b) The filter design pattern

c) The reduce design pattern

d) None of the preceding answers are correct

5. In a multithreaded program, is it always considered safe to change the values of the mutable variables of a `Singleton` object?

    a) Yes, this is correct. Scala ensures that each thread has its own copy of Singleton data.

    b) No, altering mutable variables in a `Singleton` object that are accessed by multiple threads is not safe.

Summary

In this chapter, you learned more about Scala, a language that has strong support for functional programming while being a pure OOP language at the same time. We started the chapter by installing Scala and using the `scala` command, the REPL interactive shell of Scala. You used this powerful program to try all the code snippets in this chapter. We explained the difference between imperative and functional programming. We looked at many OOP features of the Scala language and discovered that many statements are more powerful in Scala than Java's versions of the same statements. We also found out that the access modifiers of Scala and Java are similar to each other but not completely the same. You tried out some collection classes from the Scala standard library and applied generics to them. We concluded this chapter by examining functional programming in more detail.

With all the theory behind us, it's time to realize a small project with Scala. This time we will use the `scalac` compiler and sbt, Scala's build tool.

6
Scala Programming

In this chapter, we are going to do a small project in Scala, using the popular Akka toolkit. Akka is a toolkit that aims to make the creation of scalable applications on a JVM easier. It is available for both Java and Scala, but since it was built by the creators of Scala, Akka is an excellent fit for Scala.

We will build a simple program that will display a random quote from a hardcoded list of quotes. Akka is based on the Actor model, which we will explore in this chapter. To write the project we will use Scala IDE, which is available both as a standalone software package and as a plugin that could be installed on Eclipse IDE. We will use the latter. To build the project, we will use the Scala build tool. These are the topics that we will cover in this chapter:

- Scala IDE for Eclipse
- Scala Build Tool (SBT)
- SBT Eclipse for the SBT plugin
- The scalac compiler
- The Akka toolkit
- Unit testing with ScalaTest
- Writing an executable main program

Scala IDE for the Eclipse plugin

Eclipse IDE does not come with Scala support out of the box. You need to install the `Scala IDE` plugin to add Scala compatibility to Eclipse IDE. One complication is that the installed Scala IDE dictates which Scala releases would be used in Eclipse IDE. On some occasions, it takes the Scala IDE team some time to add support for the latest Scala version. After the installation, you can switch to Eclipse's new <Scala> perspective.

Installing Scala IDE for Eclipse

While Scala IDE is available on the Eclipse Marketplace, its version is often not based on the last available version. Since the installed Scala IDE version dictates which Scala release will be supported, we recommend that you install the most stable, up-to-date version from the repository sites managed by the Scala IDE team itself.

By manually adding Scala IDE's repository, Eclipse can download and install the latest stable version. You'll need to know the Eclipse version for this. You can find this by going to **Help | About** in Eclipse IDE. Usually, only the major version and minor version numbers are important. For example, on my system, the installed Eclipse version is 4.6.

 It is still possible that the latest version of Scala IDE does not support the latest Scala release. It is likely that the Scala IDE team will release updates faster on their own repositories than the Eclipse Marketplace.

Visit the Scala IDE website at `http://scala-ide.org`.

Follow these instructions to install the plugin from Eclipse IDE:

- On the Scala IDE home page, find the **update sites** link. At the time of writing this, it is located next to the prominent **Download IDE** button.
- In the list of supported Eclipse versions, find your installed Eclipse version and copy the link under the **Update site installation** heading to the clipboard:

Return to your Eclipse IDE instance if it is still running; otherwise, start a new instance. Then follow the ensuing instructions to add the repository to Eclipse:

- From the menu bar, choose **Help | Install new software...**.
- The **Install** dialog appears. The drop-down box next to **Work with** contains the list of known repository sites. Click on the **Add...** button next to this field to add the Scala IDE repository.
- The **Add Repository** dialog appears. Enter Scala IDE as the name and paste the URL you copied to the clipboard. Click on **OK** to save this repository.
- The Scala IDE repository is now selected. In the list of components that are available in the repository, find the **Scala IDE for Eclipse** entry and check it. Also, find the **ScalaTest for Scala IDE** component and check that one as well:

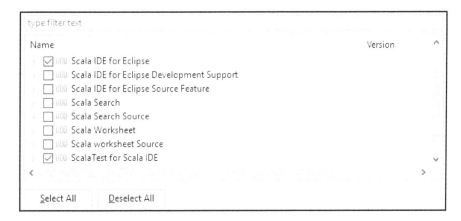

- Click on **Finish** and follow the prompts

Switching to the Scala IDE perspective

Eclipse supports a lot of different programming languages. After installing Scala IDE, Scala is one of them. Eclipse can optimize its user interface for a specific programming language or environment, by offering different perspectives. Scala IDE adds its own perspective to Eclipse. To switch to the Scala IDE perspective, do the following:

- On the upper right-hand side of the screen, there are a few buttons that represent the last used perspectives. Hover over them; one of them will have the <Scala> tooltip. Click on it:

- If the Scala perspective button is unavailable, click on the button with the Open

  Perspective tooltip and select the <Scala> perspective from the list. The button will now be added to the toolbar.

The IDE's user interface is now optimized for Scala programming.

 You can switch to a different perspective at any time. Eclipse IDE is well suited for working with projects that use different programming languages.

SBT

Although Scala projects can be built with most JVM-based build tools, including Apache Maven and Gradle (the build tool we used in Chapter 4, *Java Programming*, for our Java project), Scala has its own build tool. It is called SBT, which stands, rather predictably, for Scala Build Tool.

Scala IDE has no built-in support for SBT. As we will see, this is not a problem, as the reverse is true: we can add Eclipse support to SBT. We will create a new project using SBT and install a plugin for SBT that is capable of creating and updating Eclipse projects. We'll cover the following SBT-related topics:

- Installing SBT
- Creating a new SBT-based project
- Adding the SBT plugin to add Eclipse-related commands to SBT

Installing SBT

To install SBT, visit `http://www.scala-sbt.org` and download the latest version for your system.

For Windows, an MSI installer is available that takes care of installing and setting up the path. For other operating systems, an archive file (ZIP or TGZ) must be downloaded, extracted, and added to the path.

Like Gradle, SBT commands can be executed from the command line by specifying the commands as parameters. SBT is unique in that it also has an interactive shell option. When running SBT in interactive mode, SBT commands can run interactively, and as an additional bonus, they also support autocompletion; you just need to press the *Tab* key.

To validate the installation in the command window (Windows) or Terminal (macOS and Linux), type `sbt` and press *Enter* to start SBT in the interactive shell mode.

Creating an SBT-based Eclipse IDE project

As mentioned earlier, an important issue with the current version of the Scala IDE plugin for Eclipse IDE is that it has no support for SBT. By installing a plugin in SBT, we can generate Eclipse project files from SBT. The workflow for creating a new SBT-based project that can be opened in Eclipse IDE with the Scala IDE plugin installed is as follows:

1. Create a new SBT-based project by applying a project template.
2. Add the sbteclipse plugin to SBT.
3. From SBT, generate a new Eclipse IDE/Scala IDE project using the sbteclipse plugin.

Creating a new SBT project

The easiest way to create a new project is to let SBT generate a `Hello World` project, which includes a blank build file. This command should be run from Eclipse IDE's `workspace` directory. This is the directory that Eclipse IDE uses to store projects. If you are unsure where this directory is located, start Eclipse and try to create a Java project. It will show the path to the `workspace` directory. To create the a new SBT-based project, follow these steps:

- Start Command Prompt (Windows) or Terminal (macOS and Linux) and change the active directory to the `workspace` directory. Type the following command and press *Enter*:

    ```
    sbt new sbt/scala-seed.g8
    ```

- The first time the preceding command is entered, SBT will download some dependencies. After a while, it will ask for a project name. Type `Akka Quotes` and press *Enter*. A new project will be created in the `akka-quotes` directory.
- Change the current directory to the `akka-quotes` directory and start SBT's interactive shell by simply typing `sbt` and pressing *Enter*.
- Try the generated project by entering the following command and pressing *Enter*:

    ```
    run
    ```

Again, SBT will start downloading some dependencies on the first run. When finished, you should see a `hello` message on the console:

Exit the interactive shell by entering the command `exit` and press *Enter*.

The template used to generate the project is based on the latest stable Scala release. We must check whether this version is supported by your installed Scala IDE version. In Eclipse IDE, from the menu bar, choose **Window** | **Preferences**.

In the tree, find and expand the **Scala** entry. Then, select its **Installations** entry. Write down the full versions of all the supported built-in Scala releases of your version of Scala IDE. On my installation, the built-in versions were Scala 2.11.8 and Scala 2.10.6. In a text editor, open the generated `built.sbt` build file that was placed in the `akka-quotes` directory. In my case, the file looked like this:

```
import Dependencies._

lazy val root = (project in file(".")).
  settings(
    inThisBuild(List(
      organization := "com.example",
      scalaVersion := "2.12.1",
      version := "0.1.0-SNAPSHOT"
    )),
    name := "Hello",
    libraryDependencies += scalaTest % Test
  )
```

If the specified `scalaVersion` variable was listed in your Scala IDE's Scala installations, then everything is fine. If not, you'll have to change the `scalaVersion` entry to your version. In my case, I had to change it to:

```
scalaVersion := "2.11.8",
```

If you had to change the version, run the following commands in the command line to clean and fully recompile the project:

```
sbt clean run
```

SBT will recompile the project using the changed Scala version. Since the template is based on a minimal project, this should usually work without problems.

If you are encountering serious version conflicts with the toolchain used in this chapter, try downloading the versions as used in this book and switch over to up-to-date versions when you gain enough experience.

Loading the SBTEclipse plugin

To find out which version of the plugin you have to install, visit the project page at `http://github.com/typesafehub/sbteclipse`:

The GitHub project page has instructions to add the plugin to your project. You should look for a line that starts with `addSbtPlugin`. In my case, it mentioned the following:

```
addSbtPlugin("com.typesafe.sbteclipse" % "sbteclipse-plugin"
        % "5.1.0")
```

In the `project` subdirectory of `akka-quotes`, create a new `plugins.sbt` file and copy and paste the line from the website. SBT now knows that this plugin is required for this project.

Ensure that the file is saved in the `project` subdirectory; otherwise, SBT will not find the file.

Generating a new Eclipse IDE project with SBTEclipse

Change the active directory back to the root directory of your `akka-quotes` directory and start the SBT interactive shell again by typing `sbt` and pressing *Enter*.

SBT will download and activate the plugin. From now on, when starting SBT in this project directory, you will be able to create or update an Eclipse IDE/Scala IDE project. Run the following command that is added by the `sbteclipse` plugin:

```
eclipse
```

The `sbteclipse` plugin has now generated project files inside the SBT project's directory that Eclipse IDE with the installed Scala IDE plugin can import.

Importing the generated project in Eclipse IDE

Return to your running Eclipse IDE instance or start Eclipse IDE if it were not running previously. To import the project that SBTEclipse generated for us, follow these steps:

1. Right-click on an empty spot in **Package Explorer** on the left-hand side of the screen and select **Import...**.
2. The **Import** dialog will appear and ask you to select an import wizard. Choose the **Existing Projects into Workspace** option and click on the **Next** button.
3. Click on the **Browse...** button next to the **Select root directory** field and navigate to your `workspace` directory's `akka-quotes` subdirectory and click on **OK**.
4. The import wizard dialog's project list will now have an `akka-quotes` project entry. Click on the **Finish** button to close the dialog.

The project will now be added to **Package Explorer**. In **Package Explorer**, navigate to the `src/main/Scala | example | Hello.scala` file. Press *Ctrl + F11* to run the file; alternatively, click on the **Run** button in the toolbar or choose **Run | Run** from the menu bar. If everything goes well, you'll see the `hello` greeting in the **Console** tab:

The Scala compiler (scalac)

SBT takes care of calling the Scala compiler, `scalac`, for us when building the project, so we won't be calling `scalac` ourselves directly. Still, we need to be aware that `scalac` is used by SBT instead of the `scala` command that we used during the whole course of the previous chapter.

The most important difference is that the Scala compiler, similar to the Java compiler `javac`, requires that code is wrapped in classes. The `scala` command took care of this by creating an invisible class under the hood. The `scalac` compiler does not do this trick, so when writing Scala code in Scala IDE that is built by SBT, you're required to define classes and add your code to them.

There are two methods of doing this:

- Creating a singleton object that contains the `main()` method
- Allowing a singleton object extend the App trait

Creating a singleton object with the main() method

This is very much like Java. Since Scala does not have an equivalent for Java's `static` access modifier, you are required to use a singleton object. The method will require an array of Strings, `Array[String]` as an input parameter, and the `Unit` return type, which is similar to Java's `void` keyword:

```
object MainObject {
  def main(args: Array[String]): Unit = {
    println("Executable code here...")
  }
}
```

Creating a singleton object that extends the App trait

Instead of adding a `main()` method to a singleton object, you can use the `App` trait that Scala offers. What's unusual about the `App` trait is that you cannot override any method in it and you cannot add the `main()` method to a class that implements the `App` trait either. Instead, you simply add the executable code directly to the body of the class, like you would do with executable code in a class's primary constructor:

```
object MainObject extends App {
  println("Executable code here...")
}
```

This is the method that we will use in this chapter.

Creating an Akka project

Akka is a modular toolkit for creating robust, distributed applications. It works with the Actor model, which will be explained in more depth later, and makes great use of Scala's functional programming features. It's a huge library, so we can only demonstrate a small portion of it in this chapter.

Visit the Akka website for more information (`http://akka.io/`).

It is recommended that you have Akka documentation at your fingertips while creating this project. Visit `http://akka.io/docs/` for more information on Akka documentation.

We will cover the following topics in this section:

- Adding Akka dependencies to the SBT build file
- Updating the Scala IDE project
- Akka concepts
- Creating actors
- Creating messages
- Unit testing an actor using the ScalaTest library
- Writing a runnable application

Adding an Akka dependency to the SBT build file

In the main Akka documentation site, find the **sbt** section:

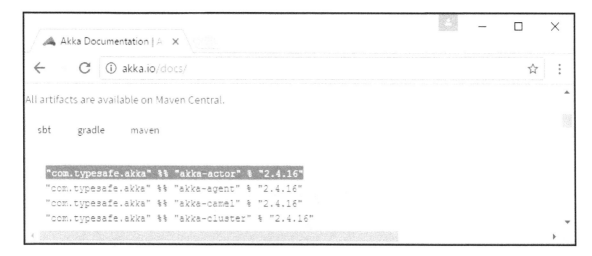

Find the `akka-actor` artifact in the list and copy the line to the clipboard:

```
"com.typesafe.akka" %% "akka-actor" % "2.4.16"
```

In Eclipse IDE, open the `build.sbt` file from **Package Explorer**. Do the following modifications:

- Add a comma to the existing `libraryDependencies` line.
- Add an empty new line, type `libraryDependencies +=`, and paste the line that was copied from the Akka documentation. Add a comma to the end of the line.

In the same list with artifacts, find the `akka-testkit` entry and repeat the same procedure as discussed just now for this line. Make sure the last line does not end with a comma; now add `% Test` to the end of the line.

After making the preceding changes, my version of the build file looked like this:

```
import Dependencies._

lazy val root = (project in file(".")).
  settings(
    inThisBuild(List(
      organization := "com.example",
      scalaVersion := "2.11.8",
      version := "0.1.0-SNAPSHOT"
```

```
        )),
        name := "Hello",
        libraryDependencies += scalaTest % Test,
        libraryDependencies += "com.typesafe.akka" %% "akka-actor"
                            % "2.4.16",
        libraryDependencies += "com.typesafe.akka" %% "akka-testkit"
                            % "2.4.16" % Test
    )
```

By adding `% Test` to a `libraryDependencies` entry, SBT will make sure that the dependency will only be used for unit testing. These dependencies will not be added to the classpath while running the main program and will also not be distributed with your project. Save the changes by pressing *Ctrl + S*.

Updating the Scala IDE project

After updating the `build.sbt` file, SBT must always run so that it can fetch dependencies and add them to the classpath. In this case, we also need to update the Eclipse IDE project files using the sbteclipse plugin; otherwise, Eclipse IDE will not see the changes.

From the command line, change the active directory to the `akka-quotes` directory. Let SBT fetch the new dependencies and update the Eclipse project by running the following command from the command line:

```
sbt eclipse
```

SBT will now download the new dependencies (and their dependencies) and also update the Eclipse IDE project accordingly. After a little while, you should see the following message:

```
[info] Successfully created Eclipse project files for project(s):
[info] Hello
```

In Eclipse IDE, right-click on the `akka-quotes` project in **Project Explorer** and select **Refresh**. If everything goes well, you should now see the `akka-actor` entry in the **Referenced Libraries** section of **Package Explorer**.

Akka concepts

Before writing our first Scala code that utilizes the Akka toolkit, let's take a look at some Akka concepts first. As mentioned earlier, Akka makes use of the Actor model. Some background information is needed before you can start writing Akka code. The following Akka concepts are covered here:

- Actors
- Actor references (`ActorRef`)
- Messages
- Dispatchers

Actors

Instead of directly calling methods on classes, in the actor model, messages are sent to an actor. In Akka, an actor is a class instance that extends the `akka.actor.Actor` trait and has a message handler. The message handler is a method that can handle all the messages that the actor supports. The actor's message handler can pass the received message to other actors, or it can create one or more new messages and pass them to other actors. It can even create new actors itself.

So far, we've seen nothing really special and no real advantages over directly calling methods on classes. One of the powerful features of Akka is that actors can not only run on a single process in a single application, but they can also run in different threads, different processes (for example, a different JVM instance). Actors can even run on completely different machines on a network. As long as the application plays by the rules, developers do not have to wrestle with classic problems related to concurrent/parallel programming, such as locking, preventing race conditions, and many other problems, that are often hard to reproduce and debug.

As mentioned, actors can create their own actors. The actor that creates other actors is the parent of the child actors and is also considered the supervisor of all the child actors. If a child actor fails, it sends a message back to its supervisor actor and that actor is responsible for handling the problem. The supervisor actor has the following options for handling the error:

- Request the child actor to resume its task, keeping its state
- Request the child actor to restart its task, clearing its state
- Stop the task permanently
- Escalate the problem; the task will fail

The easiest way to create a local actor is using the `actorOf` factory method of an `ActorSystem` instance. An `akka.actor.Props` class must be specified as a parameter that contains a reference to the actor's class. `Props` is a class that provides configuration data to the `actorOf` method. Here's an example of this:

```
import akka.actor.{ ActorSystem, Actor, Props }

val system = ActorSystem("AkkaQuote")

class MyActor extends Actor {
  def receive: Actor.Receive = { Actor.emptyBehavior }
}

val myActorRef = system.actorOf(Props[MyActor], "My-Actor")
```

There's no need to enter preceding code now.

Actor references (ActorRef)

Normally, Akka does not give direct access to actor instances. Instead, when an actor is created, an `ActorRef` instance is returned. An `ActorRef` instance is used to send messages to the actor. Note that an `ActorRef` instance does not expose the actor's internals. It is an immutable, thread-safe object and can safely be passed to other actors via messages.

One of the reasons Akka returns `ActorRef` instances instead of the instances of the `Actor` class itself is that actors can run on different machines on a network. Using the `ActorRef` reference instances, each actor can be reached, no matter whether it is running in the same process as the application or remotely on a server.

A message handler inside an actor has access to the `self` variable. This variable contains a reference to the actor's own `ActorRef` instance and `sender`, which is the `ActorRef` instance of the actor that sent the message.

 Unit tests can get full access to an actor's internals using the special `TestActorRef` class. We will demonstrate this later in this chapter.

Messages

Messages are instances of a class (which can be any class) that contains the required data. It is strongly recommended that you only have immutable data inside a message. If actors can freely change the state of a message, then typical multithreading problems might arise, which we discussed in the preceding section. Instead, the state should be handled in an actor itself. Scala's case classes are an excellent choice for messages, as these instances can easily be handled by the actor's message handler.

At this time, Akka does not guarantee that messages that are sent will also be received by the destination actors. Only Akka's persistence module (Akka's module that interacts with databases via **Object Relation Manager** (**ORM**) libraries, which we briefly discussed in `Chapter 2`, *Developing on the Java Virtual Machine*) has built-in support for making sure that a message has been received by the receiving actor. It's possible to add your own layer that will handle transmission errors on both the sending and/or receiving part, though.

Messages that are sent to an actor are stored in a queue of the receiving actor. This queue is called the actor's mailbox. Akka provides several built-in implementations for mailboxes, so actors can choose a specific one for performance reasons. It's also possible to create your own implementation if the need arises. Akka will ensure that messages inside the mailbox are handled as soon as possible by the actor.

Dispatchers

Dispatchers are a pool of threads that Akka uses for performing various housekeeping tasks. They ensure that messages that are sent by an actor are placed in the mailboxes of the receiving actors, waiting messages in the mailboxes are processed by actors, callbacks requested by the actors are called, and so forth.

Akka provides the default implementation of a dispatcher, but you can choose other implementations or even implement your own dispatchers.

Creating our first Akka actor - QuotesHandlerActor

We will write a simple Akka program that keeps an in-memory list of famous quotes. One actor will manage the list (adding new quotes and requesting a random quote) and a different actor will request a random quote and print it to the console.

Start by deleting the current files of both the main and test directories. In Eclipse's **Package Explorer**, right-click on the `example` package of `src/main/scala` and select **Delete**. When asked whether you are sure, click on the **OK** button.

Do the same with the `example` package of the `src/test/scala` directory. We'll start from scratch.

Create a new `QuotesHandlerActor` class in the `akkaquote.actor` package by right-clicking on the `src/main/scala` directory in Package Explorer and then navigating to **New | Scala Class**.

Enter the class name as `akkaquote.actor.QuotesHandlerActor.`:

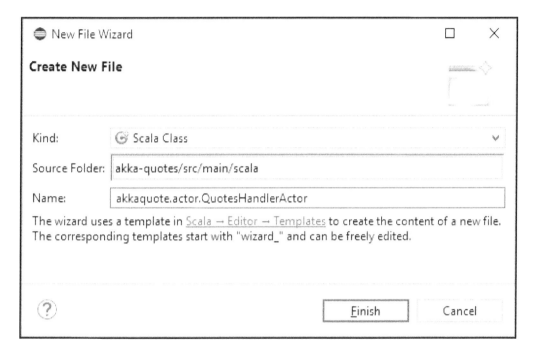

Scala IDE will now create the class and package; it will generate the following code (some empty lines removed):

```scala
package akkaquote.actor

class QuotesHandlerActor {
}
```

Place the cursor after `QuotesHandlerActor`, add a space, type `extends Actor`, and press *Ctrl* + Space bar. Scala IDE will show a list with the suggested class names:

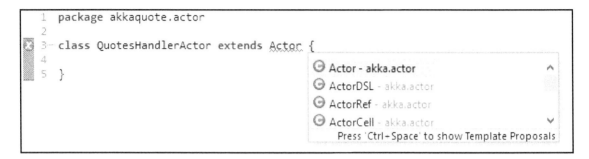

Select the `Actor` class from the `akka.actor` package and press *Enter*. Scala IDE will automatically add the corresponding import statement.

This class will hold the quotes, so let's implement a mutable list. Inside the class's body, type `val quotes = new ListB` and press *Ctrl* + Space bar. Move the cursor to `ListBuffer` (`scala.collections.mutable`) and press *Enter*:

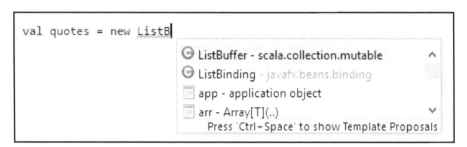

The line should read as `val quotes = new ListBuffer`.

The code should now look like this:

```
package akkaquote.actor

import akka.actor.Actor
import scala.collection.mutable.ListBuffer

class QuotesHandlerActor extends Actor {
  val quotes = new ListBuffer
}
```

Now, add two empty lines and press *Ctrl + 1* (*cmd + 1* on macOS). Scala IDE will show a list of methods that can be implemented. Select the `receive` method and press *Enter*:

```
val quotes = new ListBuffer


}        ⊙ Implement def 'receive(): Actor.Receive'
```

Scala IDE writes the method signature for us as follows:

```
def receive: Actor.Receive = {
  ???
}
```

This is the method that will handle incoming messages. We don't have any message yet that we can handle, yet Akka requires us to return a valid object. Replace `???` with `Actor.emptyBehavior`. This tells Akka that the receiver does not have any behavior and that this is intentional (for now).

Before we handle messages, we should first write them. So let's do just that.

Creating messages

As mentioned previously, message instances can be any class instance and their classes do not have to extend any trait or base class. It is strongly recommended that you use case classes, though. This is because an actor has only one `receive()` method, and all the messages are sent to that. As you will soon see for yourself, it's very convenient to use case classes' pattern matching feature to handle messages.

Create a new class, namely `Messages`, in the `akkaquote.message` package. To save some space, we will define all the public message classes in this file. Unlike Java, Scala supports adding multiple public classes to the same source file. In the file, remove the generated `Messages` class completely. We will first define the import lines and the class that defines a quote:

```
package akkaquote.message

import akka.actor.ActorRef

class Quote(val quote: String, val author: String)
```

The `Quote` class defines a quote consisting of text and the corresponding author. Both are immutable variables. Following this, add a new line and add the case classes that will define the messages that the actors in this example will use. Add the following to the end of the source file:

```
case class AddQuote(quote: Quote)
case class RequestQuote(originalSender: ActorRef)
case object PrintRandomQuote

case object QuoteAdded
case class QuoteRequested(quote: Quote, originalSender: ActorRef)
case object QuotePrinted
```

The first two classes, `AddQuote` and `RequestQuote`, are messages that can be sent to the `QuotesHandlerActor` actor we defined earlier. The third object, `PrintRandomQuote`, is a message that can be sent to the `QuotePrinterActor` actor that we will create later. The remaining three objects are messages that are sent back as a reply. Here are some noteworthy details about the preceding code:

- Notice how compact this code is. Since in Scala the primary constructor is defined in the class definition, we do not have to write code to define the fields and store its parameters. Scala takes care of this.
- None of the classes and objects need additional processing of their fields, so none of them require any body.
- Messages that do not need parameters are defined as singleton objects. This is not a requirement, but it would be a waste of memory to have multiple instances of these messages.
- Singleton objects can be case classes as well.
- Both the `RequestQuote` and `QuoteRequested` messages take an `ActorRef` instance (actor reference) as constructor parameters. The reason for this will be explained later.

One thing left to do, we must tell `QuotesHandlerActor` that it should store `Quote` instances only. We do this by using generics. Open the `QuotesHandlerActor` class and find the following line:

```
val quotes = new ListBuffer
```

Change it into:

```
val quotes = new ListBuffer[Quote]()
```

Use the *Ctrl* + Space bar key combination when entering the `Quote` class name, so that the required `import akkaquote.message` statement is added automatically.

Writing a ScalaTest-based unit test

To demonstrate how the ScalaTest unit-testing library works, we will write a unit test for one actor. Add a ScalaTest test case by right-clicking on `src/test/scala` and choosing **New | Scala Class**. Name the `QuotesHandlerActorTests` class. Remove the generated code and start by defining the required imports and the class definition itself:

```
import akka.actor.{ActorSystem, Props}
import akka.testkit.{TestKit, ImplicitSender, TestActorRef}
import org.scalatest.{Matchers, FlatSpecLike, BeforeAndAfterAll}
import akkaquote.actor.QuotesHandlerActor
import akkaquote.message.{AddQuote, Quote, QuoteAdded}

class QuotesHandlerActorTests()
extends TestKit(ActorSystem("Tests"))
with ImplicitSender with Matchers
with FlatSpecLike with BeforeAndAfterAll {

}
```

This class extends the `TestKit` class from Akka's TestKit module dependency. This class offers a lot of methods to make unit testing of Akka actors easier. By implementing the `FlatSpecLike` and `Matchers` traits, we can make use of ScalaTest's DSL, which makes it possible to write unit tests in a more natural way. Implementing the `ImplicitSender` trait ensures that the class will receive messages that the actors had sent as a reply.

It's important to properly stop the Akka system after all the tests have finished in a proper way; otherwise, memory leaks will occur. Inside the class, add the following method:

```
override def afterAll(): Unit = {
  system.terminate()
}
```

The `afterAll()` method can be overridden because the class implemented the `BeforeAndAfterAll` trait. The `system` field is a field that is inherited from the `TestKit` class.

In our test, we'll test that we can add new quotes by sending the `AddQuote` message to the `QuotesHandlerActor` actor. Add the following to the body of the class. Note that we will make use of ScalaTest's unique **domain-specific language** (DSL). It may look strange at first glance:

```
"An QuotesHandlerActor" should "add new quotes" in {
  val quoteHandlerActorRef = TestActorRef(Props[QuotesHandlerActor])
  val actorInstance = quoteHandlerActorRef.underlyingActor
                                    .asInstanceOf[QuotesHandlerActor]

  actorInstance.quotes.size should be(0)

  val quote = new Quote("This is a test", "me")
  quoteHandlerActorRef ! AddQuote(quote)
  expectMsg(QuoteAdded)

  actorInstance.quotes.size should be(1)
  actorInstance.quotes(0).quote should be("This is a test")
  actorInstance.quotes(0).author should be("me")
}
```

A lot is happening in the preceding code. Let's take a good look at it:

- The first line defines a test. The first string `"A QuotesHandlerActor"` describes which class or object is being tested, which is followed by the `should` keyword. It tells ScalaTest that this is a test; it is followed by a string describing what is being tested, in this case, `"add new quotes when receiving AddQuote message"`. After the `in` keyword, a block is opened that contains the code of the test.
- We create a `TestActorRef` object that references our `QuotesHandlerActor`. `TestActorRef` is an `ActorRef` instance that can be used for unit testing. Among other things, it gives direct access to the real `QuotesHandlerActor` actor instance that it wraps.

- We retrieve a reference to the `QuotesHandlerActor` actor instance object via the `TestActorRef` object. Now that we have a reference to the real actor's object, we can test its internals.
- Using the direct actor reference `actorInstance`, we check whether its quote's collection instance member has zero elements. If this is not the case, the test will fail.
- We send the `AddQuote` message to the `TestActorRef` instance. It will forward the message to the real actor. We do this because the `!` operator is only implemented in the `ActorRef` class. The `actorInstance` variable points to an instance of the Actor class, while `TestActorRef` is an instance of the `ActorRef` class. We create a new quote that is passed as the message's parameter.
- Because we implemented the `ImplicitSender` trait, our class receives the answer that the `AddQuote` message sent back. The `expectMsg` method checks whether the specified message has been received. It has a default interval of three seconds, which should be enough in our case.
- We then check whether there is now an element in the `quotes` list of `actorInstance` and we check whether the `quote` and `author` attributes match the quote that we sent to the message.

 Certain versions of Scala IDE have a bug regarding the `expectMsg` method. It can show an error `not found: value expectMsg`, while this method is available. If you encounter this, you can ignore this error. Scala IDE will still compile and run the code correctly.

Enough of talking, let's run the unit test by right-clicking on the `QuotesHandlerActorTests` class in **Package Explorer** and choosing the **Run As | ScalaTest** file. Not surprisingly, the test fails. The console will contain something like this:

```
Run starting. Expected test count is: 1
QuotesHandlerActorTests:
An QuotesHandlerActor
- should add new quotes *** FAILED ***
  java.lang.AssertionError: assertion failed: timeout (3 seconds) during
expectMsg while waiting for QuoteAdded
```

Switch to the **ScalaTest** tab for a summary:

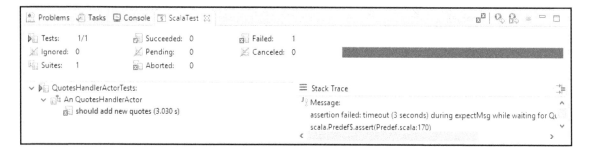

We do not handle the `AddQuote` message yet, so the `QuoteAdded` reply message has not been received by unit test script in a reasonable amount of time. Let's change that.

Implementing a message handler

In **Package Explorer**, from the `akkaquote.actor` package, open the `QuotesHandlerActor.scala` file.

Add the new required **imports**:

```
package akkaquote.actor

import akka.actor.Actor
import scala.collection.mutable.ListBuffer
import scala.util.Random
import akkaquote.message.{ Quote, AddQuote, QuoteAdded, RequestQuote,
                          QuoteRequested }
```

Replace the current implementation of the receive method with the following code:

```
def receive = {
  case AddQuote(quote) => {
    quotes += quote
    sender ! QuoteAdded
  }

  case RequestQuote(originalSender) => {
    val index = Random.nextInt(quotes.size)
    sender ! QuoteRequested(quotes(index), originalSender)
  }
}
```

Thanks to the magic of case classes and pattern matching, we can easily check which message was sent and handle each supported one accordingly. When receiving the `AddQuote` message, the passed `quote` object is added to the `quotes` list and the `QuoteAdded` message is sent back to `sender` as a reply.

This actor also handles the `RequestQuote` message. When receiving this message, it randomly selects a quote from the list and passes it to the `QuoteRequested` reply message that is sent back to the actor that sent the message. This message also contains the `ActorRef` instance of `originalSender`. This way, the receiver of this message can send a message back to the original actor that requested the quote. This is explained in more detail later.

From the `src/test/scala` directory, open the `QuotesHandlerActorTests.scala` file again and run the test again by right-clicking on the filename and choosing **Run As | Scala-Test**. It should now pass. Congratulations! You did it.

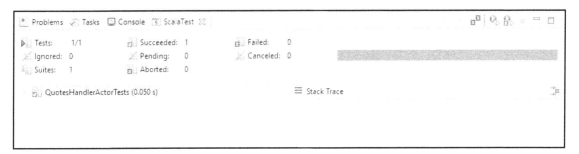

Creating QuotePrinterActor

We will now create an actor that will request a quote from `QuotesHandlerActor` and print the returned quote to the console. It will work as follows: when it receives the `RequestQuote` message, it will send it to `QuotesHandlerActor`. As we have seen, `QuotesHandlerActor` will reply by sending a `QuoteRequested` message, which would contain a random quote. When this message has been received, it will print the message to the screen. To save space, we will not be unit testing this class.

Note that not unit testing in a production environment because of time constraints is usually a very bad idea.

Create a new class, namely `akkaquote.actor.QuotePrinterActor`. First, add the import statements and the body:

```
package akkaquote.actor

import akka.actor.{ Actor, ActorRef }
import akkaquote.message.{ PrintRandomQuote, RequestQuote,
                            QuoteRequested, QuotePrinted }

class QuotePrinterActor(val quoteManagerActorRef: ActorRef) extends
     Actor {
}
```

What's noteworthy is that this class has a primary constructor that passes an `ActorRef` instance. Using an `ActorRef` object, we can send messages to the actor using the `!` operator.

In the class's body, add the message handler:

```
def receive: Actor.Receive = {
  case PrintRandomQuote => {
    val originalSender = sender
    quoteManagerActorRef ! RequestQuote(originalSender)
  }

  case QuoteRequested(quote, originalSender) => {
    System.out.println('"' + quote.quote + '"')
    System.out.println("-- " + quote.author)
    originalSender ! QuotePrinted
  }
}
```

When `QuotePrinterActor` receives the `PrintRandomQuote` message, it sends the `RequestQuote` message to `QuoteManagerActor` using the `quoteManagerActorRef` actor reference instance that was passed via the constructor. This actor is supposed to send a `QuoteRequested` message as a reply with a random quote.

When the `QuoteRequested` message is received, it prints it to the console.

What may seem complicated is that the sender is added to the `RequestQuote` message. Let's look at this in detail now. When the **PrintRandomQuote** message is received, its sender is the actor that sent the **PrintRandomQuote** message to **QuotePrinterActor**. We don't know which actor this will be at this point. Let's call it **Actor X** for now. Visually, the flow will look like this in a UML sequence diagram:

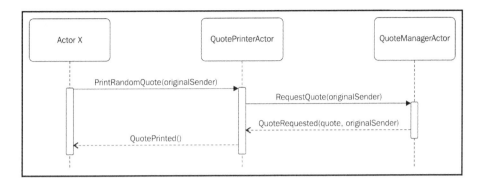

A reference to the **Actor X** actor is added to the **RequestQuote** message in the form of **originalSender. QuoteManagerActor** simply forwards the **originalSender** reference to the **QuoteRequested** reply message, which is sent back to the **QuotePrinterActor** actor. After printing the quote to the console, the **QuoteRequested** handler can now let **originalSender** (**Actor X**) know that a message has been printed by sending the **QuotePrint** message to the actor. If it had used the **Sender** actor reference instead of the **originalSender** actor reference, it would have sent the **QuotePrinted** message back to **QuoteManagerActor,** which is not what we want.

The main application

We will create a simple console-based application that adds some quotes to the collection and then prints a random one. It will communicate by sending messages to actors. A message handler inside actors is not supposed to block, meaning it should not run code that takes time to complete in the same thread. Our actors adhere to this rule; both actors process messages directly and return immediately.

To demonstrate the working of both the actors, we will do something different for the main program. When sending a message to an actor, we will let the program wait for the reply before continuing with the program. We do this to ensure that all the quotes are added before we request one to be printed. We also want to print the quote before stopping the Akka system and the program.

The *ask* pattern takes care of this. It sends a message to an actor and returns immediately, without waiting for a reply. Its return value is called a `Future` object. A `Future` object can be run by a dispatcher on a separate thread and run without blocking the Akka application. Among other things, we can also wait on code that runs inside `Future` (pause the program) until an answer is received or a timeout occurs. We will do the latter in this example.

Add a new `Singleton` object by right-clicking on the `akkaquote` package and choosing **New** | **Scala Object**. Change the code so it looks like this:

```
package akkaquote

import akka.actor.{ ActorSystem, Props, ActorRef }
import akka.pattern.ask
import akka.util.Timeout
import scala.concurrent.Await
import scala.concurrent.duration.DurationInt
import scala.language.postfixOps
import akkaquote.actor.{ QuotePrinterActor, QuotesHandlerActor }
import akkaquote.message.{ Quote, AddQuote, RequestQuote,
                           PrintRandomQuote }

object Main extends App {

}
```

That are a lot of import statements. The classes of the `akka.actor` package are fundamental to Akka actors. The `akka.pattern.ask` package has to be imported; otherwise, the `ask` method, or the similar `?` operator, is not recognized. The `ask` method is an expensive command, and Akka designers wanted to ensure that programmers would be aware of this. The `Await` class is needed to wait for a `Future` object to finish. Importing the `Timeout`, `DurationInt`, and `postfixOps` classes is needed to set the interval using the postfix notation.

Let's start by initializing Akka and the actors. Place the following code inside the object's body:

```
val system = ActorSystem("AkkaQuote")
val quoteActorRef = system.actorOf(Props[QuotesHandlerActor],
                                   "quotesActor")
val quotePrinterActorRef = system.actorOf(Props(new
                            QuotePrinterActor(quoteActorRef)),
                            "quotesPrinterActor")
```

Then add the code that will initialize the timeout value and add three quotes to `QuotesHandlerActor`:

```
implicit val timeout = Timeout(10 seconds)

val future1 = quoteActorRef ? AddQuote(new Quote("Hello world",
                                        "Various book authors"))
val future2 = quoteActorRef ? AddQuote(new Quote("To be or not to be",
                                        "W. Shakespeare"))
val future3 = quoteActorRef ? AddQuote(new Quote(
                  "In the middle of difficulty lies opportunity",
                  "A. Einstein"))

Await.result(future1, timeout.duration)
Await.result(future2, timeout.duration)
Await.result(future3, timeout.duration)
```

When you use the ? operator (remember that importing the `akka.pattern.ask` package is required as otherwise, the ? operator will not be available), a `Future` object is returned. For each message, we wait for a reply or a timeout to occur. If a timeout happens, then an exception will be thrown. Add the final code of this small application:

```
val future4 = quotePrinterActorRef ? PrintRandomQuote
Await.result(future4, timeout.duration)

system.terminate()
```

Finally, we send the `PrintRandomQuote` message to `QuotePrinterActor` using the actor's `ActorRef` instance. Again, we wait until a message is sent back as a reply or a timeout occurs. Finally, we stop the Akka system by calling the `terminate()` method.

 Again, due to a bug, certain versions of Scala IDE may not recognize the `system.terminate()` method and will show an error on the corresponding line: **value terminate is not a member of akka.actor.ActorSystem**. The code will run and compile fine, though.

The program will then exit gracefully and properly release all the resources.

When running the application by pressing *Ctrl + F11*, you should see one of the quotes printed to the console:

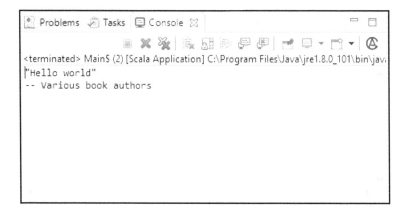

Summary

In this chapter, we covered a lot of technologies. We installed the Scala IDE plugin for Eclipse IDE so that we could write Scala code in Eclipse IDE and enjoy many of Eclipse's features. To build the project, we installed SBT. We installed the sbteclipse plugin for SBT because Scala IDE does not have built-in support for SBT. SBTEclipse creates and updates Scala IDE projects that use an SBT build file.

We learned about the `Actor` model, a model where various actors send messages to each other. Each actor has a single method that handles all the messages. Instead of communicating directly with actor instances, actor references called `ActorRef` instances are used. If you use `ActorRef` instances, the code wouldn't care much whether an actor is running locally or remotely on a network. We wrote a unit test using a DSL to test the internals of an actor. Finally, we wrote the main program that used `ask-pattern` and `Future` objects to wait for replies.

In the next chapter, we will take a detailed look at Clojure, a Lisp language implementation for JVM. Clojure will be interesting for fans of Scala, as its is also specialized in the functional programming paradigm.

7
Clojure

Clojure is a language that is rather different from the other languages covered in this book. It is a language largely inspired by the Lisp programming language, which originally dates back to the late 1950s. Lisp stayed relevant by being up to date with both technology and times. Common Lisp and Scheme are arguably the two most popular Lisp dialects in use today. Clojure is a dialect of Lisp, but its design is influenced by both.

Unlike Java and Scala, Clojure is a dynamic language. Variables do not have fixed types and when compiling, no type checking is performed by the compiler. When a variable is passed to a function that is not compatible with the code in the function, an exception will be thrown at runtime. What's also noteworthy is that Clojure is not an object-orientated language (OOP), unlike all the other languages in this book. Clojure still offers interoperability with Java and JVM, as it can create instances of objects. And, as we will soon see, it can also generate classes to let other Java-compatible languages on the JVM run the bytecode compiled by Clojure.

We will cover the following topics here:

- Installing Clojure
- Clojure's interactive shell - Read-Eval-Print-Loop (REPL)
- Clojure language basics
- Working with classes
- Clojure agent system

Installing Clojure

From the official project's website (`https://clojure.org/`), download the latest version:

It is recommended that you have the documentation available while trying the examples in this book. Both the online official documentation and the community-driven documentation sites are recommended:

- `http://clojure.org/reference/`
- `http://clojure-doc.org`

At the time of writing, the latest version is Clojure 1.8.0. Extract the archive and write down the full path to the directory where you've extracted the archive; you'll need it to create a start script.

To validate the installation, start the interactive shell. In the Command Prompt (Windows) or Terminal (macOS and Linux), replace the directory with Clojure's main directory and type the following command (replace the version number with your installed version):

```
java -jar clojure-1.8.0.jar
```

The preceding command is fine to test the shell, but it should not be used to run real Clojure code. The reason is that when using the -jar option, no custom classpath can be set. This is explained in full detail in Chapter 2, *Developing on the Java Virtual Machine*. We'll show a better way to run the shell.

If everything goes smoothly, something similar to the following should appear on the console:

```
Clojure 1.8.0
user=>
```

Type the following code and press *Enter* to exit:

```
(System/exit 0)
```

This code runs the standard exit method from the java.lang.System class to gracefully stop the current JVM instance.

Creating a start script

Unlike many other JVM languages, Clojure's distribution does not contain start scripts for common operating systems. The easiest way to run Clojure is to create a start script manually and add the script to a directory that is in the path of your operating system.

The start scripts we'll discuss next specify a fixed classpath. If you create an application in Clojure that requires additional classes on the classpath, it is recommended to create a custom start script for that program.

Creating a start script on Windows

Using your favorite text editor, create a file with the following line:

```
java -cp c:\PATHTO\clojure\clojure-1.8.0.jar clojure.main
```

Replace `c:\PATHTO\clojure` with the path to your Clojure installation. Also, replace the version number with your installed version.

Type `path` in the command window to see the directories in the path. Alternatively, refer to `Chapter 2`, *Developing on the Java Virtual Machine*, for instructions on how to add other directories to the path. Save the file to a directory that is in your path and call it `clojure.bat`.

Creating a start script on macOS and Linux

Create a file with the following content to a directory that is on your path:

```
java -cp /path/to/clojure/clojure-1.8.0.jar clojure.main
```

Replace `/path/to/` with the path to your Clojure installation. Also, replace the version number with your installed version. Save the file to a directory that is in your path and call it `clojure.sh`. Make the file executable by entering the following command in the Terminal, change the active directory to the directory where you stored `clojure.sh`:

```
chmod +x clojure.sh
```

Clojure's interactive shell (REPL)

Using the startup script, you can now run Clojure's REPL interactive shell from Clojure by simply running a simple script. Unlike Scala's `scala` REPL interactive shell, Clojure's REPL does not have its own custom commands. As we have already seen, to gracefully exit, you have to call the `java.lang.System` class's `exit()` method by typing (`System/exit 0`):

Clojure does not come with a standalone compiler command. Instead, it generates and executes JVM bytecode in memory while executing Clojure code. To generate class files that will be saved in a directory on the filesystem, which can be used by other JVM languages, you'll have to call ordinary Clojure functions. We will demonstrate this functionality in the next chapter.

Clojure language

Since Clojure is so different from many mainstream programming languages, we'll place more emphasis on the basics of Clojure than for other languages in this book. Here are the basics we'll discuss:

- Syntax
- Expressions
- Defining variables
- Defining functions
- Data structures (numerals, strings, and collections)
- Iteration over arrays and loops
- Conditions

Syntax

Lisp and Clojure both adhere to the *code is data and data is code* principle. This property of Lisp is called *homoiconicity*, which means that a language's syntax is similar to its program structure. Among Lisp's built-in datatypes is a list. This list type is used when writing code. After you define a list, you can add expressions to it. An expression contains a function reference and its parameters. When closing a list, the list is evaluated dynamically at runtime. Basically, entire programs are represented by Clojure's internal data structures. Clojure has a process, called *the reader*, that reads and evaluates each entry in the list and creates certain data structures that are passed to the compiler. Let's look at a simple example of an expression:

```
(println "Hello" "from Clojure!")
```

Feel free to enter this in Clojure's REPL shell. The REPL shell will print the following to the console:

```
Hello from Clojure!
nil
```

The (and) characters start and end a list. In this case, the content of the list is a single expression that can be read and evaluated by the reader. The expression consists of a call to Clojure's `println` function. The `println` function is called a **variadic** function, which means that it consumes all the remaining elements in the list as input parameters. It is somewhat similar to Java's `varargs` keyword, which we briefly looked at in Chapter 3, *Java*. In this case, there are two parameters; both were evaluated before they were passed to the `println` function. The `println` function prints the passed strings to the console and does not return anything itself (the function would have been declared with the `void` keyword in Java); therefore, its call is evaluated to `nil`, which is similar to Java's `null`. Unlike Java, function calls in Clojure always evaluate to something.

You might ask yourself what would be the advantage of using data structures that contain code (we will mainly focus on expressions in this chapter) instead of simply defining a fixed language syntax that is parsed by the compiler using a traditional parser. The answer is that special functions can be written that directly manipulate the code by simply modifying its data structures. These special functions are called *macros*. Macros dynamically alter or enhance the existing code by simply manipulating the lists that contain the expressions. This opens up a lot of new possibilities. Creating new macros is a rather advanced topic that is not part of the scope of this book. We will focus on the functions and macros that Clojure provides.

Expressions

An expression starts with a function call and is followed by its parameters. As we will soon see, expressions can be nested.

Unlike many mainstream languages, Clojure does not have the concept of operators. Instead, it simply provides functions that return the result of a calculation. For example, there's the + function that consumes and adds up all the numeric values that are specified in the same list:

```
(+ 10 20 30)
```

It returns 60.

Each expression in Clojure evaluates to a single value. An expression is placed in a list; the first entry in the list is the function, and all the other entries in the list are its parameters. Parameters are evaluated before being passed to the function. This makes it possible to add nested expressions for parameters that need some processing:

```
(+ 10 ( * 3 5 ))
```

The preceding expression will be evaluated in the following order:

```
(+ 10 ( * 3 5 ))
(+ 10 ( 15 ))
(+ 10 15)
(25)
```

The second parameter, which is a list, is evaluated to 15. Note that 15 is passed as the second parameter to the + function. The expression, therefore, results in 25. Clojure does not have any notion of operator precedence; it just evaluates lists with expressions from left to right. Therefore, nested lists are often required in calculations.

The following table sums up the most important arithmetic functions:

Function	Description	Example
+	Add the values	(+ 10 20) → 30
-	Subtract the values, from left to right	(- 50 25) → 25
*	Multiply the values	(* 10 20) → 200
/	Divide the values (see "Numeric types," discussed in a bit, for more information)	(/ 25 5) → 5
quot	Quotient operation	(quot 13 4) → 3
rem	Remainder operation	(rem -13 4) → -1
mod	Modulus operation	(mod -13 4) → 3
inc	Increase the value by one	(inc 41) → 42
dec	Decrease the value by one	(dec 43) → 42
max	Returns maximal value	(max 100 20 30) → 100
min	Returns minimal value	(min 0 -1 30) → -1

Defining variables

Clojure is not a pure functional programming language. It can create variables that can point to different data structures over time, which means there can be side effects. Variables are defined by the def function:

```
(def var-name)
```

When no value is specified, the variable is unbound. A variable can point to a value by defining it at the same time the variable is defined. A new global binding is created that lets the variable name point to the specified value:

```
(def var-name "This is a value")
```

The variable var-name now points to the This is a value string. To let it point to a different value, you can use the def function again:

```
(def var-name 100)
```

Other references to var-name are not changed. Only the code that from now on could read var-name will see the new value: 100.

It is possible to bind variables on a per-thread basis so different threads can have their own copy of the variable, but this is outside the scope of this chapter.

Defining functions

The easiest way to create a function is to use the defn function:

```
(defn greet [name] (println (str "Greetings, " name "!")))
```

The greet function defined earlier can be called in the usual way:

```
(greet "reader of this book")
```

This line is printed to the console: Greetings, reader of this book!. A few notes about the defn function:

- Its first parameter is the name of the function
- The second parameter must be a vector object containing the function's input parameters. Use an empty vector [] array if you don't need parameters

- The third parameter is the expression that is evaluated and returned by the function
- It returns the last expression of the function. In this case, it is `nil` because `println` evaluates to `nil`

If you want the `greet true` value, instead of `nil`, it should be the last entry in the list, and it should not be put between parentheses because the `true` value is not a function:

```
(defn greet [name] (println (str "Greetings, " name "!")) true)
```

Data structures

In the Scala chapters, we've already seen that immutable data is the cornerstone of functional programming. Instead of functions that alter data, functions return new copies of that data so that the existing instances of that data are not changed. We have seen this with immutable lists in Scala as well. When using the + operator to add a new element to an immutable list, a new list is returned and the existing list is left alone.

At first sight, it may seem wasteful to have multiple separate, copies of the same data eating up precious memory, slightly modified in each copy. In reality, Clojure makes use of complex data structures that make intelligent use of reference fields. In a copy of modified data, only the data that has been changed takes up new space; .

Imagine we create a simple list with four elements:

We update the second item in the list. Clojure creates a new list. In the new list, all the entries point to the original version, except for the second item:

Updated List		Original list
		→ Item 1
Updated item 2		Item 2
		→ Item 3
		→ Item 4

Since the data of each version is immutable and will never change, these references will always be valid.

This technique is called **persistent data structures**, not to be confused with persistent database objects that are used in an **Object Relation Manager (ORM)**.

Clojure's data structures are good JVM citizens. They follow JVM conventions as described in the first and second chapter. They implement `hashCode()` and `equals()` methods so they can be used in ordinary Java collections, such as `HashMap` instances. Also, they use JVM interfaces to hide implementation details from their callers. Clojure's collection classes implement iterators so they can be used in `for` loops. The Clojure team has put in a lot of effort to offer good compatibility with the Java ecosystem, and therefore, with the most other popular JVM languages as well.

Numeric types

For performance and efficiency reasons, Clojure uses JVM's primitive types as the default type for numeric types, rather than the wrapper classes that were covered in the previous chapters. Clojure uses the long type as the default type for whole numbers. If a value fits in a primitive long variable, Clojure will create primitive longs even when integers are used. For floating point values, Clojure uses primitive double variables by default. As we will see later, Clojure also has built-in support for classes from the standard Java class library that support larger values and/or precision as well.

It must be noted that Clojure has built-in support for primitive wrapper classes, though. For instance, when using the `java.lang.Integer` class, Clojure will automatically autobox it to a primitive integer.

When a calculation results in a value that is not equal to a whole integer number, a `Ratio` object is returned instead. This is a rather unique feature of Clojure. Let's look at an example:

```
(/ 1 3)
```

In most languages, dividing 1 by 3 using two integer values would simply result in 0 (also an integer). In Clojure, somewhat surprisingly, this is returned:

```
1/3
```

This is a `Ratio` class instance, which is a normal JVM class defined in Clojure's runtime library. The `Ratio` class keeps the numerator and denominator in separate fields. If you want a double precision result instead, without dealing with a `Ratio` object at all, you should change at least one of the integers to a double value:

```
(/ 1 3.0)
```

This would return the more familiar 0.3333333333333333 primitive double value.

If you want to know the integer quotient and modulus, you could use the `quot` and `mod` functions:

```
(quot 42 10) (mod 42 10)
```

These functions would result in 4 and 2, respectively.

Along with the built-in primitive `long` and `double` datatypes, Clojure also provides its own `BigInt` type, which can store much larger numbers than a primitive `long` variable. Clojure also has built-in support for Java's `BigDecimal` class from the `java.math` package of the Java class library. By prefixing an integer value with the letter N, Clojure converts it into a `BigInt` instance:

```
(+ 100 1N)
```

This results in 101N. When at least one input parameter of an operator function is a `BigInt` instance, the result of the calculation will also be a `BigInt` instance. `BigDecimal` works in a similar way. By prefixing a value with the letter M, a value is converted into a `BigDecimal` instance:

```
(+ 555 0.4169M)
```

This results, unsurprisingly, in 555.4169M.

Clojure's documentation says that its standard arithmetic functions can throw an exception when whole values that cannot fit in a primitive long variable value are used. This is indeed the case:

```
(* 123 1234567890123456789)
```

The preceding code throws an exception: `ArithmeticException integer overflow clojure.lang.Numbers.throwIntOverflow`. All the arithmetic functions that were mentioned in the table in the *Expressions* section have a variant with an additional apostrophe (`'`) suffix. These functions will convert a result value into a `BigInt` instance when necessary:

```
(*' 123 1234567890123456789)
```

In case you're wondering, the preceding expression returns `151851850485185185047N`.

Strings and characters

Like Scala, Clojure uses the standard JVM (`java.lang.String`) class for its strings. Clojure's math functions do not work on strings. While many languages use the addition operator (often +) to concatenate two strings, Clojure's + function does not support strings. Instead, the `str` function has to be used:

```
(str "Good" "night!")
```

The preceding expression evaluates to `Goodnight!`.

Clojure offers many of its own functions that are dedicated to strings. Many of those are declared in the `clojure.string` namespace. For example, to convert a list into a `String`, the `join` function of the `clojure.string` library can be used:

```
(clojure.string/join "/" ["10", 20, 30M, 40N])
```

This results in `10/20/30/40`. The parameter specifies the separator that will be added between the elements. Even though the list contains values of several different types (string `"10"`, integer 20, 30M BigInt, and 40N BigDecimal), they are all converted into strings.

It's a recommended practice to import the `clojure.string` library with `require`:

```
(require '[clojure.string :as str])
(str/join, "/" [1, 2, 3])
```

Here's a list of other common functions in the `clojure.string` namespace. The examples in this table assume that the `clojure.string` library has been loaded with the `(require '[clojure.string :as str])` line demonstrated above:

Name	Description	Example input → output
blank?	Returns `true` when the passed string is nil, empty, or it only contains whitespace characters. Otherwise returns `false`.	`(str/blank? " ")` → `true`
capitalize	Converts the first character of string into an uppercase character and all the others to lowercase	`(str/capitalize "JVM rules")` → `"Jvm rules"`
ends-with?	Returns whether the string ends with the specified character or string	`(str/ends-with? "Hi" "i")` → true
last-index-of	Returns a zero-based index of the last occurrence of the string or null when not found	`(str/last-index-of "HELLO" "L")` → 3
lower-case	Returns a copy of the string with all the characters converted into lowercase	`(str/lower-case "HeLlO")` → `"hello"`
replace	Replaces a substring in an input string with another substring	`(str/replace "HELLO" "ELLO" "i!")` → `"Hi!"`
reverse	Probably not too surprising, but this returns a reversed version of the input string	`(str/reverse "!iH")` → `"Hi!"`
split	Refers to split strings using a regular expression; note that regular expressions are prefixed with # in Clojure	`(str/split "a-b-c" #"-")` → `["a" "b" "c"]`

split-lines	Refers to split strings on either end-of-line characters as used by Windows (*CR* + *LF* or run) or Linux's (and many other popular operating systems) LF n character	`(str/split-lines "A\nB\r\nC")` → `["A" "B" "C"]`
trim	Removes the leading and trailing whitespace characters (Space bar, *Tab*, CR, and LF)	`(str/trim " A\nBC\t\n")` → `"A\nBC"`
upper-case	Returns the input string with all the characters converted into uppercase	`(str/upper-case "abC")` → `"ABC"`

Note that the library has more functions than described here, so be sure to read its documentation.

Clojure does not use the primitive char fields for characters. Characters in Clojure are `java.lang.Character` instances and can be created by prefixing the character with a backslash:

```
(println \H \e \l \l \o)
```

This prints H e l l o to the console. The passed parameters to the `println` function are not strings; therefore, no double-quotes are required. Instead, each individual character is converted into a `java.lang.Character` class instance, and the `println` function simply prints all the class instances that are specified from left to right.

It's also possible to use the `char` function if you know the UTF-16 code point of a character:

```
(println (char 65))
```

This prints A because the ASCII character #65 has A and the UTF-16 encoding is compatible with the classic ASCII character set. Note that in the preceding example, additional parentheses are required as function parameters are evaluated before being passed to the function. If you leave them away, a reference to the `char` function would be printed along with 65.

Collections

Like Scala, Clojure provides its own implementations of its collection classes. This was necessary to provide immutable and persistent collections (as explained earlier, persistent in this context means that new copies in a collection make use of the references to earlier copies of the data in order to keep the memory safe).

Clojure provides interfaces for its collections, and it decides which implementation of a class is used. Clojure may even decide to change implementations when calling certain functions. Since all the collections implement the same interfaces, this should normally not be an issue.

We will look at the following collection types:

- Lists
- Vectors
- Sets
- HashMaps

Lists

A normal list is created with the `list` function:

```
(list "item 1" "item 2")
```

A list implements Clojure's `ISeq` interface, an interface that all the Clojure collections implement. Lists can be iterated (iterating will be discussed later in this chapter) but are not optimized for index-based retrieval of items, unlike a vector, which we will discuss shortly. Clojure provides the `nth` function that iterates over the list to find the specified item. It is not very efficient as it has to iterate through the collection to find the item:

```
(nth (list "item A" "item B" "item C") 2)
```

Here we asked `nth` to iterate through the list to retrieve the third (index is zero-based) item. It returns `item C` as expected. This is how **nth** works:

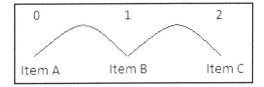

Imagine the penalty you'll come across when you have a list with hundreds of elements. Luckily, we will see that Clojure has a data structure that is more appropriate when indexing is needed.

If you want to create a new list by adding new items to an existing list, you can use the `conj` function. Here's an example of this:

```
(conj (list 10 20 30) 40 50)
```

Surprisingly, this new list is returned as `(40 50 10 20 30)`. The reason is that lists, by design, are optimized for adding items to the head of the list, which means the start of the list.

Vectors

A vector is quite comparable to Java's `ArrayList` class. Like an `ArrayList` object and unlike lists, vectors are optimized for retrieving items at certain indexes. You can create a vector using the `vector` function:

```
(vector 10 20 30)
```

The preceding code returns `[10 20 30]`. You can also create a vector with brackets. The following code works as well:

```
[10 20 30]
```

We did not add parentheses to the preceding example because that would require adding a function call.

Although the `nth` function can be used to retrieve an item from a specified index, this is not recommended. As discussed earlier, the `nth` function iterates through the collection to find the item. When using vectors, it is much better to use the `get` function. The `get` function, which does not support lists, retrieves the item by directly reading the reference:

```
(get [10 20 30] 1)
```

The preceding expression simply returns `20`.

Vectors are optimized to add items to the tail of the collection. So this time, no surprises when adding items to a vector:

```
(conj [10 20 30] 40 50)
```

It returns [10 20 30 40 50].

Sets

Sets are a collection of values where each value is unique. When a value is added to a set that is already in the set, then the value is not added again. To create a hash set (a type of set that does not preserve the original order of the added elements), use the following literal notation:

```
#{ 10 20 30 }
```

The returned set may have the values in different order, in my case, #{20 30 10} was returned.

To create a sorted set that retains the order of the added elementsthe sorted-set function can be used:

```
(sorted-set 10 20 30)
```

The returned set should now have the same order: #{10 20 30}. It should be noted that a sorted set is more expensive than a hash set.

Like vectors, the get function can be used to retrieve a value from a set, and the conj function can be used to add values to a set.

Hash-maps

Similar to vectors, hash-maps can be created using the hash-map function and {}. The following code is equivalent:

```
(hash-map :key1 "value1", :key2 "value2")
```

```
{:key1 "value1", :key2 "value2"}
```

The commas to separate key/value pair are optional but recommended to make the code more readable. As most standard HashMap implementations, the order of key/value pairs will not be predictable. On my machine, the following was printed as output: {:key2 "value2", :key1 "value1"}.

In the preceding example, both the keys are keywords. Keywords are created by prefixing the name with the colon (:) character. It is not required to `hash-map` keys, but it is recommended that you them when possible and feasible because they are very efficient and make very fast lookups possible. Keywords evaluate to themselves, so when you enter `:key1` in REPL, you'll see `:key1` printed as output.

To retrieve a value from a `HashMap`, you can use the familiar `get` function, which you also used to retrieve items from a vector:

```
(get { :key1 "value1", :key2 "value2" } :key2)
```

This will return `"value2"`.

When using keywords as keys, you can omit the `get` function call to retrieve a value from a `HashMap`:

```
(:key1 { :key1 "value1", :key2 "value2" })
```

This returns `"value1"`.

To create a new `hash-map` object that contains updated key/value pairs, use the `assoc` function:

```
(assoc { :k1 "v1", :k2 "v2" } :k3 "v3", :k2 nil)
```

This creates the following new `hash-map`: `{:k1 "v1", :k2 nil, :k3 "v3"}`.

To merge two hash-maps, use the `merge` function:

```
(merge { :k1 "v1", :k2 "v2" } { :k2, nil, :k3 "v3" })
```

This returns `{:k1 "v1", :k2 nil, :k3 "v3"}` as well.

To check whether `hash-map` currently holds a key, use the `contains?` function:

```
(contains? { :k1 "v1", :k2 "v2" } :k3)
```

Since the map does not contain any entry with the `:k3` keyword as the key, it returns `false`.

Iteration over arrays and loops

Clojure's `for` function is very powerful. In its most simple form, it just iterates over a collection:

```
(for [x ["A" "B" "C"]]
 x)
```

It returns a new list `("A" "B" "C")`.

Adding multiple iterators in a for loop is possible:

```
(for [x [1 2 3],
      y [100 200]]
 (+ x y))
```

As always, commas are optional. This returns a new list: `(101 201 102 202 103 203)`.

By adding the `:let` keyword, a function can be defined that defines a new local and is called for each iteration. The local can only be used inside the body of the for loop and cannot be modified:

```
(for [x [10 20 30]
      :let [y (* 2 x)]]
 (list x y))
```

This returns a new list containing three lists: `((10 20) (20 40) (30 60))`

You can add the `:while` keyword with a function that either returns true or false. The iteration stops when this function returns false:

```
(for [x [10 20 30]
      :let [y (* 2 x)]
      :while (<= y 40)]
 (list x y))
```

This returns a list: `((10 20) (20 40))`.

Finally, you can add a condition by adding the `:when` keyword. The expression must return either `true` or `false`. When true, the value is added to the list; otherwise, the value is ignored. The iteration continues when a value is ignored:

```
(for [x (range 10)
      :let [y (* x x)]
      :when (= (mod y 2) 0)]
 y)
```

The preceding function returns `(0 4 16 36 64)`. The `(range 10)` function generates a sequence from `0` to `9` (inclusive).

Conditions

We looked at some conditions briefly when specifying the `:while` and `:when` keywords to the for function. Again, instead of offering operators, Clojure offers ordinary functions that simply evaluate to either true or false. All the functions mentioned in the following table are variadic. In this case, this means you can specify at least two values and more. Here are the most important functions:

Function	Description	Example input → output
`==`	Returns true if all the specified parameters represent the same value	`(== 42 42.0 42M 42N)` → `true`
`not=`	Returns true if one of the specified parameters is not equal to the next one	`(not= 1 1 2)` → `true`
`<`	Returns true if each passed parameter is smaller than the next one	`(< -1 5 10)` → `true`
`>`	Returns true if each parameter is larger than the next one	`(> 10 5 -1)` → `true`
`<=`	Returns true if each passed parameter is either equal to or smaller than the next one	`(<= 5 5 6)` → `true`
`>=`	Returns true if each passed parameter is either equal to or larger than the next one	`(>= 6 6 5)` → `true`
`and`	Logical AND	`(and (> 6 5) (< -1 10) )` → `true`
`or`	Logical OR	`(or (== 3 10) (> 5 3))` → `true`
`not`	Logical NOT	`(not (== 1 5))` → `true`

It also offers the logical `if` function:

```
(if (< 100 10) "This is true" "This is completely false")
```

When the first parameter evaluates to `true`, the second (evaluated) parameter is returned; otherwise, the third is returned. In this case, the expression obviously evaluates to `"This is completely false"`. A few notes about the `if` function:

- Here `nil` is evaluated to `false`.
- It is not required to specify the else part (the third parameter). When not specified and the condition returns `false`, the expression evaluates to `nil`.

Working with Java classes

As will be known by now, Clojure is not an object-orientated language. The Clojure team added several features to Clojure to ensure that Clojure can properly consume and create classes from the Java class library and other JVM libraries.

To create an instance of a class, two forms are supported. First, to do this, use `new`:

```
(def x (new java.util.ArrayList () ))
```

Here we define a variable that points to an `ArrayList` instance. By passing an empty `list` `()` method, we do not pass any parameter to its constructor. A different way to create an instance is to add a dot to the class name:

```
(def x (java.util.ArrayList. () ))
```

Note the dot added to `ArrayList`. There's no functional difference between the two ways.

> Think twice before using mutable collections in a Clojure program. Since Clojure is a functional programming language, it is usually a much better idea to use Clojure's immutable collections whenever possible.

To call methods on the instance of an object, you can prefix the method name with a dot, followed by the instance and the method's parameters:

```
(.add x 10)
```

The `add` method returns `true`. To see the content, simply enter x in REPL and press *Enter*. It will print `[10]`.

A convenient way to call multiple methods on a single instance is to use the `doto` macro:

```
(doto x (.add 20) (.add 30) (.add 40))
```

The `doto` macro returns the instance of the object, so it prints `[10, 20, 30 40]`.

Class attributes (static fields) can be accessed by specifying the fully qualified class name, the forward slash, and the member name:

```
(java.lang.Integer/MAX_VALUE)
```

This will return `2147483647`.

Here's another example where we use the static `out` field of the `java.lang.System` class to print a message:

```
(.printf System/out "Hello %s!!n" (into-array String (list "world")))
```

It evaluates to something like `#object[java.io.PrintStream 0x4ea5b703 "java.io.PrintStream@4ea5b703"]` (the values will be different on your machine).

The preceding snippet shows multiple tricks:

- The `java.lang` package is imported by Clojure implicitly. Therefore, it was not necessary to use the fully qualified `java.lang.System` class name.
- The second argument of the `PrintStream` class's `printf` method is a string array (`String[]`). We convert a list with a single entry into a string array using Clojure's `into-array` function.
- The `printf` method returns the `PrintStream` object. Therefore, the expression evaluates to the object displayed earlier.

Creating simple Java classes with deftype and defrecord

Clojure offers `deftype` and `defrecord` macros that can be used to dynamically generate Java classes with feature constructor and fields. These classes can be used to define types that hold simple data. Here's an example of the `deftype` macro usage:

```
(deftype Position2D [x y])
```

It defines a `Position2D` class with two fields: `x` and `y`. To instantiate an object based on this class:

```
(def position (Position2D. 5 10))
```

This creates the `position` variable with `x=5` and `y=10` instance fields. Note the required dot after the `Position2D` class name. We've already explored this syntax in the previous topic.

When you specify one or more Java interfaces during the process of specifying the class with either macros, it can also add methods to the generated class; however, it can only add those methods that are defined in an interface. Let's say we will be implementing a closeable resource, which implements the `java.io.Closeable` interface of the Java class library:

```
(deftype SomeCloseableResource []
  java.io.Closeable
  (close
   [this]
   (println "Closing resource...")))
```

The `java.io.Closeable` interface defines one method called `close()`. This method takes no parameters, but in Clojure, it is required to define the variable that will contain the reference to the instance, which in Java is called `this`.

 Java automatically defines the `this` variable on instance methods, but in Clojure, you will have to specify the variable manually yourself for each method.

Here's an example that demonstrates the `close()` method:

```
(def resource (SomeCloseableResource.))
(.close resource)
```

The preceding code will print the `Closing resource...` text to the console.

The `defrecord` macro has the same syntax as that of the `deftype` macro, but it has the following most important differences:

- Classes defined with `defrecord` feature a persistent map, which introduces extensible fields. Additional keys that were not defined when defining the class can be added to the object.
- Mutable fields are optionally supported for classes that are defined with `deftype`; the fields in classes defined with `defrecord` are always, by design, immutable.

Here's a simple example of a class defined with defrecord; it demonstrates that its class implements a map-like interface:

```
(defrecord Record [:field1 :field2])
(def rec (Record. "value1" "value2"))

(contains? rec :field2)
```

The expression will evaluate to `true`.

Managing states with agents

To safely manage a mutable state in a multithreaded program, Clojure offers agents. Each agent is responsible for managing one object that contains its state. Most often, a state object will be stored in one of Clojure's own immutable data structures. To change the state of a particular agent, an action can be sent to it. Actions are ordinary, non-blocking functions that are executed by the agent. The return value of the action will replace the current state of the agent.

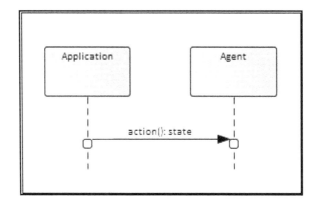

Agents run in a thread provided by an internal thread pool that is managed by Clojure. They are built to be responsive; Clojure will never place locks while handling actions. The agent's state can safely be read at any time by other code, no matter on which thread it is running. An action is sent to the agent asynchronously and is picked up later by the agent's thread. The agent's thread will execute the action and its result value will become the agent's new state.

It is possible to add a validator to an agent. A validator is a function that validates the new state and can either accept it or reject it. If a validator is added to an agent, the action is first sent to the validator. If it accepts the new state, the action's response will become the new agent's state. If the validator rejects the action, then the action's return value is discarded and an exception is thrown.

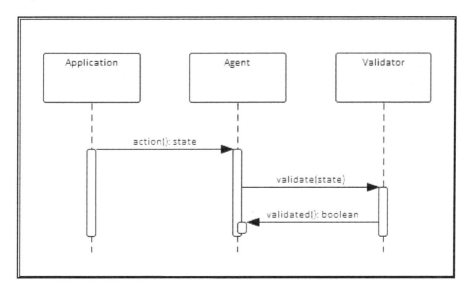

It's also possible to add watchers to an agent. If watchers are present, they will be called once the agent's state is successfully changed. When exceptions are thrown, the errors will be cached by the agent. The agent will stop accepting actions until the agent is restarted.

Because agents run in threads provided by a thread pool, the JVM will not shut down while agents are running. To ensure that resources are freed correctly, the agents must be shut down properly using the functions provided by Clojure.

Agent example

An agent is created with the `agent` function. Let's create a hypothetical agent that will hold the state of an invoice. To keep it simple, we will only store the customer name and a Boolean flag indicating whether the invoice is being processed:

```
(def invoice-agent (agent (hash-map :name nil, :isProcessed false)))
```

This creates an agent and we store a reference in the `invoice-agent` variable. As the agent's state, we keep an immutable map containing the customer name (initially empty) and a flag indicating whether the invoice is being processed (initially `false`).

Let's create two actions for this agent:

* An `update-customer-name` action to update the customer name
* An `update-processed` action to update the invoice's `isProcessed` flag

Remember that actions are ordinary functions that will return the new agent state. As input, they will receive the current state from the agent. Here's the code for the two actions:

```
(defn update-customer-name [state name] (assoc state :name name))
(defn update-processed [state flag] (assoc state :isProcessed flag))
```

Both the functions will automatically receive the current agent's state from the agent. As their second parameter, they will get the new value of the customer name or the flag indicating whether the invoice is being processed. Both the functions return an updated copy of the agent state's HashMap. Review the *Hash-map* section for a description of the `hash-map` and `assoc` functions. This returned value will become the new state.

Let's test the agent by setting the customer name:

```
(send invoice-agent update-customer-name "Your Name")
```

The `send` function's first parameter is the agent instance that will receive the action. The second parameter is the action, and all other parameters are the parameters of the action, excluding the first parameter (in our case, `state` for both actions). The action and its parameters are sent to the agent, but the `send` function is returned before the action is processed by the agent. Since the agents run on a separate thread, it is not predictable when the action will be processed. However, since this isn't a busy application with many threads running concurrently, chances are high the action will be processed shortly after you press *Enter*. The `send` function returns the agent instance, but we ignore it since we already have the reference, thanks to our `invoice-agent` variable.

To check the current agent's state, enter the name prefixed with `@`:

```
@invoice-agent
```

The expression should evaluate to `{:name "Your Name", :isProcessed false}`.

It worked! Let's add a validator that will reject an action when the name is set to nil while the invoice is being processed. The validator function receives the new state and returns true when it accepts the change; otherwise, it will reject the change by returning false:

```
(defn validator-invoice [state]
  (if
    (and
      (get state :isProcessed)
      (clojure.string/blank? (get state :name)))
    false
    true)
)
```

The `blank?` function from the `clojure.string` library returns `true` if the string is `nil`; it returns `false` otherwise. Let's add a validator to the agent. We do this using the `set-validator!` function:

```
(set-validator! invoice-agent validator-invoice)
```

Update the processed flag to true, and after a short while, request the current state:

```
(send invoice-agent update-processed true)
@invoice-agent
```

You should see that the agent is now being processed: `{:name "Your Name", :isProcessed true}`.

Let's see whether the validator works by resetting the name to `nil`:

```
(send invoice-agent update-customer-name nil)
@invoice-agent
```

You'll see the name was not reset to `nil`. The validator prevented it. You can check whether the agent has an error with the `agent-error` function:

```
(agent-error invoice-agent)
```

When a validator refuses a message, a traceback is automatically thrown by the agent system. Therefore, the following is returned (cut for brevity):

```
#error {
  :cause "Invalid reference state"
  ...
}
```

Note that the agent will not accept new actions until the agent is restarted. Actions that are received in the meantime are held in a buffer. To restart the agent, simply call the `restart-agent` function:

```
(restart-agent invoice-agent (hash-map :name nil, :isProcessed false)
:clear-actions true)
```

The state of the restarted agent must be specified. If you want the agent to handle the actions that were buffered while the agent did not respond, specify false after the optional `:clear-actions` keyword parameter.

To properly shut down the agent system, execute the `shutdown-agents` function:

```
(shutdown-agents)
```

Agent threads will now be stopped and no longer respond to actions.

Style guide

The Clojure team did not publish an official style guide on their website, but there's a community-driven document available at `http://github.com/bbatsov/clojure-style-guide`.

Some of the more important rules discussed in the document are:

- For indentation, generally use two spaces.
- In a function definition with `defn`, place the function name and input parameters on a single line and the body on a new line:

```
(defn function1 [input]
( ...function calls here... )
```

- When a parameter does not fit on one line, align it vertically. Use one space:

```
(defn function2 []
  (str
     "Hello"
     " and goodbye"))
```

- Don't put commas between elements in a list.
- Use good taste when coding hash-maps. When you have multiple key/value pairs on the same line, use a comma to separate them.
- Do not put trailing parentheses on their own line (in the `function2` example we just saw, the last line closed both the parameters and the function blocks).
- Linux newlines (LF) are preferred before Windows's end-of-line characters (*CR + LF*).
- Lines up to 80 characters are preferred.

Quiz

1. Is Clojure a pure functional programming language?

    a) Yes, it's a pure functional programming.

    b) No, it's a functional programming language but not a pure one because it allows state changes.

    c) No, but Clojure is a pure OOP language.

    d) No, Clojure is not a functional programming language.

2. Will this code run in the Clojure REPL?

    ```
    (10)
    ```

    a) Yes, this is valid code. It will return 10.

    b) No, the last entry in the list must be a function.

    c) No, this will not run because the first element in the list is not a function.

    d) None of the preceding options.

3. What is the default type that Clojure uses for whole numbers if it can fit in the data type?

    a) Primitive long value.

    b) The `java.lang.Long` wrapper class instance.

    c) Primitive integer value.

    d) The `java.lang.Integer` wrapper class instance.

4. What is the printed output of the following program?

```
(println + 25 25)
```

    a) It prints `50`.

    b) It prints a reference to the + function, followed by `"25 25"`.

    c) An exception is thrown.

    d) None of the preceding options.

5. If you need an iterable list collection and need random access to its elements, would you choose a list or a vector?

    a) Vector

    b) List

    c) Both the vector and list are fine

    d) None of the preceding options

Summary

In this chapter, we looked at the Clojure language, a language that is quite different from the other languages covered in this book. After writing a lot of one-line expressions in the REPL environment, I hope you discovered that learning the Clojure syntax is not that difficult at all. By just creating lists that contain expressions, often nested in multiple lists, one can write surprisingly readable code. We also learned that Clojure is a functional programming language and that its most important data structures are immutable. Unlike Java, Clojure is not an object-orientated language at heart, but it offers very good compatibility with the JVM platform. We created some instances of JVM objects and called methods and read fields from them. Finally, we looked at agents, a safe way to manage states in a multithreading application. We even wrote a simple application to try them out.

Now that you know the most important rules of Clojure, you are ready to write a real application.

8
Clojure Programming

In the previous chapter, we covered how to program Clojure by entering code directly in its REPL. While this works well, even for smaller projects, having the code placed in multiple source files is a must. Writing projects is the main focus of this chapter, and we will use Eclipse IDE again for writing code, thanks to the **Counterclockwise** plugin that adds Clojure compatibility to Eclipse IDE. The most popular build tool for Clojure projects is called **Leiningen**, and we will use it a lot during the course of this chapter.

We will build two projects. One project will focus on monads, which are used a lot in functional programming languages. We will explore this subject by applying test-driven development. We will also create a very simple web application using Luminus, a popular micro web framework for Clojure. Here's a list of what we will cover in this chapter:

- The Counterclockwise plugin for Eclipse IDE
- Leiningen's build tool
- Creating executable programs in Clojure
- Creating a Counterclockwise project in Eclipse IDE
- Exploring monads by applying test-driven development
- The Luminus web framework

The Counterclockwise plugin for Eclipse IDE

To add Clojure support to Eclipse IDE, a plugin is required. In the Clojure world, this plugin is called Counterclockwise. It is available in a standalone version as well, which does not require an existing Eclipse IDE installation. As with all the other languages covered in this book, we will provide the installation instructions for the plugin version in this chapter. This results in one Eclipse IDE installation that will support all the languages.

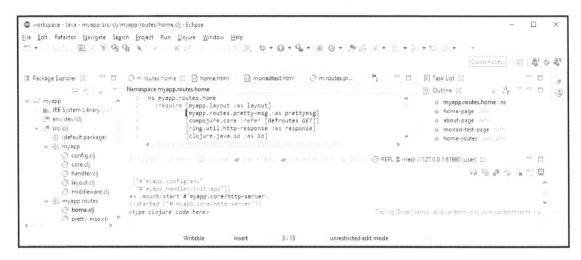

It is recommended that you read Counterclockwise's documentation at `http://doc.ccw-id e.org`.

Installing the Counterclockwise plugin

We will use the Counterclockwise version provided on the **Eclipse Marketplace**. Follow this procedure to install it on your Eclipse IDE installation:

1. From Eclipse IDE's **Help** menu, choose **Eclipse Marketplace....**

2. In the search bar, enter `counterclockwise` and press *Enter*. Find the latest
   version of Counterclockwise that credits the Counterclockwise team and click on
   its **Install** button.

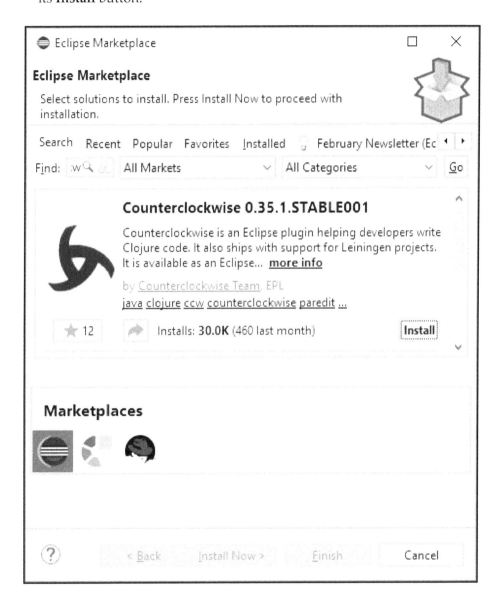

3. If you agree with the license terms, accept them and click on **Finish**. The installation may take longer than the time it took for other plugins covered in the book. Like many other plugins by independent teams, the Counterclockwise installation files are currently not signed. This results in a security warning when the dialog box appears; click on **OK** to confirm the installation.

4. When prompted to automatically restart, click on **Yes**.

Switching to the Java perspective

Unlike many other language plugins, the Counterclockwise plugin does not add a dedicated Clojure perspective to Eclipse IDE. Instead, it expects the developer to activate the Java perspective. On the top-right corner of the Eclipse IDE window, find the Java perspective button and click on it:

If it is not visible, choose the **Open Perspective** button on the toolbar. A dialog with the available perspectives will appear. Find and click on the Java perspective:

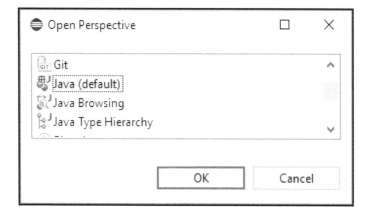

 You'll need to repeat this step every time you want to do Clojure programming and activate a different perspective in the meantime.

As we will see during the course of this chapter, Counterclockwise still adds several Clojure-related elements to the Java perspective's user interface when creating new or opening existing Counterclockwise projects.

Leiningen's build tool

Leiningen is the de facto build tool used for Clojure development. The project's tagline speaks for itself:

> *For automating Clojure projects without setting your hair on fire.*

The Counterclockwise plugin bundles Leiningen as part of its installation, but the bundled version is out of date at the time of writing this book. We, therefore, recommend you to install the latest version manually. We'll show how to configure Counterclockwise so that it can use your Leiningen installation.

Refer to the Leiningen website at `http://leiningen.org` for more information.

Installing Leiningen

Leiningen's installation procedure is straightforward. In the project's main website, find the **Install** section. Here you can download an install script for Linux and macOS and a version for Windows. Place this script in a directory. Follow these steps to run the script:

1. In the Command Prompt (Windows) or Terminal (macOS/Linux), change the active directory to the subdirectory where you stored the script.
2. Execute the downloaded script (in Linux/macOS, you'll have to add executable rights by `chmod +x SCRIPTNAME`). You should see a message stating that the JAR file could not be located in the `.lein` subdirectory in your home directory:

   ```
   C:\Users\USERNAME\.lein\self-installs\leiningen-2.7.1-standalone.jar
       can not be found.
   You can try running "lein self-install"
   or change LEIN_JAR environment variable
   or edit lein.bat to set appropriate LEIN_JAR path.
   ```

3. Execute the `lein self-install` command. It will download a JAR file and place it in the directory noted earlier.

4. When you now execute the `lein` command, it will display a list of options.

5. Place the directory where you stored the script in your operating system's path or copy the script to a directory that is already in your path.

Test your installation by entering the `lein repl` command from any different active directory. This will start Clojure's REPL. Enter any Clojure expression, such as:

```
(+ 1 2)
```

You should see 3 printed to the console. Leiningen adds the exit command to the REPL, so you can now quit the REPL by typing `exit` and pressing *Enter*. You should see the cheerful **Bye for now!** message printed to the console.

Configure Counterclockwise to use a different Leiningen installation:

1. In Eclipse IDE, in its menu bar, choose **Window | Preferences**.

2. The Preferences dialog appears. In its left bar, expand **Clojure | General**. Click on the **Browse...** button, next to the **Leningen jar (empty = use embedded):** label. The lein installation script installs Leiningen to a directory called `.lein` (note the dot prefix) in your user's home directory. You'll find the JAR file in its self-installs subdirectory. On my system, the filename was `leiningen-2.7.1-standalone.jar`:

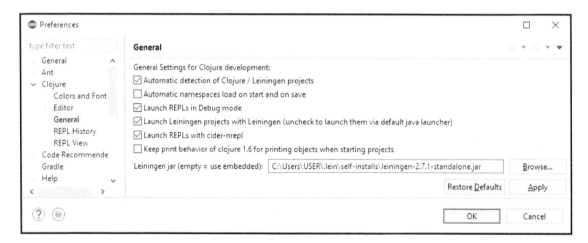

3. Click on **OK** to acknowledge and close the **Preferences** dialog.

4. Restart Eclipse IDE manually to apply the change.

Creating executable programs in Clojure

Until now, we have only entered snippets of code in Clojure's interactive REPL shell. As mentioned in the previous chapter, Clojure is not bundled with a standalone compiler program. To create executable programs in Clojure, you'll have to call an ordinary Clojure macro in your code that will instruct the built-in compiler to generate JVM `.class` files. This macro only generates class files when Clojure compiles code and does nothing when you run code that is already compiled.

Compiling to class files without Leiningen

Let's start by creating an executable class without the build system. You'll appreciate Leiningen more when you experience the difference. Let's create this small project with a normal text editor instead of using Eclipse IDE. Create the `testproject1` root directory to hold the example files, and start by creating the required subdirectories:

- `com`
- `com\example`
- `classes`

Before Clojure writes class files, you'll have to generate JVM classes. One of the options is to define a namespace and add the `:gen-class` keyword to it. Store the following source file in the `com\example` directory and call it `main.clj`:

```
(ns com.example.main
  (:gen-class :name com.example.Main))
  (defn -main [] (println "hi!"))
  (compile 'com.example.main)
```

The namespace specified as the first parameter of the `ns` function is only used by Clojure, but it is a good practice to let it match the JVM package name closely. Note that in Clojure, it is considered a good practice to use lowercase names for namespaces only. It is important that the Clojure script's filename and directory structure match the Clojure namespace. This is similar to Java, where the Java source code is supposed to follow the package structure. Therefore, the `main.clj` file must be stored in the `com\example` directory. The `:gen-class` keyword is specified as a parameter to the `ns` function, followed by the `:name` parameter, which specifies the fully qualified JVM class name. `M` is specified as the class's name, indicating `Main`, in order to adhere to JVM conventions.

After this, a main method is added to the class. By prefixing the method name with a dash, -, Clojure will know that this the method that will be added to the `com.example.Main` class. It's actually possible to specify a different prefix, which can be handy when defining multiple classes in one file. Clojure has built-in logic to compile methods called `main` to the JVM's `static void main(String[] args)` variant. The method's body simply prints a greeting.

Finally, the `compile` macro is called. As a parameter, a reference to the Clojure namespace that must be compiled is specified. Note the single quote and no ending quotes. This is not a typo. By prefixing a name with `'`, it becomes a symbol. A symbol is not evaluated right away and is passed right to the function or macro.

To compile this code, make sure the project's root directory (the directory containing the `classes` and `com` subdirectories) is the active directory, then run the following command in the Command Prompt or Terminal:

```
java -cp ".;.\classes;c:\PATHTO\clojure\clojure-1.8.0.jar" clojure.main
com\example\main.clj
```

Replace `PATHTO\clojure` with the path to your Clojure JAR file and replace the version number with your installed version. Linux and OS X users need to use `:` separators between the classpath directories instead of `;`.

Clojure compiles the code and writes the generated class files to its classes directory. The classes directory must be in the classpath; otherwise, the compiler would crash. If you take a look at the classes directory, you'll see that Clojure generates multiple class files. This is because some support classes are necessary for Clojure's internal infrastructure. You don't have to worry about them; just make sure you put them on the classpath when running your application. It's time to run the application now. Change the active directory to the classes directory and run the following command:

```
java -cp ".;c:\PATHTO\clojure\clojure-1.8.0.jar" com.example.Main
```

Follow the same instructions provided by the previous Java command regarding the path to Clojure's path and directory separators to use on your operating system. You should see the `hi!` message.

The process is complicated mostly because of the classpaths that need to be set. As we will see in the next section, Leiningen makes this process much easier.

Compiling projects with Leiningen

This time, we let the Leiningen build tool take care of all the details. First, we let Leiningen create an empty skeleton project for an app, then we will compile and run it.

Let's get started by creating a new directory as the project's root directory and make sure this is the active directory. Type the following command to generate an empty skeleton project, based on a template provided by Leiningen:

```
lein new app testproject2
```

Leiningen will create a new `testproject2` directory containing the project files based on its `app` template. Other templates provided by the Leiningen team include one for libraries (this is the default when not specifying any template). It's even possible to create your own templates.

Examine the content of the generated directory. It generated `doc` files where you can store your documents. The `src/testproject2` directory will contain your project's source files. One `core.clj` file has been placed there that contains a Hello World-like script. Other directories include the `test` directory to hold unit tests and `target` to hold compiled files. A file called `project.clj` was placed in the root directory of the project. This file contains the build file that Leiningen uses to build the project. We will take a more detailed look at this file later.

Make sure the project's root directory (the one containing the `project.clj` file) is the active directory. Run the project by issuing the following command:

```
lein run
```

It displays `Hello, World`. As you can see, there is no hassle when Leiningen is used to run your project. There's no need to manually specify complex classpath entries. Finally, we will compile the project. The `app` template conveniently configured the `uberjar` task, which not only compiles the code to class files but also places them in a JAR file. Again, from the project's root directory, run the following command:

```
lein uberjar
```

It creates a `target/uberjar` subdirectory where two jar files are placed. Its `classes` subdirectory contains individual class files. One of the JAR files has a bigger file size and is called `testproject-0.1.0-SNAPSHOT-standalone.jar`, while the other is much smaller and is called `testproject-0.1.0-SNAPSHOT.jar`. The difference is that the smaller version does not contain Clojure's runtime library, while the standalone version is a self-contained JAR file, including all the required dependencies. Change the current directory to `target/uberjar`. Let's see if the latter one works:

```
java -jar testproject-0.1.0-SNAPSHOT-standalone.jar
```

Yes, you should be greeted by your computer, again.

It's interesting to note that the `src/testproject2/core.clj` source file does not contain a call to Clojure's compile function. A call to the compile function is not required when using Leiningen's compilation tasks; Leiningen handles the compiling internally.

Creating a new Counterclockwise project

Now that we've tried out Leiningen, we are ready to build our first project in Eclipse IDE using the Counterclockwise plugin:

1. In Eclipse IDE, right-click on an empty spot in **Package Explorer** and choose **New | Other**....
2. The **Select a wizard** dialog appears. Choose **Clojure | Clojure Project** and click on **Next**.
3. Choose the `exploring-monads` project name. Make sure the `default` Leiningen template is selected:

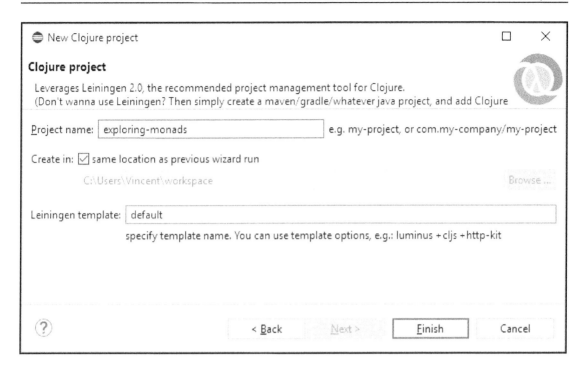

4. Click on **Finish** to generate the project.

 Note that you can choose any other template supported by Leiningen here. There's one caveat: Counterclockwise's built-in Leiningen version is used to generate projects, and this version can be out of date. As we will see later in this chapter, this can be resolved by creating a project on the command-line.

The creation process of the project will take some time. When finished, take a look at the created project by expanding it in **Package Explorer**. Its directory structure should look familiar.

Open the `src/exploring_monads/core.clj` file and add the following line to the bottom of the file:

```
(foo "I'm tired of hearing: ")
```

To verify the installation, click on the project name in the Package Explorer and Eclipse IDE's run button on the toolbar. A window might be displayed asking you to choose the run configuration. Choose **Clojure application** and click on **OK**:

Counterclockwise will now load Clojure's REPL. This might take a short while. When it has finished loading, a new tab will be added containing the REPL. Now that the REPL is running in Eclipse IDE, you can run the code by clicking the `core.clj` file in the **Package Explorer** and pressing the run button on the toolbar again. You should see a rather rude message--I'm tired of hearing: Hello, World!--printed to the console.

Clojure REPL in Eclipse IDE

Clojure's source code of a project is run inside a Clojure REPL instance running inside Eclipse. The REPL screen is split into two subwindows. The upper window contains the output of the REPL, while the lower half can be used to enter commands. When you press enter, the command is printed to the upper window and evaluated and the output is printed:

You can run multiple instances of the REPL at the same time. To run an additional instance, click on the project name once again, press the **Run** button on the toolbar, and choose Clojure Application when prompted to select **Run Configuration**. Counterclockwise will ask whether to start a new REPL tab or use the last one to run the project's scripts. Click on **OK** to start a new instance and cancel to run them in the last loaded instance.

The REPL remains in the last activated namespace. By pressing *Ctrl + Alt + N (cmd + alt + N* on macOS), you'll activate the current namespace of the editor in the REPL.

If you get a message indicating that a command cannot be found in the current context when entering a command in the REPL, try pressing the *Ctrl + Alt + N (cmd + alt + N* on macOS) key combination to switch the namespace.

Updating the project's Clojure version

The default version of Clojure that is chosen may be older than the latest current version. Since we've chosen to use the latest Leiningen version in Counterclockwise, it's possible to update the Clojure version. From **Package Explorer**, open the `project.clj` build file. Take care that you choose `project.clj` and not the `.project` file that is in the same directory. The latter file contains the Eclipse project file definition. As mentioned earlier, this is the Leiningen build file that is used to build and run the project. On my system, the file looked like this:

```
(defproject exploring-monads "0.1.0-SNAPSHOT"
  description "FIXME: write description"
  :url "http://example.com/FIXME"
  :license {:name "Eclipse Public License"
            :url "http://www.eclipse.org/legal/epl-v10.html"}
  :dependencies [[org.clojure/clojure "1.6.0"]]
  :main ^:skip-aot exploring-monads.core
  :target-path "target/%s"
  :profiles {:uberjar {:aot :all}})
```

Here, we can observe that Leiningen uses Clojure's source code to define the project and its build requirements. This is the difference with build tools, such as Maven, which uses XML files to store this information. Actually, Clojure's *code is data and data is code* principle is neatly demonstrated here. The build file is defined using Leiningen's `defproject` macro, which accepts some specific keywords (words that start with a colon) and their corresponding values, as parameters.

The parameters of the defproject macro include a lot of metadata, such as the project description, project URL, and license. The :main key specifies that the main function that is called when running the program is defined inside the exploring-monads.core namespace, which translates to the core.clj file in the src/exploringmonads subdirectory. The :dependencies key specifies the current dependencies. Currently, the only dependency of this project is Clojure 1.6.

The :aot references deal with Clojure's **ahead of time** (**AOT**) compiling feature. It determines which namespaces are compiled to class files when using one of the compile tasks. If you specify the :all value, it means that all the namespaces are compiled; in this case, this is applicable when the uberjar task is used. It is a convention to skip the AOT feature for the main function by specifying the ^:skip-aot metadata setting.

To update the Clojure version that will be used in this project, do the following:

1. Simply change the version number in the :dependencies section. When the book went to press, version 1.8.0 was the latest version of Clojure that was available, so I changed 1.6.0 to 1.8.0.
2. Save the file by pressing *Ctrl* + *S* (*cmd* + *S* on macOS). Counterclockwise will immediately update the project and replace the Clojure version with the version you specified.
3. Close the REPL by pressing the Close icon on its tab. Open the core.clj file again and press the Run icon on the toolbar. You should now see a REPL tab that is powered by the newer Clojure version.

Adding a dependency

We're going to use the monads library. Visit the project's website at https://github.com/clojure/algo.monadsto check the version and dependency details that we will have to supply to Leiningen.

At the time of writing this, the last version is 0.1.6. Leiningen's dependency information is available on the home page. In my case, it was:

```
[org.clojure/algo.monads "0.1.6"]
```

Open the `build.clj` file in Eclipse and add the new dependency by adding the preceding code's vector to the `:dependencies` vector. The `:dependencies` line should now look like this:

```
:dependencies [[org.clojure/clojure "1.8.0"],
               [org.clojure/algo.monads "0.1.6"]]
```

When saving the file by pressing *Ctrl + S*, Counterclockwise will immediately update the project. When expanding the Leiningen dependencies' entry in **Package Explorer**, you'll see the `algo.monads` library listed there:

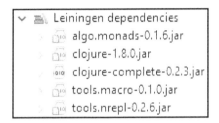

Exploring monads by applying test-driven development

Monads are used in functional programming to build simple components. They are used to chain a series of operations in a safe way. Each component encapsulates a value and makes sure that the next component that is called could handle its output as input. For example, if component A generates `nil` (null) as output and the next component in the chain cannot handle `nil` as input, the computation of the chain will be stopped automatically.

In Haskell, a pure functional programming language, monads are used prominently. Still, they can be useful in other functional programming languages as well. We will take a brief and very high-level look at monads here and skip a lot of complex theory and background information.

We'll create a simple monad that will return a fancy (well, kind of) formatted message. It adds a number of asterisks before and after the passed string. Open the `src/exploring-monads/core.clj` file and replace the code with the following main code that we will be unit testing. We'll start with a dummy implementation of the `pretty-msg` function so that we can check whether our API is correct before committing to it:

```
(ns exploring-monads.core)
(use 'clojure.algo.monads)
(defn pretty-msg [msg asterisk-amount]
    (str ""))
```

Save the file. We will now define the source file that will store the unit tests. Open the `test/exploring-monads/core_test.clj` file and replace its content with the following code:

```
(ns exploring-monads.core-test
  (:require [clojure.test :refer :all]
            [exploring-monads.core :refer :all]))

(deftest test-sane-parameters
  (testing "pretty-msg with with sane parameters"
    (is (= (pretty-msg "test" 3) "***test***"))))
```

Here, we define the `exploring-monads.core-test` namespace that will contain our test cases. The `:require` keyword adds references to the `clojure.test` and `exploring-monads.core` namespaces. Finally, we define our first test case. We will cover this test case in more detail after running the test.

To send the content of a file to the running Clojure REPL instance, you can use the *Ctrl + Alt + S* (Windows/Linux) or *cmd + alt + s* (macOS) key combination.

To run our updated code, do the following:

1. Open the `src/exploring-monads/core.clj` file and press *Ctrl + Alt + S* (*cmd + alt + S* on macOS)
2. Open the `test/exploring-monads/core_test.clj` file and press *Ctrl + Alt + S* (*cmd + alt + S* on macOS) again.
3. Switch the active namespace of the REPL tab by pressing *Ctrl + Alt + N* (*cmd + alt + n on macOS*)

The running Clojure instance has now compiled the code. One of the features that most IDEs offer on the JVM but Counterclockwise lacks is built-in support for unit testing. One way to run the unit test is by executing the run-tests function manually in the REPL. Enter the following line in Clojure's REPL tab to run the tests:

```
(run-tests)
```

> You could add the run-tests call to the script for convenience so that it runs automatically when the REPL evaluates the script. This is not recommended, however, as this will cause conflicts when you use Leiningen's built-in test command.

This should print the following output:

```
Testing exploring-monads.core-test
FAIL in (test-sane-parameters) (core_test.clj:7)
pretty-msg with with sane parameters
expected: (= (pretty-msg "test" 3) "***test***")
 actual: (not (= "" "***test***"))

Ran 1 tests containing 1 assertions.
1 failures, 0 errors.
{:test 1,
 :pass 0,
 :fail 1,
 :error 0,
 :type :summary}
```

The line showing actual: (not (= "" "***test***")) shows what's wrong. An empty string "" was returned by the pretty-msg function instead of the expected **test*** string. Since we are still happy with the API of pretty-msg, we can now implement the pretty-msg function to make the test pass. We will use a monad for this. Open the src/monad_test/core.clj file and replace the existing function with the following:

```
(defn pretty-msg [msg asterisk-amount]
  (domonad identity-m
           [a asterisk-amount
            b (clojure.string/join (repeat a "*"))
            c (str b msg)]
           (str c b)))
```

A monad, by definition, contains a `bind` function. This *bind* function makes sure that the output value of one component can be used as input of the next component, and as we will soon see, it can be used to take decisions. In this example, we'll only use the prebuilt monad types, provided by the `clojure.algo.monads` library, that have built-in `bind` functions. In the preceding example, we use the `identity-m` monad type that does have a `bind` function, but we use the one that does not process values in any way or make any decisions based on the values. We will use a different monad type, which uses its `bind` function, later and use that opportunity to explain the `bind` function principle in more detail.

Save the file and run it by pressing *Ctrl* + *F11*. It's time to run the test again. Open the `test/monad_test/core_test.clj` file one more time. Press *Ctrl* + *Alt* + *S* and run the `(run-tests)` function in the REPL again. Things should now look better than the previous attempt:

```
Testing exploring-monads.core-test
Ran 1 tests containing 1 assertions.
0 failures, 0 errors.
{:test 1, :pass 1, :fail 0, :error 0, :type :summary}
```

Now that we know that the monad works as expected, let's take a detailed look at the main code in the `src/monad_test/core.clj` file:

1. First, we import the monads library.
2. We create a function that takes two parameters: `msg` contains the message and `asterisk-amount` contains the number of asterisks that will be printed before and after the message.
3. In the function's body, the `domonad` macro is called, and the `identity-m` monad type is specified, which we will explain in more detail later.
4. We start a vector that will contain the components of the monad.
5. The first component is bound to the local `a`. It is bound to an integer that represents the amount of asterisks that will be added before and after the message.
6. The second component is bound to the local `b` and bounds to the result of the expression that follows. Assuming `a` will be bound to 3, `b` will be bound to the string `***`.

7. The third component is specified and its value will be bound to `c`. It joins the result of `b` with the `msg` parameter that contains the message. This was the last component, hence the vector will be closed. Assuming that `msg` contains `test` and `a` is bound to `3`, `c` will now hold the `***test.` value.

8. Finally, as a result of the monad, `c` is joined with `b`. In our example, `c` holds the `***test` value and `b` holds `***`.

Therefore, the string that `pretty-msg` returns in the unit test is `***test***`.

A few things can be concluded when you look at the preceding code:

- Each component in a monad can use the value of the previous components.
- The first parameter of the `domonad` macro is the monad type; we used the built-in `identity-m` type here. We will look at other available types in a bit.
- The second parameter is a vector containing the components. Each result of a component is bound to a local.
- The third parameter is the expression. The evaluated expression is the monad's return value if the whole chain of components is completed successfully.

Let's do an experiment. What happens when we specify `nil` as a number? We would like it to simply return `nil` in that case. Add a new test case to the test script `test/monad_test/core_test.clj` to find this out:

```
(deftest test-nil-amount
  (testing "pretty-msg with with amount=nil"
    (is (= (pretty-msg "JVM" nil) nil))))
```

Run the test script again by pressing *Ctrl* + *Alt* + *S* (*cmd* + *alt* + *S* on macOS) and running `(run-tests)` in the REPL. You should now see that a test caused an error (cut for brevity):

```
ERROR in (test-nil-amount) (RT.java:1241)
pretty-msg with with amount=nil
expected: (= (pretty-msg "JVM" nil) "***JVM***")
actual: java.lang.NullPointerException: null
```

This happens because the `repeat` function, which is called in the second component of the monad, does not accept `nil` (`null` in Java) and throws `NullPointerException` in that case. Our current monad type, `identity-m`, accepts all the values and assumes that the next component can use the values of the previous component. One of the other built-in monad types is the `maybe-m` type. The `maybe-m` monad type will stop executing the chain of components when a component evaluates to `nil`.

Some background information is in order: as explained earlier, all monads have a *bind* function. This *bind* function can be used to convert the output data of the previous component of a monad and convert it in such a way that it could be used for the next component. However, it can also be used to make certain choices based on returned values. The *bind* function is automatically called by the library. While the `identity-m` monad that we used earlier has a *bind* function, it does not process data in any way or make decisions based on the values. The `maybe-m` monad type, on the other hand, has an internal *bind* function that is defined as follows (you do not have to enter this definition; it is provided by the `clojure.algo.monads` library that we are using):

```
...
fn m-bind-maybe [mv f] (when-not (nil? mv) (f mv))
...
```

The preceding code is nested in a list that is not shown. Do not worry about the `fn` macro that defines a function. The `clojure.algo.monads` library calls the `m-bind-maybe` function after a component is finished. When calling it, the first parameter `mv` will contain the output value of the previous component, while the second parameter `f` is the function that will contain the implementation of the next component to be called. As can be seen in the preceding code, it only calls the component (represented by the function `f`) if the `mv` value is not `nil`. Therefore, the execution of the chain of components stops when a component returns `nil`. While the bind function of a monad is often used to convert data, in the case of the `maybe-m` monad type, it is used to decide whether the next component could be called based on the previous component's output value. This is also a valid use case of the bind function.

In the `src/monad_test/core.clj` file, change the monad type from `identity-m` to `maybe-m`. The function should look as follows:

```
(defn pretty-msg [msg asterisk-amount]
  (domonad maybe-m
         [a asterisk-amount
          b (clojure.string/join (repeat a "*"))
          c (str b msg)]
         (str c b)))
```

Save the file and run the main program again by pressing *Ctrl + F11*. Since we did not change the test code, it's not necessary to send the unit test code to the REPL. Simply run the (run-tests) expression in the REPL. This time, no exception will be thrown and the monad will simply evaluate to nil and pass the test. The maybe-m type exits the chain of components when one of the components evaluates to nil. When this happens, nil is returned. Therefore, clojure-test now returns:

```
Ran 2 tests containing 2 assertions.
0 failures, 0 errors.
```

Explicit conditions can be added to a monad. You can add a condition by adding the :when keyword to the component's vector. For example, to stop the execution when the passed message string is not a string with at least one character, add the following condition as the last entry to the component's vector:

```
(defn pretty-msg [msg asterisk-amount]
  (domonad maybe-m
           [a asterisk-amount
            b (clojure.string/join (repeat a "*"))
            c (str b msg)
            :when (> (count msg) 0)]
           (str c b)))
```

If the condition returns true, then the execution runs normally. Otherwise, the execution of the monad is stopped and nil is returned. This condition can be added to all the monad types and is evaluated right before the result expression is evaluated.

Before we leave the subject of monads, it should be mentioned that, by definition, a monad also has a *unit function* (often called *return* or *result* function). This function can be compared with a constructor of a class that takes input parameters. The unit function initializes the monad and makes sure that the first component can use the passed data, commonly by converting the data. Like the *bind* function, the *unit* function is provided by the clojure.algo.monads library, and in the case of both the identity-m and maybe-m monad types, it does not process the passed input values in any way.

By creating your own monads, which make intelligent use of the *unit* and *bind* functions and the expression that is returned upon the completion of a monad, you can create different monad types that can easily be combined (chained) with other monads.

The Luminus web framework

Luminus is a microframework for quickly building powerful web applications in Clojure. It is fully configurable and has strong built-in database support, both for traditional SQL and NoSQL databases. Getting started is easy, especially if you use one of the built-in Leiningen templates. It is strongly recommended that you consult the documentation while playing around with Luminus. You can find this at `http://www.luminusweb.net`.

In the following sections, we will be creating a new project based on the `myapp` template and then run and explore it.

Creating a Luminus project

As we have seen, Counterclockwise can generate projects based on Leiningen templates. There's an issue when creating projects, though. Counterclockwise uses its built-in Leiningen version that can be older than the latest version. At the time of writing this book, Counterclockwise throws exceptions while generating a project based on the `luminus myapp` template. This problem can be solved by creating a project with the latest Leiningen release and importing the project manually in Counterclockwise. We will do this in this chapter.

On the command-line, replace the active directory with your Eclipse `workspace` directory and enter the following command:

```
lein new luminus myapp
```

Change the active directory to `myapp`, then issue the following command:

```
lein run
```

Leiningen will fetch the required dependencies on the first run of the project. After a while, you should see the messages that the HTTP server would start. The default port used by Luminus's built-in HTTP server is 3000. Using your favorite browser, visit the web application that now runs this:

```
http://localhost:3000
```

You should see a screen that looks like this:

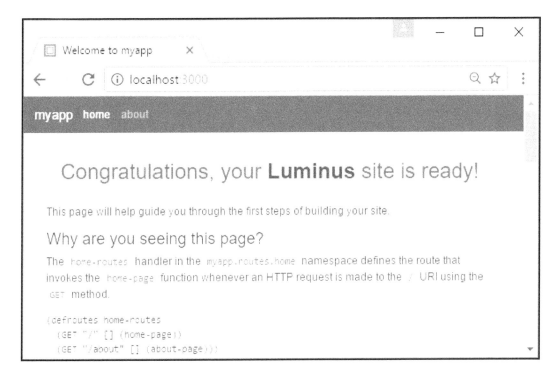

Read the text on this initial page thoroughly. It contains a great introduction to the framework. Also, click on the **about** link.

Importing the project in Counterclockwise

To import the Leiningen project and generate a Counterclockwise-compatible Eclipse IDE project, do the following:

- In Eclipse IDE, right-click on an empty spot on **Package Explorer** and choose **Import...**. The **Import** dialog will be displayed. Choose the **Projects from Folder or Archive** option and click on the **Next** button.
- In the window that is now displayed, click on the **Directory...** button next to the **Import** source field. Navigate to the `workspace` directory (usually in your user's home directory) and choose the `myapp` subdirectory. Make sure the **Search for nested projects** and **Detect and configure project natures** options are checked. Click on the **Finish** button.

Eclipse IDE will detect that this project is compatible with Counterclockwise and generate a corresponding Eclipse IDE project.

To run the project in Eclipse IDE, start the REPL by clicking on the project name in Package Explorer and the **Run** button on the toolbar. A dialog may pop up asking which project type you want to choose; again, choose **Clojure Application**. Once the REPL has started, simply enter the following command in it:

```
(start)
```

Switch to the **Console** tab. You should see a message stating the server has started. The HTTP server is not started by default. To start the server, switch back to the REPL tab and enter the following command:

```
(mount/start #'myapp.core/http-server)
```

Now you can visit the page again at port 3000. To stop the server, click on the terminate button on the Console's tab.

Exploring the Luminus project

The following table lists the most important files and directories that were generated for this project:

File	Description
project.clj	As always, project.clj is the Leiningen build file.
profiles.clj	This is used to hold data that is required to run the system on your system, such as database connection credentials. This file is configured to be excluded from the Git version control manager.
src/myapp/config.clj	This is the configuration file. The generated file tries to load settings from either command-line arguments, Java system properties, or the configuration files in the env subdirectory. For the following scenarios, different configurations can be defined: dev (settings used while developing), prod (settings used for production), and test (settings used while running unit tests).
src/myapp/core.clj	This contains the main method, in other words, the JVM entry point function. It contains the code that is called when starting the server.

`src/myapp/layout.clj`	This file contains the logic that will render views. The default implementation ensures that the templates in the /resource subdirectory can be loaded by the template engine. Also, it defines the error page that is loaded when an exception is thrown.
`src/myapp/middleware.clj`	Middleware are wrapper functions that processes requests, before the request handler is called. One of the middleware functions that is generated for the `myapp` template is the one that protects the application against a well-known web attack.
`src/myapp/handler.clj`	This file determines which routes are available and which middleware is loaded in each specific route. Since URLs are linked to a route (see next file), it is possible to share middleware with multiple URLs.
`src/myapp/routes/home.clj`	In this file, URLs are defined. For each URL, a handler function is defined that will be called when the URL is requested. The handler function can make use of the template engine to render pages. A group of URLs is linked to a route.
`resources/`	This directory contains static assets. Only the files and subdirectories in the resources/public directory are made available to the HTTP server; all the other files are only for internal use by the application.
`resources/templates/`	This directory holds HTML templates that are used by `src/myapp/routes/home.clj`. Luminus uses the Selmer templating system as its default template engine for HTML files.
`resources/public/`	As mentioned earlier, everything in this directory is made available to the HTTP server. This is the directory where the frontend files must be stored: images, JavaScript files, CSS stylesheets, and so forth.

Adding a page to the web application

As an exercise, let's add a new page to the application. Here are the requirements:

- The page's URL must be `/monadtest`
- It should make use of the existing `home-routes` route. This route calls middleware that protects the application against specific web attacks.
- It will use an HTML page with a form that renders the entered text using the `pretty-msg` function

The page will make use of the `pretty-msg` function that we wrote in the *Exploring Monads* section.

In the `project.clj` build file, add the `org.clojure/algo.monads` dependency by copying and pasting its dependency line from the `exploring-monads/project.clj` file to the dependencies section of the `myapp/project.clj` file. After saving the file, Counterclockwise will fetch the dependency and add it to the project.

We must now copy the `exploring-monad` project's `core.clj` file and rename it:

- From the `exploring-monads` project, copy the `src/exploring-monads/core.clj` file by selecting the file in **Package Explorer**, then right-click on it and choose **Copy**.
- Right-click on the `myapp` project's `src/clj/myapp.routes` directory and choose **Paste**.
- Right-click on the pasted `src/clj/myapp.routes/core.clj` file and choose **Refactor | Rename**. Enter the `pretty_msg.clj` filename (note the underscore instead of dash) and click on **OK**.
- Open the `pretty_msg.clj` file and change its namespace definition from `(ns monad-test.core)` to `(ns myapp.routes.pretty-msg)` and save the file.

Open the `myapp.routes.home.clj` file. In its `:require` block, add the following entry:

```
[myapp.routes.pretty-msg :as prettymsg]
```

Also, import the POST request method. Do so by finding the following line in the same `:require` block:

```
[compojure.core :refer [defroutes GET]]
```

Add the POST method to it so it looks like this:

```
[compojure.core :refer [defroutes GET POST]]
```

Now we can write the handler function that will be called when the /monadtest URL is requested. It will render an HTML page and two variables to the page: prettymsg, which will contain the formatted message, and msg, which will contain the original message. In the myapp.routes.home.clj file, add the following above the line that starts with (defroutes home-routes:

```
(defn monad-test-page [msg]
    (layout/render
        "monadtest.html" {:prettymsg (prettymsg/pretty-msg msg 10)
                          :msg msg }))
```

In the defroutes home-routes block, add two entries to define a URL for our new page:

```
(defroutes home-routes
  (GET "/" [] (home-page))
  (GET "/about" [] (about-page))
  (GET "/monadtest" [] (monad-test-page nil))
  (POST "/monadtest" [msg] (monad-test-page msg)))
```

We added the entries to the home-routes block. This means that both a GET and PUT request to the /monadtest URL will make use of the home-routes route, which calls middleware that helps to protect our application. Save the changes in the file.

Finally, add the HTML page. Right-click on the **resources/templates** directory in **Package Explorer** and choose **New | Other**. In the wizard, choose **General | File** and click on **Next**. Enter the monadtest.html filename. Let's start by defining the form where the user will enter the sentence. Add the following content and then save the file:

```
{% extends "base.html" %}
{% block content %}
    <div class="row">
        <div class="col-sm-12">
            <form name="input" action="/monadtest" method="POST">
                {% csrf-field %}
                Message: <input type="text" name="msg" value="{{ msg }}">
                <input type="submit" class="btn" value="Submit">
            </form>
        </div>
    </div>
{% endblock %}
```

It's a pretty standard HTML template. Variables passed to the template can be substituted in the generated output using the `{{ variable name }}` syntax. The most notable thing about the preceding code is probably the `{% crsf-field %}` line. The middleware that the `home-routes` route calls provide protection against *Cross-Site Request Forgery* (CSRF) attacks, a common exploit of websites and applications. When submitting forms using Luminus, an invisible `<input>` field must be specified in the HTML that contains a token that was generated by the framework. The `{% csrf-field %}` macro takes care of this.

Add the row that will render the HTML output. Add the following just below the last `</div>` element:

```
<div class="row">
  <div class="col-sm-12">
    <p><h1>{{ prettymsg }}</h1></p>
  </div>
</div>
```

Make sure no existing `myapp` instance is running. If applicable, terminate the current session on the Console tab and close the existing REPL tab by pressing its Close icon. Run the project by clicking on the `myapp` project in **Package Explorer** and pressing the Run icon on the toolbar. Choose **Clojure Application**. When the REPL is loaded, enter `(start)`. Switch back to the REPL tab and enter the `(mount/start #'myapp.core/http-server)` command.

In your favorite browser, visit the new URL:

`http://localhost:3000/monadtest`

If everything goes well, you should see a page where you can enter a message and submit it:

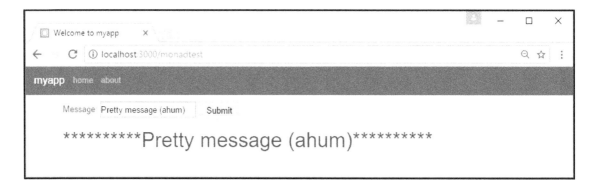

Summary

We started by installing the Counterclockwise plugin in Eclipse IDE. While not as feature-rich yet as some other Eclipse plugins covered in this book, it served us quite well. We installed Leiningen, the most popular build tool in use by Clojure developers. As promised in the previous chapter, we also covered how to compile class files with and without using the Leiningen build tool. We even tried Leiningen's `uberjar` task that conveniently generates a JAR file containing all the dependencies. We created our first project where we explored the monads subject by applying test-driven development using the `clojure.test` unit testing framework. After this, we created a Luminus micro web framework project, based on a built-in template, that we imported to Eclipse IDE. We added a page that accepts text input and shows the entered text using the function that we created in the monads section.

The next language that we will cover is Kotlin. Kotlin is, like Java, a static, strongly typed programming language. Code written in the Kotlin language is often much more compact than Java, while is still very readable.

9
Kotlin

Kotlin is a language that is designed by JetBrains. JetBrains is the company behind popular IDEs for a wide variety of languages, including Java (IntelliJ), Python (PyCharm), PHP (PhpStorm), and many others. Their IDEs are offered in both commercial and a free community edition (which often has fewer features but is still very usable). Kotlin is, like Java, a statically typed language that is orientated towards object-oriented programming (OOP), but it also allows procedural programming. Like many modern OOP languages, it has many features inspired by functional programming. We'll cover the following topics here:

- Installing Kotlin
- Kotlin's Read-Eval-Print-Loop interactive shell
- Kotlin language fundamentals
- OOP in Kotlin
- Procedural programming in Kotlin
- Style guide
- Quiz

Installing Kotlin

Visit the Kotlin website to download the Kotlin compiler. There are several ways to download or run the compiler:

- Running snippets in the online version of Kotlin
- Downloading the compiler

The most suitable installation for trying out the examples in this book would be downloading the standalone version. At the time of writing this book, it is downloadable from GitHub. You will find this link at `http://kotlinlang.org`.

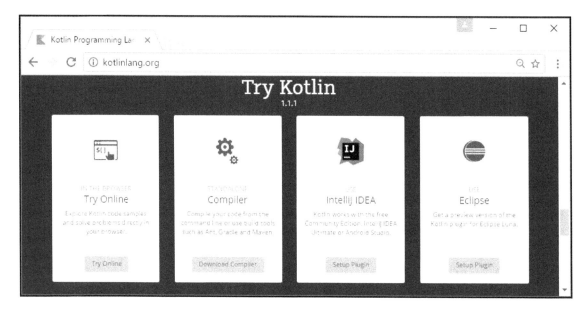

To download the latest standalone compiler release, follow these instructions:

1. On the home page, scroll down until you find the **STANDALONE Compiler** box and the **Download Compiler** link. This link will lead you to an article containing instructions on downloading the latest standalone compiler release, including a link to the GitHub page.
2. On the GitHub repository site, scroll down to the **Downloads** section where you will find the ZIP file of the latest release. Download the ZIP file. When this book went to press, 1.1 was the latest version and the ZIP file was called **kotlin-compiler-1.1.zip**.

The procedure for installing Kotlin is very similar to installing other languages covered in this book:

1. Extract the files.
2. Place its `bin` directory on your path.

To validate the installation, try running the `kotlinc-jvm` launch script (`kotlinc-jvm.bat` for Windows and `kotlinc-jvm` for Linux and macOS). It will start the interactive shell, also known as REPL, as we have seen in previous chapters:

```
Command Prompt - kotlinc-jvm                                    —    □    ×
C:\>kotlinc-jvm
Welcome to Kotlin version 1.1.0 (JRE 1.8.0_112-b15)
Type :help for help, :quit for quit
>>> :quit_
```

Type `:quit` to exit the shell.

 Developers of various REPL shells do not agree on a common command set. As we have seen in previous chapters, Scala and Clojure (when using Leiningen to start the shell) use `:exit` to exit the shell, while Kotlin's REPL uses `:quit`.

Launch scripts

Kotlin comes with several launch scripts for popular operating systems. Since the Kotlin compiler can compile to multiple targets (JVM and JavaScript), for each target, a separate launch script is available. Currently, JVM is the default target, so you can also use the general `kotlinc` launch script to compile your Kotlin code. Here's an overview of the launch scripts in the `bin` directory:

Windows launch script	Linux/macOS launch script	Description
`kotlinc.bat`	`kotlinc`	This launches the default Kotlin compiler implementation (JVM is the default target).
`kotlinc-jvm.bat`	`kotlinc-jvm`	This launches the Kotlin compiler that compiles Kotlin code to JVM bytecode. It is also used to launch the REPL when no command-line options are specified.

kotlinc-js.bat	kotlinc-js	This launches the Kotlin compiler that compiles Kotlin code to JavaScript code, which can be used inside the frontend of a web application. No REPL is available for this compiler.
kotlin.bat	kotlin	This is a script that can be used to run the main() function of a class file that is compiled by the Kotlin compiler. It automatically adds the Kotlin runtime library to Java's classpath.

Since this book focuses on JVM, the JavaScript target use case is not covered further in this book.

Kotlin is now an official language on the Android platform, meaning that Google considers Kotlin a first-class language for Android software development. Kotlin is bundled with newer versions of Android Studio IDE. As explained in the first chapter, while Android uses Java, this use case is not explored in this book.

Kotlin's REPL interactive shell

Like two of the previous languages covered in this book, Scala and Clojure, Kotlin also has a REPL interactive shell that can be used to try Kotlin snippets interactively. As covered in the previous section, the REPL can be started by starting the compiler launch script without parameters (you can add the .bat extension on Windows, but this is not required):

```
kotlinc-jvm
```

You can also choose to simply launch the kotlinc launch script, as JVM is Kotlin's default compilation target.

The REPL shell implements a few built-in commands. In the Kotlin REPL, there's no need to call a Java class library method to exit the shell:

Command	Description
`:help`	This shows a help screen containing the built-in REPL commands.
`:quit`	This is used to exit the REPL.
`:dump bytecode`	This dumps the Java bytecode of all the code generated during the current session in a readable text format. It is not useful to most end users but will be interesting to advanced developers who want to study Java bytecode.
`:load FILE`	This loads a file (replaces `FILE` with a full path to a file containing the Kotlin source code) in the current REPL instance.

At the time of writing this, Kotlin's REPL seems to have some serious reliability problems, especially on the Windows platform. When copying and pasting code, it often does not accept code that would compile fine when running a standalone compiler. Also, from time to time, the program seems to hang when compiling perfectly fine code. Hopefully, these problems will be solved in a future release. The code in this chapter has been written in such a way that it should work with the REPL.

 If you encounter problems when entering your own code in the REPL, try placing the code in a source file with the `kt` extension, then use the REPL's `:load` command to load and process the file. Beware, Windows users must convert the source files to Linux's **end of lines** (**EOL**) format.

When using the `:load` command on Windows systems, it is required that you use a text editor that can save files in Linux's EOL format, as the `:load` command does not accept Windows's *CR + LF* end of line format at the time of writing this. One free open source editor that can do this is Notepad++, which can be downloaded from `http://notepad-plus-plus.org`:

```
class PropertyDemo1 {
    var mutableProperty: Int = 0
}

val p1 = PropertyDemo1()
println(p1.mutableProperty)
p1.mutableProperty = 24
println(p1.mutableProperty)
```

Before saving, from Notepad++'s menu bar, go to **Edit** | **EOL Conversion** | **Unix (LF)**:

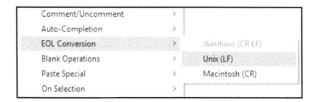

The example files that can be downloaded from the Packt website have been saved in the Linux EOL format to make running them easier.

Kotlin language fundamentals

It is advisable that you have the Kotlin reference documentation available while learning Kotlin. You can find it by clicking on the **LEARN** link on its homepage or by visiting `http://kotlinlang.org/docs/reference/`.

We'll cover these topics in this section:

- Defining local variables
- Defining a function
- Kotlin's types
- Loops

Defining local variables

Local variables are defined with either `var` or `val`:

```
var aMutableNumber = 24
val anImmutableNumber = 42
```

The difference is that variables defined with `var` are mutable, while variables defined with `val` are immutable. A type can optionally be defined:

```
var aMutableString: String = "A type can optionally be specified..."
val anImmutableString: String = "...no matter whether you are using
                                  var or val"
```

The available types are discussed later in the *Kotlin's types* section of this chapter. Variables cannot be assigned to `null` (nothing) without taking precautions. Kotlin has a unique typing system that dictates some rules when working with variables that can optionally be `null`. This will be covered in the *Kotlin's types* section as well.

A variable can be defined inside a function, class, or when programming a procedural language at the top level of the code. All these use cases are covered in the relevant sections.

You can handle literal values as follows:

- Whole numbers without a suffix are Int
- Long values need the L suffix
- Hexadecimal notation can be used for `Int` and `Long` by prefixing the hex value with 0x
- Binary notation can be used for whole numbers as well by prefixing the binary value with 0b
- Floating point numbers without a suffix are `Double`
- Floating point numbers with f or F are `Float`
- Both Float and `Double` values can be written in scientific notation

Here are some examples:

```
val thisIsAnInt = 42
val thisIsALong = 1000L
val hexInt = 0xFF
val binaryLong = 0b10101100L
val thisIsADouble = 149.16
val thisIsAFloat = 501.19e2f
```

Kotlin does not have Java's new keyword to instantiate objects. Instead, in Kotlin, the class name is used like a function:

```
class A (i: Int) {
}
val a = A(25)
```

In the preceding example, `class A`, with a primary constructor that takes `Int` as an input parameter, is defined. It is then instantiated by simply following the class name with values for the constructor parameters.

Defining a function

A function is defined with the `fun` keyword:

```
fun functionName() {
}
```

Of course, arguments can be specified. Specifying the type is required:

```
fun functionNameWithParameters(i: Int, j: Int) {
  println(i * j)
}
```

When no return type is specified (as in both examples earlier), the function gets `Unit` as its default return value. `Unit` is comparable to Java's `void` with the difference that a `Unit` return value can be evaluated and put in a variable:

```
fun noReturnValue(x: Int, y: Int): Unit {
val f = noReturnValue(1, 2)
println(f)
```

The preceding snippet will print `kotlin.Unit` when this code is entered in the REPL. Here's an example that returns an integer, which is an `Int` in Kotlin:

```
fun returnsAnInt(x: Int, y: Int): Int {
 return x * y
}
val f = returnsAnInt(10, 10)
println(f)
```

One-line functions can be defined using the = operator instead of brackets (`{ }`). One-line functions are not required to explicitly set the function's return type; this is inferred from the code:

```
fun alsoReturnsAnInt(x: Int, y: Int) = x * y
```

Kotlin's types

One of the unique features of Kotlin is its type system, especially the handling of `null` references. These are the topics we will discuss in this section:

- Kotlin basic types
- Strings
- Null safety handling
- Conversions
- Collections and generics

Kotlin basic types

Kotlin does not use JVM's data types directly; instead, it wraps them around their own types. One of the reasons is that Kotlin has support for multiple compilation targets (currently, JVM, Android, and JavaScript). Using their own types, they can make sure that the features are the same across different platforms. Kotlin is still fully compatible with JVM code that uses popular JVM datatypes, such as primitive types and common classes, for example, `java.lang.Integer` and `java.lang.String`. The reason is that the Kotlin compiler automatically converts between the JVM's types and its internal types when calling Java code.

Here is a table containing Kotlin's most important basic types and its fully qualified type names and their JVM equivalents:

Kotlin type name	Kotlin's fully qualified type name	JVM equivalent
Byte	kotlin.Byte	Primitive byte
Byte?	kotlin.Byte?	java.lang.Byte
Double	kotlin.Double	Primitive double
Double?	kotlin.Double?	java.lang.Double
Float	kotlin.Float	Primitive float
Float?	kotlin.Float?	java.lang.Float
Int	kotlin.Int	Primitive int
Int?	kotlin.Int?	java.lang.Integer
Long	kotlin.Long	Primitive long

Long?	kotlin.Long?	java.lang.Long
Short	kotlin.Short	Primitive short
Short?	kotlin.Short?	java.lang.Short
Any	kotlin.Any	java.lang.Object
String	kotlin.String	java.lang.String

I will explain the meaning of the question mark after the type names in more detail in a bit. For now, it's sufficient to know that only variables of a type that have a question mark after their name are allowed to be a null reference. Variables of types that have no question mark are never allowed to be null.

It's interesting to note that Kotlin types behave like ordinary classes (for example, each type seemingly offers its own methods); however, internally, many of the preceding types directly use JVM's primitive types whenever possible. This is fully handled under the hood by the compiler and this improves performance a lot, as Kotlin does not have to autobox primitive values all the time.

Strings

The kotlin.String type is remarkably powerful and easy to use. It can be used like Java's java.lang.String class:

```
val s: String = "Hello!"
```

There's also the raw string, which can be multiline:

```
val s: String = """
raw string"""
```

In a raw string, characters cannot be escaped by a backslash, unlike in normal strings (\n for newline and for tab, for instance).

There's also support for String templates:

```
var favoriteBar = "FooBar"
println("Your favorite bar's name $favoriteBar consists of
    ${favoriteBar.length} characters")
```

This will print `Your favorite bar's name FooBar consists of 6 characters.`

Be aware that `String` templates are not supported on raw strings.

Null safety handling

As mentioned several times, Kotlin guards against errors caused by reference variables that are assigned to `null`. When using normal types, Kotlin refuses to compile code when `null` is assigned to a variable.

This will not compile, for example, the following:

```
var currentTime = java.util.Date()
// LINE BELOW WILL NOT COMPILE
currentTime = null
```

Remember that Kotlin does not require (or even support) the `new` keyword to instantiate classes. The following error will be thrown when you run the preceding snippet:

error: null can not be a value of a non-null type Date

To make this code compile, the variable's type name has to be added with an additional question mark:

```
var currentTime: java.util.Date? = java.util.Date()
// Line below will now compile fine
currentTime = null
```

Before you can call methods or access other members from `currentTime`, you'll have to let the compiler know that you are fully aware that its reference may or may not be `null`. For example, the following code will not compile:

```
var currentTime: java.util.Date? = java.util.Date()
// LINE DOES NOT COMPILE
var seconds = currentTime.getTime()
```

The following error is thrown:

```
error: only safe (?.) or non-null asserted (!!.) calls are allowed on a
nullable receiver of type Date?
```

Even though we agree that currentTime is not a null reference in this snippet, we have to tell the Kotlin compiler that we know that currentTime could potentially be null. There are several possibilities:

- Adding a conditional check
- Using the safe call operator ?.
- Using the Elvis operator ?:
- Using the !! operator

Option 1 - Adding a conditional check

By simply adding an if statement, you can tell the compiler that you are aware that the reference variable might be null:

```
fun test() {
    var currentTime: java.util.Date? = java.util.Date()
    println("Line below will now compile fine")
    var seconds = if (currentTime != null) currentTime.getTime() else 0
    println(seconds)
}
test()
```

The compiler sees that you are aware that the instance variable can be null and happily compiles the code. When used this way, the if condition returns either the result of currentTime.getTime() or 0. In the preceding case, the output of currentTime.getTime() will be printed when calling test(), because currentTime is not a null reference.

Note that this only works when the compiler is sure that the variable cannot be reached by any thread other than the thread that is running the code. Since currentTime is defined inside a function, this is true. If currentTime were a public field of a class, then the compiler would still refuse to compile the code since the value could potentially be changed by a different thread between the if (currentTime != null) check and the currentTime.getTime() call. In those cases, you'll have to use one of the other options; otherwise, the compiler will fail with an error message.

Option 2 - Using the safe call operator ?.

Kotlin offers the ?. (question mark, followed by a dot) operator, which is a safe call operator. It returns null if the reference is a null reference; otherwise, it calls the method or accesses the member:

```
var currentTime: java.util.Date? = null
var seconds = currentTime?.getTime()
println(seconds)
```

When it calls test(), it will print null because, when it executes currentTime?.getTime(), Kotlin sees that currentTime is a null reference. If currentTime had been pointed to a java.util.Date instance, it would have printed the getTime() method's output.

A nice feature of the ?. operator is that it can be chained. Here's a hypothetical example:

```
member1?.member2()?.member3()
```

If either the member1 attribute is a null reference, or the member2 method returns null, the whole expression is simply evaluated to null. If the output of both member1 and member2 is not null references, then the output of the member3 method will be returned.

Option 3 - Using the Elvis operator ?:

The if statement used in the first example can be rewritten with the Elvis operator ?:, which is a bit shorter:

```
var currentTime: java.util.Date? = null
var seconds = currentTime?.getTime() ?: -1
println(seconds)
```

The preceding snippet will print -1. This is because currentTime?.getTime() returns null (the safe call operator ?. returns null, as currentTime is a null reference). Therefore, the -1 literal after the Elvis operator ?: is returned. If currentTime were a reference to a java.util.Date instance, it would have printed the output of getTime().

Option 4 - Using the !! operator

To quote the official documentation: *this operator is meant for NullPointerException-lovers.*

By adding the !! operator to a variable name, you tell the Kotlin compiler to completely skip the null safety system. If the instance variable is a null reference and the code tries to call a method or access a member, Kotlin will throw NullPointerException, similar to what Java would have done in the same situation:

```
fun test() {
    var currentTime: java.util.Date? = null
    println("Next line compiles, but throws exception when running")
var seconds = currentTime!!.getTime()
    println(seconds)
}

test()
```

Conversions

In Java, conversions automatically take place when the compiler is sure that no precision loss will occur. For example, this is valid in Java:

```
// Java code
int a = 1000;
long b = a;
```

Since int can be stored in long without the loss of precision, Java automatically converts int to long. Kotlin does not automatically convert variables. It requires the programmer to convert variables manually:

```
val a: Int = 1000
val b: Long = a.toLong()
```

For conversions, each numeric type (`Int`, `Long`, and so forth) in Kotlin has the following methods:

- `toByte()`
- `toChar()`
- `toDouble()`
- `toFloat()`
- `toInt()`
- `toLong()`
- `toShort()`

Collections and generics

Like Scala and Clojure, Kotlin provides its own implementations of collection classes. Both immutable and mutable variants of common collection classes are available. Kotlin's generics implementation is very similar to that of Java. This table sums up the available interfaces and the functions that must be called to create instances of a class from the Kotlin runtime library that implements the interface:

Interface	Description	Function to create the instance
`List<T>`	Provides methods for immutable lists	`listOf`
`MutableList<T>`	Provides methods for mutable lists	`mutableListOf`
`Set<T>`	Provides methods for an immutable set	`setOf`
`MutableSet<T>`	Provides methods for a mutable set	`mutableSetOf`
`Map<K, V>`	Provides methods for an immutable map	`mapOf`
`MutableMap<K, V>`	Provides methods for a mutable map	`mutableMapOf`

For full documentation on all the available methods and properties of each type, refer to the API Reference section in the Kotlin documentation. Here are some examples that demonstrate the methods of some of the types listed in the preceding table. Let's start by looking at an immutable list:

```
val someImmutableInts: List<Int> = listOf(10, 20, 3
println("$someImmutableInts --> ${someImmutableInts.size} elements")
```

The preceding snippet prints `[10, 20, 30] --> 3 elements`. Other methods that are available in Kotlin's `List` interface include `contains()`, `indexOf()`, `isEmpty()`, `lastIndexOf()`, and `subList()`. The `List` interface has various functional programming functions as well, which are called extension functions. We will cover extension functions in the next chapter:

```kotlin
val mutableDoubles: MutableList<Double> = mutableListOf(3.14, 1.0,
                                                        25.5)
mutableDoubles.add(1, -1.99)
mutableDoubles.removeAt(0)
println(mutableDoubles)
```

The preceding code will print `[-1.99, 1.0, 25.5]`. Other common functions of the `MutableList` interface include `addAll()`, `clear()`, and `remove()`. They are used to remove a specific element:

```kotlin
val mapNumbers: Map<String, Int> = mapOf("one" to 1, "ten" to 10,
                                         "thirty" to 30)
println(mapNumbers["thirty"])
for ((key, value) in mapNumbers) {
  print("$key = $value ")
}

println()
```

This example prints `30` and `one = 1 ten = 10 thirty = 30`. Other common methods include `keys()`, `values()`, `containsKey()`, `containsValue()`, `getOrDefault()` (new in version 1.1), and `isEmpty()`.

Loops

Kotlin knows all the common loop statements, such as `for`, `while`, and `do...while`.

Let's start by looking at a `for` loop example:

```kotlin
val items = listOf(10, 20, 30)
for (i in items) {
  println(i)
}
```

No surprises at all. It prints `10 20 30`, each entry on a new line.

There's also a `while` statement. As always, the condition is checked first. If it evaluates to `true`, no iteration takes place; otherwise, it starts looping until the condition evaluates to `true` or the `break` method is called:

```
var x = 10
while (x > 20) {
  println("Hello")
  x++
}
```

The example prints nothing, as `x` is not larger than `20`.

Also, the `do...while` variant is available:

```
var y = 0
do {
  y++
  if (y == 2)
    continue
  println(y)
} while (y % 5 != 0)
```

This prints `1, 3, 4, 5`.

Like Java and many other popular programming languages, Kotlin supports both the `break` and `continue` statements in all loop constructions to stop the iteration and skip the current iteration, respectively.

OOP in Kotlin

Kotlin is first and foremost an OOP language. We will look at all the basics here:

- Defining packages
- Importing members
- Defining classes and constructors
- Adding members to classes
- Inheritance
- Visibility modifiers
- Singleton and companion objects
- Data classes
- Lambdas and inline functions

Defining packages

Packages are defined with a package statement, which works in a way that is very similar to Java:

```
package com.example
```

Unlike Java and Clojure, the source code's directory structure does not have to match the package names used in Kotlin. You are free to organize the source code in any way you wish.

 You should not use the package statement in Kotlin's interactive REPL shell as this environment does not support the creation of packages.

Importing members

Kotlin's import statement is very similar to that of Java:

```
import java.util.ArrayList
import java.io.*
```

One nice difference is that you can specify an alias, which is very handy when you encounter name clashes:

```
import java.io.File as JavaFile
val f = JavaFile("test.txt")
```

Defining classes and constructors

Classes are defined with the class keyword:

```
class ClassName {
}
```

The primary constructor can be specified as part of the header:

```
class Point constructor(x: Int, y: Int) {
}
```

You can omit the constructor keyword:

```
class Point (x: Int, y: Int) {
}
```

If you want the code to be executed when a class is instantiated, you can specify a block with the init keyword:

```
class Point (x: Int, y: Int) {
  init {
    println("Executable code here...")
  }
}
```

You can use the constructor parameters in the init block and the properties that are defined in the same class (we will cover how to add properties to a class shortly). If you want to use constructor parameters inside methods as well, you'll have to prefix them with either val (for immutable properties) or var (for mutable parameters):

```
class Point (val x: Int, val y: Int) {
  override fun toString(): String { return "${x}, ${y}" }
}
val p = Point(-30, 50)
println(p)
```

This will print -30, 50. It's often a good idea to make constructor parameters immutable using val, so think twice before making them mutable with var, unless you really need it for your design choices.

When specifying the constructor keyword, you can also specify an access modifier of the primary constructor. This is not possible when the constructor keyword is omitted (the constructor is implicitly public then):

```
class Customer private constructor(id: Int) { }
```

When no constructor is explicitly specified, a default public and parameterless constructor is generated automatically. If you don't want this automatically created constructor, you can explicitly create a private constructor that takes no parameters, for example:

```
class Customer private constructor()
```

We will look at the available access modifiers later. Adding one or more secondary constructors is possible as well:

```
class Customer(val name: String, val country: String?) {
  constructor(name: String) : this(name, null) {
      println("Name: " + name)
      println("Country: " + country)
  }
}

var c = Customer("Your Name")
```

The preceding snippet will print `Name: Your name` and `Country: null`. A secondary constructor is required to call the primary constructor either directly (as the example earlier) or indirectly. Indirectly, it calls a different secondary constructor that calls the primary constructor either directly or indirectly.

Adding members to classes

We will now look at how to add members to classes:

- Adding functions
- Adding the main point entry function
- Adding properties

Adding functions

While functions are referred to as methods in Java, they are simply called functions in Kotlin. Since we have already looked at functions, for instance, methods, there are no surprises here:

```
class MethodDemo {
  fun instanceMethod(i: Int): Int {
      return i*i
  }
}

var demo = MethodDemo()
println(demo.instanceMethod(5))
```

Interestingly, Kotlin does not have a keyword for generating static methods (class methods). As an alternative, you can place functions outside any class (this topic is covered in the *Procedural programming in Kotlin* section). You can also generate static functions using object companions, which will be discussed later as well.

The main entry function

As we have seen previously, in Java, you can add `static main(String[] args)`, which acts as the entry point of an application. In Kotlin, the methods inside classes are automatically instance methods, so adding the following function to a class will not work:

```
// The main() function below is a normal instance method
// and CANNOT act as application's entry point
class A {
  fun main(args : Array<String>) {
    println("Executable code here...")
  }
}
```

There are two possibilities to define a `main()` entry point in Kotlin:

- Place the `main()` function as a top-level function of the source code (not inside any class). This is discussed in the *Procedural programming in Kotlin* section.
- Add the `main()` function to a companion object and add the `@JvmStatic` annotation. This is demonstrated in the *Singleton and companion objects* section.

Adding properties

Classes in Kotlin cannot have standalone variables; instead, properties are added to a class. A property is a variable with a matching getter and/or setter (this depends on whether the property is both readable and/or writable). Kotlin can generate default getter/setters for a property, but you can also provide your own implementation for both.

Here's an example of a property that is mutable (can be read and written to). It is mutable because the `var` keyword is used to declare the property:

```
class PropertyDemo1 {
  var mutableProperty: Int = 0
}

val p1 = PropertyDemo1()
println(p1.mutableProperty)
p1.mutableProperty = 24
println(p1.mutableProperty)
```

The `mutableProperty` property is initialized to 0. Since no explicit getter and setter implementations are provided, the Kotlin compiler will automatically generate a getter and setter function for the `mutableProperty` property. To access the property, you can simply use the property name without the *get* and *set* prefixes. Kotlin automatically calls the generated getter and setter functions, which are called accessors in Kotlin.

Properties are required by the Kotlin compiler to be either initialized at the same time as a declaration (as in the preceding example), or initialized in an `init { }` block.

Here's an example of a read-only property. A read-only property is declared using the `val` keyword:

```
class PropertyDemo2 {
  val readOnlyProperty: Int = 1000
}

val p2 = PropertyDemo2()
println(p2.readOnlyProperty)
```

If you try to execute something like `p2.readOnlyProperty = 1234` in the preceding example, an exception similar to the following will be thrown: `java.lang.IllegalAccessError: tried to access field Line35$PropertyDemo2.readOnlyProperty from class Line39`. Like mutable properties, a read-only property must be either explicitly initialized when being declared, or initialized in an `init { }` block.

As mentioned, a property can implement its own accessors (getters and setters). Here's a mutable property with its own getter/setter accessors:

```
class PropertyDemo3 {
  var customProperty: Int = 1000
  get() { field + 1 }
  set(value) { field = value }
p3.customProperty = 10
println(p3.customProperty)
```

The `field` keyword is used to access the generated field, which the Kotlin documentation calls the *backing field*.

It is possible to hide the setter accessor by making it `private`:

```
class PropertyDemo4 {
  var anotherProperty: Int = 314
    private set
}

var p4 = PropertyDemo4()
println(p4.anotherProperty)
```

The `anotherProperty` property does have a setter function (Kotlin's default implementation), but it is hidden since it is private. The getter is automatically created as always and is public. It is not possible to make the getter private, however. The getter must match the property's own access modifier, which is called a visibility modifier in Kotlin and is discussed in more detail later.

Inheritance

Like most popular languages on the JVM platform, Kotlin allows a class to extend up to one super class only. A class that does not implicitly inherit another class inherits from Kotlin's `kotlin.Any` class. This class is similar to Java's `java.lang.Object` class, but note that they are two different classes.

Classes created without an explicit modifier are always `final` and cannot be inherited. To inherit a class, the parent class must be prefixed with the `open` keyword:

```
open class Person(name: String)
class Customer(name: String, department: String) : Person(name) {
}
```

If a child class does not have a primary constructor, the `super` keyword must be used to call a constructor from the parent class:

```
open class Person(name: String)
class Customer : Person {
  constructor(name: String) : super(name)
}
```

To inherit a method, the `override` keyword must be used:

```
open class ParentClass {
  open fun greatMethod() {
    println("greatMethod in parent class")
  }
}
```

```
class ChildClass: ParentClass() {
  override fun greatMethod() {
    super.greatMethod()
  }
}
```

Note that a function is `final` by default and must explicitly have the `open` access modifier.

Interfaces

Interfaces in Kotlin are similar to those in Java 8. They can contain both abstract functions (functions without implementation) and concrete default implementations of functions:

```
interface NameOfInterface {
  fun functionWithoutImplementation()
  fun functionWithImplementation(i: Int) {
    // Default implementation here...
  }
}
```

It's also possible to declare properties, both with and without implementation:

```
interface InterfaceWithProperties {
  var propertyWithGetterAndSetter: Int
  val propertyWithGetterOnly: String
  val propertyWithDefaultImplementation: Double
    get() = 0.0
}
```

It's not possible to have backing fields in an interface, so the `field` keyword cannot be used inside an interface. It's therefore not possible to provide a default implementation of a setter accessor in an interface.

Kotlin uses the same syntax that is used for inheriting classes for implementing interfaces:

```
class DemoClass : NameOfInterface, InterfaceWithProperties {
  override fun functionWithoutImplementation() {
    println("but now it has a implementation")
  }
  override var propertyWithGetterAndSetter: Int = 0
  override val propertyWithGetterOnly: String = "test"
}
```

The order of the class and/or interfaces does not matter, but it's probably a good idea to have the super class as the first entry (if any), followed by the interfaces that the class implements.

Visibility modifiers

In Kotlin, functions and properties can be defined outside a class. This is called the top level of a package and is explained in more detail in the *Procedural programming in Kotlin* section. Different visibility modifiers (called *access modifier* in Java) are available for top-level declarations and class members. Kotlin's visibility modifiers are listed below:

Visibility modifier	Available for	Description
public	Top-level declarations and class members	This is Kotlin's default visibility modifier when no visibility modifier is explicitly added. It has the same meaning as Java's public access modifier: the declaration is available everywhere.
private	Top-level declarations and class members	Here, the definition is only visible to the code in the same file.
internal	Top-level declarations and class members	Here, the definition is visible only to the code inside the same module. A module can be a group of Kotlin files that are compiled together, for example, all of the Kotlin source code of a specific project.
protected	Class members only	This is the same as Java. The members are seen only by the class and its subclasses; they are invisible to any other classes.

Kotlin does not have a visibility modifier that is comparable to Java's package-private member (Java's default access modifier when no access modifier is specified).

Singleton and companion objects

Kotlin's `object` is very similar to Scala's `object` keyword. It creates a singleton:

```
object ThisIsASingleton {
  fun coolMethod() = println("Not so cool, after all")
}

ThisIsASingleton.coolMethod()
```

An instance of this class is created automatically and its members are available using the object's name.

You can create a singleton object inside a class and add the companion prefix:

```
class NormalClass {
  companion object CompanionObject {
    var i = 100
    fun yetAnotherCoolMethod() {
      i = 50
    }
  }
}

NormalClass.CompanionObject.yetAnotherCoolMethod()
println(NormalClass.i)
println(NormalClass.CompanionObject.i)
```

As demonstrated here, the members of a companion object can be reached using the `NormalClass.CompanionObject` reference or simply using the `NormalClass` class name only, which still references its companion object `CompanionObject` internally. The preceding snippet will print `50` twice.

> The companion object's name is not required when not specified explicitly. Kotlin will simply call it *Companion*.

A companion object is available only via its parent class (`NormalClass` in this case), not via a reference variable. The following code does not compile:

```
var i = Normalclass()
// DOES NOT COMPILE
i.CompanionObject.yetAnotherCoolMethod()
```

The following exception will be raised: `error: nested companion object 'CompanionObject' accessed via instance reference`.

The reason for the error is that the members of the companion object behave very similarly to Java's static members. Since the companion object is a singleton object, there's only one instance of this object that is shared with all the instances of its parent class. To make it obvious that you are not dealing with normal instance variable fields and functions, Kotlin forbids accessing the companion objects via a reference variable.

It should be noted that companion objects or their members are not static members technically. Internally, they are still normal instance members, but since they are instantiated automatically before a program can start using them, they behave like static members. It is possible to generate real static methods in a companion object using the `@JvmStatic` annotation:

```
class StaticDemo {
  companion object {
    @JvmStatic fun realStaticMethod() {
      println("Real static method...")
    }
  }
}

StaticDemo.realStaticMethod()
```

Again, the method can be called by simply using the parent class name. Kotlin will make sure that the companion object's static `realStaticMethod()` method is called.

Fields inside an object or companion object can be compiled to a real JVM static field by prefixing them with the `const` keyword:

```
class StaticFieldsDemo {
  companion object {
    const val CONSTANT_VALUE = 3
  }
}
```

This is the equivalent of `public static final int CONSTANT_VALUE = 3;` in Java.

You may wonder why you would want to make a real static method or static field as companion object members already behave like static . One reason could be that this is useful for classes that are to be called by other JVM languages, such as Java.

A good example of a real static method would be the JVM's entry point method of an application, called the `main()` method. By design, this method must be `static`. If you want to define the entry point inside a class, then the only option in Kotlin is to create a companion object and use the `@JvmStatic` annotation:

```
class MainDemo {
  companion object {
    @JvmStatic fun main(args: Array<String>) {
      println("This is the main method")
    }
  }
}
```

Data classes

If you want to create a class to just hold a few fields, data classes are extremely useful. We have seen in Chapter 3, *Java*, that creating a **Plain Old Java Object** (**POJO**) class in Java requires a lot of code for defining the fields and two methods (a getter and a setter) for each field. In Kotlin, data classes are provided that automatically provide generated properties for each field. Let's look at an example:

```
data class Computer(val brand: String, val cpu: String, var memoryGB:
Int, var harddiskSizeGB: Int)
```

This single line generates a class that looks like this:

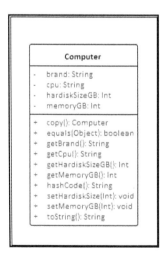

A data class is accessed in the code like an ordinary Kotlin class. The primary constructor takes all the fields as parameters:

```
var pc = Computer("Dell", "Intel Core i5", 8, 1024)
println(pc.brand)
pc.memoryGB = 4
```

The generated class created by the compiler will automatically create a getter function for each field (and an additional setter function for each mutable field that was prefixed with the `var` keyword instead of `val`). It will also automatically add implementations of common JVM methods, including `equals()`, `hashCode()`, and `toString()`.

As always, in Kotlin, you do not write the get/set prefix when accessing the properties; this was demonstrated in the snippet earlier.

What's also generated is a `copy()` function. This handy function allows you to make a copy of a data class and specify some fields that you want to modify in the created copy:

```
var pc2 = pc.copy(brand="HP", memoryGB=16)
println(pc2)
```

This will create, predictably, a copy of the `Computer` data class instance referenced in the `pc` variable, but the brand is changed to `HP` and the memory is upgraded to 16 GB.

 Data classes can implement interfaces and (as of Kotlin version 1.1) extend other classes.

Lambdas and inline functions

Like most other languages covered in this book, it is possible to pass lambda functions as arguments in Kotlin, also called lambda functions. Let's assume we have an application that has enough rights to reboot the server. When this function is called, you'd probably want to log this somewhere. Here's the header of the shutdown function:

```
fun shutdown(logger: (m: String) -> Unit) {
  logger("The server is about to shutdown. There's no way back.")
  println("Code to shutdown the application here...")
}
```

The `shutdown` function takes one argument, named `logger`, which is a function that takes one String as an input value (note that the name `m` is not used) and does not return anything (`Unit`). Before shutting the server down, the `shutdown()` function calls the passed `logger` function. It does not know any implementation details of the `logger` function; all it knows is that it takes a single string containing the message that must be logged and that it does not return anything.

The caller of the `shutdown()` function could pass a lambda by directly passing the `logger` function's body when calling `shutdown()`:

```
shutdown({ msg: String -> println("Logged message: '$msg'") })
```

Here, the lambda simply prints `msg` to the console.

Passing a function to another function is a rather expensive process. Functions are internally defined as objects. A lot is going on under the hood when the `shutdown()` function calls the `logger()` function, and this takes up some processing time. Since a lambda function has access to members of its parent class, one of the things that happens is that copies of those member variables are passed to the lambda function. Usually, that is not a big problem nowadays, but when speed really matters, Kotlin has a neat trick: inline functions. By adding the `inline` prefix to a function that takes a lambda as an input value--as the `shutdown` function in our preceding example--internally, the Kotlin compiler simply rewrites the code in such a way that it no longer calls the lambda; it simply copies the lambda's implementation to the function itself, instead.

This may sound confusing, so let's look at an example. Let's add the `inline` prefix to our `shutdown()` function:

```
inline fun shutdown(logger: (m: String) -> Unit) {
    logger("The server is about to shutdown. There's no way back.")
    println("Code to shutdown the application here...")
}
```

When calling the lambda function, the code that will call the inline function will invisibly be rewritten by the compiler. As an example, look at this example code that calls the shutdown function:

```
fun closeConnectionsAndShutdown() {
    println("Code that shutdowns active connections omitted...")
    shutdown({ msg: String -> println("Logged message: '$msg'") })
}
```

The preceding code will be rewritten by the compiler to something that resembles this:

```
fun closeConnectionsAndShutdown() {
    println("Code that shutdowns active connections omitted...")
    val msg = "The server is about to shutdown. There's no way back."
    println("Logged message: '$msg'")
    println("Code to shutdown the application here...")
}
```

This version of `shutdown` will execute faster than the original one.

Procedural programming in Kotlin

While Kotlin is a pure OOP language, it also supports procedural programming. This means that functions and variables can be defined without placing them explicitly in classes, unlike Java and compiled Scala code. (As we have seen earlier, Scala does not require functions and variables to be placed in classes when using its REPL; it requires this when using the standalone `scalac` compiler.)

When not using Kotlin's REPL interactive shell to write programs, you'll make use of the Kotlin compiler. When you use the compiler to compile your source code, you can place both the functions and properties at the top level of a source file. We have been doing this for a while now in this chapter:

```
fun function1 {
    println("function1 is running...")
}
var property1: String = "default value of property1"
```

It's not possible to place executable code at the top level in the source code, though. Executable code must always reside in a function. To create a JVM application that is executable with either the `java` or `kotlin` command, a `main()` function must be defined. When a function is defined that has the following signature, the Kotlin compiler will compile it as a static method so that it can be used as the JVM entry point function:

```
fun main(args : Array<String>) {
    // Executable code here...
    function1()
    println(property1)
}
```

Since the JVM platform always works with classes, what happens under the hood is that the Kotlin compiler compiles the source code to a class file that acts as a wrapper around the code of the source file. The class will be given the same filename as the source file, appended with the `Kt` suffix. So, if your source file is called `CoolProject.kt` and starts with the `package com.example` line, the fully qualified name of the generated class would be `com.example.CoolProjectKt`.

Note that Kotlin's REPL does not execute the `main()` method automatically. To run this example, save the source code in a file called `procedural_programming.kt` and run the following commands in your Command Prompt (Windows) or Terminal:

```
kotlinc-jvm procedural_programming.kt
kotlin Procedural_programmingKt
```

What happens is the following:

- The `kotlinc-jvm` compiler compiles `procedural_programming.kt` to a JVM-compatible `Procedural_programmingKt.class` file containing the Java bytecode.
- The class inside the class file is called `Procedural_programmingKt`, as described a bit earlier.
- The `kotlin` commands act as a shortcut for the JVM's `java` command. It makes sure that the Kotlin runtime library is added to the classpath. Since the class has a main entry function, the JVM is able to run the application.

Style guide

The Kotlin documentation includes the *Coding Conventions* topic. The most important rules of this topic are:

- Use Java conventions when in doubt
- Use four spaces for indention
- There's a space before and after a column when specifying a class and superclass, for example, `class X : Y()`
- There's no space when declaring variables, for example, `val x: Int`
- Do not specify the optional `Unit` return type for methods that do not return anything

Quiz

1. Which answer best describes Kotlin?

   a) It's a statically typed functional programming language with some OOP features

   b) It's a statically typed OOP language with some functional programming features

   c) It's a dynamically typed functional programming language with some OOP features d) It's a dynamically typed OOP language with some functional programming features

2. Does Kotlin allow us to inherit multiple parent classes?

   a) Yes, a class in Kotlin can extend any number of classes

   b) No, a class in Kotlin can extend only up to one other class

3. When not explicitly specifying a superclass when declaring a class, what will be its superclass?

   a) It will have no super class

   b) `java.lang.Object`

   c) `kotlin.Object`

   d) `kotlin.Any`

4. Will this code run in the Kotlin REPL; if not, why?

   ```
   var k: Int = null
   ```

   a) Yes, this will run without errors

   b) No, an error will occur because Kotlin's type system will not allow `null` values for the `Int` type

   c) No, a mutable variable defined with `var` can never be initialized with null

   d) Kotlin uses the `nil` keyword instead of `null` for null references

5. Which of the following cannot be declared at the top level of a Kotlin source file?

    a) Functions

    b) Properties

    c) Executable code

    d) All of the preceding options

Summary

We started the chapter by downloading Kotlin from its home page and installing it. We examined the REPL and used it to learn some Kotlin fundamentals, such as defining functions and variables. We quickly found out that Kotlin has many features that are similar to Java, but it requires much less boilerplate code for common situations and is often easier to use. We learned about Kotlin's unique type system, especially when it comes to handling null references. We learned the most important OOP-related subjects, such as defining classes, adding functions and properties to it, and even adding a JVM entry point function to it. Also, some more advanced features were discussed, such as singleton and companion objects, data classes, and lambda functions. Finally, you learned that Kotlin can be used for procedural programming as well; you also looked at Kotlin's coding conventions.

In the next chapter, we will create a Kotlin project together that is powered by Oracle's advanced JavaFX desktop GUI framework, and we will use the popular Apache Maven JVM build system to build the project.

10
Kotlin Programming

In this chapter, we are going to write a small desktop GUI application in Kotlin using the JavaFX toolkit. While we mostly used Kotlin's REPL in the previous chapter, we will now be using the Eclipse IDE again for writing code. Just as was the case with both Scala and Clojure, we will need to install a plugin to do this. As this plugin is available in the Eclipse Marketplace, the installation process is a breeze.

As a build tool, we will be using Apache Maven, a build tool that was originally created for Java but can be extended with plugins to support other languages, such as Kotlin. It builds projects by reading an XML file that defines all dependencies and plugins to use during different phases and goals of the building process. We'll use a preconfigured template provided by the Kotlin team as the template for this project. Here's the list of topics that will be covered:

- Kotlin for the Eclipse IDE plugin
- Apache Maven
- Creating a JavaFX desktop GUI application

Kotlin for the Eclipse IDE plugin

The Kotlin language was designed by a team at JetBrains, the company behind popular commercial IDEs and their free community editions. It will not be a surprise that their popular IntelliJ IDEA IDE for JVM software development offers very good built-in Kotlin support. JetBrains, in their quest for widespread use of Kotlin, are also developing a plugin that adds Kotlin compatibility to the Eclipse IDE. We will be using this plugin during this chapter.

Installing the Kotlin plugin for the Eclipse IDE

Installation couldn't be simpler, as it is available on the Eclipse Marketplace. At the time of writing, the version on the Marketplace was fully up to date with the latest available version on their website. The installation procedure should feel rather familiar by now:

1. From the Eclipse IDE's **Help** menu, select the **Eclipse Marketplace...** option.
2. Enter `Kotlin` in the **Find** field and press *Enter*.
3. Look for the `Kotlin Plugin for Eclipse` entry (which credits JetBrains) and click its **Install** button:

4. Follow the prompts. The Eclipse IDE will give a security warning and ask whether you want to continue. If you agree that it's not a problem that JetBrains did not sign the installer, acknowledge by choosing **Yes**. Also, accept the license if you agree with it. Finally, the Eclipse IDE will ask if it can restart; choose **Yes**.

That's all! Kotlin support is now added to the Eclipse IDE.

Switching to Kotlin perspective

The Kotlin plugin for Eclipse offers its own perspective, so that you can switch to an user-interface that is optimized for Kotlin programming. At the top-right toolbar of the Eclipse IDE's window, find the button with the Kotlin tooltip:

If it is not visible, find the button with the Open Perspective tooltip, which is on the same toolbar, and click it. A dialog with a list with all supported perspectives is opened. Select the **Kotlin** perspective and click **OK**:

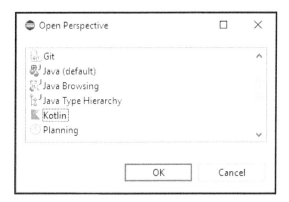

The Eclipse IDE's user interface is now fully optimized for development in the Kotlin language.

Apache Maven

Kotlin developers on the JVM often use ordinary build tools that are used generally in the JVM world and Java especially. Two popular build tools that Kotlin developers use are Gradle from Gradle Inc. and Maven by the Apache Software Foundation. Both Gradle and Maven can both manage dependencies and build projects. As we have already covered Gradle back in `Chapter 4`, *Java Programming*, when we developed a small Java application, we will use Apache Maven in this chapter.

Maven is a build tool that uses a XML build file for building a project. Maven closely follows the convention over configuration paradigm. If you can follow its conventions, you won't need to alter the build file too often, but things can get quite complex (or even immensely problematic) once you need to break free and need custom actions when building your project. For most popular actions plugins can be added to the system, that add new functionality and/or actions to the build process. It can be challenging to find the right plugin that does exactly what you need. For Kotlin development, the Kotlin Maven plugin has to be added, so that Maven knows how to compile Kotlin code.

The Eclipse Kotlin plugin does not support creating a Maven-based project from its GUI, but as Maven support is built in to the Eclipse IDE, a project can be created manually and then imported in the Eclipse IDE. The following subjects are covered in this section:

- Installing Apache Maven
- Downloading a preconfigured Kotlin starter kit
- Importing the project in the Eclipse IDE

Installing Apache Maven

Since Maven is a tool that is used in lots of existing JVM-based projects, it's a good idea for aspiring JVM developers to install this tool anyway, regardless of whether you plan to use Maven in Kotlin projects in the future. Learn more about Maven by visiting the project's homepage:

```
http://maven.apache.org
```

The installation procedure of Maven is very similar to the other JVM tools covered in this book:

1. Visit the Maven's project homepage to download Maven. From the homepage's **Download** section, find a nearby download mirror from the list and download the latest version. At the time of writing, this was version 3.5.0. Windows users should download the ZIP file (at the time of writing, it was called `apache-maven-3.5.0-bin.zip`), while Linux and macOS users should download the `tar.gz` archive (at the time of writing, `apache-maven-3.5.0-bin.tar.gz`).
2. Extract the archive to a convenient directory on your system
3. Add the `bin` directory to your system's path.

To validate the installation, type `mvn --help` in a Command Prompt (Windows) or Terminal window (macOS and Linux). A long list with the options should be printed to the console window:

```
Command Prompt                                    —    □    ×

C:\>mvn --help

usage: mvn [options] [<goal(s)>] [<phase(s)>]

Options:
 -am,--also-make                   If project list is specified, also
                                   build projects required by the
                                   list
 -amd,--also-make-dependents       If project list is specified, also
                                   build projects that depend on
                                   projects on the list
 -B,--batch-mode                   Run in non-interactive (batch)
                                   mode
 -b,--builder <arg>                The id of the build strategy to
                                   use.
 -C,--strict-checksums             Fail the build if checksums don't
                                   match
 -c,--lax-checksums                Warn if checksums don't match
```

Downloading a preconfigured Kotlin starter kit

The Kotlin teams offers a starter kit that contains a preconfigured project for both Gradle and Maven. It can be retrieved from the Kotin's team official GitHub repository:

```
https://github.com/JetBrains/kotlin-examples
```

By visiting the GitHub page in your favorite browser, you can download a ZIP file containing the latest version of the master branch of the repository. Unzip this file in your Eclipse's workspace directory:

If you have Git installed, you can also checkout the file by typing `git clone https://github.com/JetBrains/kotlin-examples` inside your Eclipse's workspace directory.

Let's test your Maven installation by compiling and running the project. In your Command Prompt (Windows) or Terminal window (macOS and Linux), change the active directory to `kotlin-examples/maven/hello-world` and run the following command:

```
mvn compile
```

This will start Maven and execute the build file's `compile` goal. Maven will fetch all dependencies required to compile the project, including the Kotlin Maven plugin and start compiling the project source files. It should return a successful completion of the task. Maven created a `target` directory, containing a `classes` subdirectory which contains the compiled class files.

The build file that is included in the maven starter's kit is configured in such a way that it can also be launched by using Maven. To run the project. Run the following command to launch the project:

```
mvn exec:java
```

Although it is a Kotlin project, it can use Maven's default `java` execution task, as the normal JVM `java` command is used to launch the application:

```
Command Prompt                                                    —    □    ×
[INFO] -------------------------------------------------------------------
[INFO] Building hello-world 1.0-SNAPSHOT
[INFO] -------------------------------------------------------------------
[INFO]
[INFO] >>> exec-maven-plugin:1.2.1:java (default-cli) > validate @ hello-world >>>
[INFO]
[INFO] <<< exec-maven-plugin:1.2.1:java (default-cli) < validate @ hello-world <<<
[INFO]
[INFO] --- exec-maven-plugin:1.2.1:java (default-cli) @ hello-world ---
Hello, world!
[INFO] -------------------------------------------------------------------
[INFO] BUILD SUCCESS
[INFO] -------------------------------------------------------------------
[INFO] Total time: 1.270 s
[INFO] Finished at: 2017-03-29T00:28:31+02:00
[INFO] Final Memory: 8M/184M
[INFO] -------------------------------------------------------------------
C:\Kotlin\kotlin-examples\maven\hello-world>
```

Among Maven's own output, you should see (yet again) the `Hello, World` greeting.

Importing the project in the Eclipse IDE

As Maven is such a household name in the JVM world, all Java editions of the Eclipse IDE have built-in Maven support. Therefore, importing the project in the Eclipse IDE is a breeze:

1. In the Eclipse IDE, right-click on an empty spot in the **Package Explorer** and choose **Import...**.
2. The **Import** dialog appears. Choose the **Projects from Folder or Archive** option.
3. Click on the **Directory** button next to the **Import Source** field. Navigate to your workspace directory (usually in your operating system's home directory), find the `kotlin-examples-master` directory, and navigate to its `maven` subdirectory. Select its `hello-world` directory and choose **OK**.
4. Finally, click **Finish** to import the project.

Since the Eclipse IDE knows the conventions as dictated by Maven, it will be able to properly import the project and map the most important Maven tasks to the proper GUI elements. Let's test if it works as expected. From the **Package Explorer**, expand the `hello-world` project entry and from the `src/main/kotlin` entry, open the `Hello.kt` file. Change the `Hello, world!` greeting to something different, save the file, and click the launch icon on the toolbar. It should have the Run Hello.kt tooltip:

You should see your modified message now in Eclipse's **Console** tab. The Eclipse IDE was able to compile the file and run the `main()` function from the `Hello.kt` file.

Exploring the pom.xml build file

Before continuing, let's take a look at the Maven build file, which is usually called `pom.xml`. From the **Package Explorer**, open the `hello-world` project's `pom.xml` file. By default, an overview page is displayed, but since we want to look at the XML file itself, click the `pom.xml` tab that is displayed at the bottom of the same window. The raw XML file is now displayed:

```
      M hello-world/pom.xml ⊠                                                      ⬜ ⬜
  1   <?xml version="1.0" encoding="UTF-8"?>
  2   <project
  3         xsi:schemaLocation="http://maven.apache.org/POM/4.0.0 http://maven.apache.org/xsd/maven-4.0.0.xsd"
  4         xmlns="http://maven.apache.org/POM/4.0.0" xmlns:xsi="http://www.w3.org/2001/XMLSchema-instance">
  5
  6       <modelVersion>4.0.0</modelVersion>
  7
  8       <groupId>org.jetbrains.kotlin.examples</groupId>

Overview  Dependencies  Dependency Hierarchy  Effective POM  pom.xml
```

POM is an abbreviation for **Project Object Model**. Version 4.0.0 of the POM file format has been the current version of the format since Maven 2.

We will discuss some important elements from this file:

```
<project
 xsi:schemaLocation="http://maven.apache.org/POM/4.0.0
 http://maven.apache.org/xsd/maven-4.0.0.xsd"
 xmlns="http://maven.apache.org/POM/4.0.0"
 xmlns:xsi="http://www.w3.org/2001/XMLSchema-instance">
   ...
</project>
```

This is the root node of a POM. As mentioned earlier, version 4.0.0 is the current version:

```
<groupId>org.jetbrains.kotlin.examples</groupId>

<artifactId>hello-world</artifactId>

<version>1.0-SNAPSHOT</version>
```

The `groupId` is a string that should identify your project. It should follow JVM package name conventions. The `artifactId` defines the filename of the JAR file that is created, without the version number. The version is defined using the `version` element:

```
<properties>
  <kotlin.version>1.0.3</kotlin.version>
  <junit.version>4.12</junit.version>
  <main.class>hello.HelloKt</main.class>
  <project.build.sourceEncoding>UTF-8</project.build.sourceEncoding>
</properties>
```

Properties are key/value pairs. The element name defines the key, while the value is the content. It's a convention to define dependency version numbers as properties, so that you only have to change a property when updating a version, instead of searching and replacing multiple XML elements:

```
<dependencies>
  <dependency>
    <groupId>org.jetbrains.kotlin</groupId>
    <artifactId>kotlin-stdlib</artifactId>
    <version>${kotlin.version}</version>
  </dependency>
  ...
</dependencies>
```

The `<dependency>` elements between the `<dependencies>` elements define each dependency of the project. One of the dependencies is the **Kotlin Standard Library** (`kotlin-stdlib`). It uses the value of the `kotlin.version` property for specifying the version:

```
<build>
    <sourceDirectory>${project.basedir}/src/main/kotlin</sourceDirectory>

<testSourceDirectory>${project.basedir}/src/test/kotlin</testSourceDirectory>
    <plugin>
      <artifactId>kotlin-maven-plugin</artifactId>
      <groupId>org.jetbrains.kotlin</groupId>
      <version>${kotlin.version}</version>
      ...
    </plugin>
    ...
</build>
```

The bulk of the build file consists of entries between the `<build>` and `</build>` tags. Several plugins are defined; the plugin displayed here is the `kotlin-maven-plugin` plugin, which adds Kotlin support to Maven. Maven has several phases, and each Maven plugin can alter phases and define goals.

Goals are specified as arguments to Maven when using the `mvn` command on the command-line. For example, when you ran `mvn compile` on the command-line, you specified the `compile` goal.

Updating the build file in Eclipse

At the time of writing this book, Kotlin 1.1 was available, while the starter kit defined 1.0.3 as the Kotlin version. To change this, I changed the `kotlin.version` property from 1.0.3 to 1.1.0:

```
<properties>
  <kotlin.version>1.1.0</kotlin.version>
  ...
</properties>
```

At default, the Kotlin compiler compiles Java 1.6 bytecode. It is recommended to also add the following property, so that more efficient Java bytecode will be generated by the compiler:

```
<properties>
  <kotlin.version>1.1.0</kotlin.version>
  <kotlin.compiler.jvmTarget>1.8</kotlin.compiler.jvmTarget>
  ...
</properties>
```

An issue with the Eclipse IDE is that it defaults to Java version 1.5 platform when the Java compiler is not explicitly set in the Maven build file. Since our project will not use the Java compiler, this is not a real problem.

 This means that the warning `Build path specifies execution environment J2SE-1.5...` will be displayed in the **Problems** tab for both the main project and test resources during the development of this project, unfortunately.

After editing the `pom.xml` file, Eclipse must refresh the project. Do this by right-clicking the project name and choosing **Maven | Update Project**. In the dialog that appears, just click on **OK**.

Creating a JavaFX desktop GUI application

We will be building a simple desktop application in Kotlin, that makes use of the JavaFX GUI desktop toolkit. JavaFX is the newest GUI toolkit that is supplied with most popular versions of the **Java Runtime Environment** (**JRE**). JavaFX is supplied with Java for Windows, macOS, and desktop-based Linux versions. JavaFX was initially supplied with the Java SE Embedded 8 version that is preinstalled on the Raspberry Pi's Raspbian operating system, but unfortunately Oracle removed it from later updates. It is also not available for Solaris users.

 Oracle made the source code of JavaFX for Java SE Embedded available via an open source license, so advanced users can still compile and run JavaFX-based applications on the Raspberry Pi. This use case is out of scope of this chapter, though.

It's strongly recommended to have the JavaFX documentation nearby while developing the project in this chapter. It can be found at the following link:

```
http://docs.oracle.com/javase/8/javase-clienttechnologies.htm
```

Kotlin is an excellent fit for JavaFX development. As Kotlin can access attributes of a class by their attribute name, you don't need to call getter/setter methods in Kotlin, but instead you can access attributes as you would access, a field and this makes the code quite a bit cleaner. Under the hood, Kotlin still calls the same setter/getter methods. Here's a simple example, first in Java, then the same code in Kotlin:

```java
// Example Java code. Do not enter this in Eclipse

@Override
public void start(Stage stage) {
  stage.setTitle("Kotlin JavaFX Demo")
  stage.setScene(new Scene(new Pane(), 300.0, 300.0))
}
```

In Kotlin this is written as follows:

```kotlin
// Example Kotlin code. Do not enter this in Eclipse

override fun start(stage: Stage) {
  stage.title = "Kotlin JavaFX Demo"
  stage.scene = Scene(Pane(), 300.0, 300.0)
}
```

While perhaps not a very big deal, you'll probably agree that the Kotlin code is a bit cleaner and more readable. Luckily, as we will see soon, the Kotlin plugin for the Eclipse IDE shows attributes in its auto-complete suggestions.

Preparing the project

We will be customizing the project that we imported in the Eclipse IDE in the previous section. To prepare the project, do the following:

1. From `src/test/kotlin`, delete the `HelloTest.kt` file by right-clicking the file and choosing **Delete...**.
2. From the `src/main/kotlin` entry, rename the `Hello.kt` file to `App.kt`, by clicking `Hello.kt` on the **Package Explorer** and pressing *F2*.
3. Open the `pom.xml` file again, find the `<properties>` section and change the `<main.class>hello.HelloKt</main.class>` property to `<main.class>javafxdemo.AppKt</main.class>`. This is the class that will contain the `main()` JVM entry-point method in our program.
4. Refresh the Maven project again by right-clicking project name and choosing **Maven | Update Project**.

Creating a runnable application

From `src/main/kotlin`, open `App.kt`. Replace its content with the following:

```
package javafxdemo
fun main(args: Array<String>) {
}
```

Place the cursor after the package statement and add a new blank line. Type the following:

```
class KotlinJavaFXDemo :
```

Type `Appl` and press *Ctrl* + Space bar (*cmd* + Space bar on Apple machines); the Eclipse IDE will show a popup window with suggestions:

Find the `Application` class from the `javafx.application` package in the list and double-click it or press *Enter*. An import statement will be added and the `Application` class name will be written for you. Now add `()`, so that our subclass automatically calls the parameter-less constructor of the `javafx.application.Application` parent class. The code should now look this:

```
package javafxdemo

import javafx.application.Application

class KotlinJavaFXDemo : Application() {
}

fun main(args: Array<String>) {
}
```

`Application` is a class from the JavaFX toolkit. It is an abstract class that has several concrete methods and one abstract method. The definition of the abstract method in Java is:

```
// Java code
public abstract void start(Stage primaryStage)
```

A JavaFX-based application is supposed to extend the `Application` class and implement its `start()` method; therefore, we must provide its implementation in our `KotlinJavaFXDemo` class. Put the cursor inside the `KotlinJavaFXDemo` class definition and press *Ctrl + 1* (for macOS users: *cmd + 1*) and choose **Implement Members**:

```
class KotlinJavaFXDemo : Application() {

}           ◈ Make 'KotlinJavaFXDemo' abstract
fun m ◈ Implement Members
```

 Ctrl + 1 (or *cmd + 1* on macOS) is the shortcut for the Eclipse IDE's *Quick Fix* command, which can provide easy fixes for common issues.

The class should now look like this:

```
class KotlinJavaFXDemo : Application() {
  override fun start(primaryStage: Stage?) {
    TODO()
  }
}
```

Unfortunately, this does not automatically add the required `Stage` import statement, so place the cursor before the question mark of the `Stage?` class name and press *Ctrl* + Space bar (*cmd* + Space bar on macOS) and choose the `Stage` class from the `javafx.stage` package. The import statement will now be added.

Remove the question mark after the `Stage` type, as this is a method provided by JavaFX and it should never be null, then replace the `start()` function implementation with the following code. For each class name, use the *Ctrl* + Space bar (*cmd* + Space bar on macOS) shortcut to use the auto-complete feature and always select the corresponding class from the `javafx` package:

```
override fun start(primaryStage: Stage) {
    primaryStage.title = "Kotlin JavaFX Demo"
    val pane = Pane()
    val scene = Scene(pane, 500.0, 500.0)
    primaryStage.scene = scene
    primaryStage.show()
}
```

A lot is happening in the preceding code, let's take a more detailed look at it:

- A `Stage` object is the top-level container of a JavaFX application. A main window is automatically created by JavaFX by default, and a reference to this window (which is a `Stage`), is passed to the start method.
- We change the `title` (caption) of this main window to **Kotlin JavaFX Demo**. By default, the window caption is empty.
- A `Pane()` object is created. A `Pane` is an object that can have children objects. Each child object can be a GUI element, which will all automatically be rendered when the pane renders itself.
- We create a `Scene` object. A `Scene` object contains the root object that contains all children that will be drawn. In this case this may look useless, since we only have one `Pane()` object, but we will see soon that usually a window has multiple objects. We tell JavaFX that we want our scene to take up 500 pixels horizontally and vertically.
- The `Scene` is assigned to the `primaryStage` window. JavaFX now knows the required size and creates a dialog that has a size of 500x500 pixels.
- Finally, the `primaryStage` window is made visible.

JavaFX usually uses primitive double variables to specify positions and sizes, instead of integers.

We still need to implement the JVM `main()` entry point function. To start a JavaFX application, we must call the public, static `launch` method of the `Application` class. Replace the implementation of the `main()` function with the following code:

```
fun main(args: Array<String>) {
    Application.launch(KotlinJavaFXDemo::class.java)
}
```

 Make sure that this function is not placed inside the class block, otherwise it will be a normal instance method. Only if this method is not inside any class, Kotlin will compile it to a static method that can be used as the JVM entry-point method.

The `launch` method is a static method of the `Application` class, so in Kotlin this means that it can only be accessed by using the `Application` class name. As a parameter, a reference to the Java class that extends the `Application` class must be specified, in Kotlin this is done by casting it to a `class.java` object.

As we have seen in the previous chapter, when a method is placed at the top-level (not in any class), Kotlin creates a class that consists of the source code filename followed by the `Kt` suffix. So, in this case, the `main` method will be placed in the `AppKt` class in the `javafxdemo` package. This is also the class that we specified as main class when we prepared the `pom.xml` build file.

You should now be able to run the program by pressing *Ctrl + F11* (*cmd + F11* for macOS users) or pressing the launch icon on the toolbar. An empty window should appear:

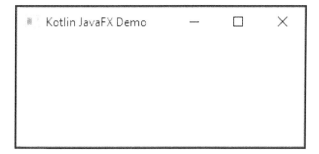

Not very exciting, so let's start by printing something to it.

Writing an extension function

Kotlin offers an interesting feature called an extension function. An extension function is a function that is attached to a specific type, called the receiver type. The receiver type is the class where the function will be added to. Objects that are instances of that class can call this function like any other method of the class. The only difference is that code must import the function before it can call them. Inheriting the receiver type's class is not needed, and therefore, extension functions can be added to any class, even classes that are closed (final in Java). Let's add an extension function to JavaFX' `Pane()` class, that prints a message in a somewhat fancy way.

In the **Package Explorer**, right-click on the `src/main/kotlin` entry and choose **New Kotlin File...**. Enter `javafxdemo.extensions` as package and `PaneExtensions` as file name. A new file will be created, containing the relevant package statement. Add the following function to this file:

```
import javafx.scene.layout.Pane
fun Pane.prettyPrint(y: Double, text: String) {
}
```

By prefixing the function name with the `Pane` class name and a dot, Kotlin knows that the declared function is an extension function that will be made available on all instances of the `Pane()` class, including its subclasses. Code that imports this extension function (we will learn how to do this soon), will be able to call this function in the following way:

```
// Example code (do not enter this in the code)
val pane = Pane()
pane.prettyPrint(50.0, primaryStage.title)
```

To the code that does the `prettyPrint` call, it seems like `prettyPrint` was a normal method of the `Pane()` class. The code inside `Pane.prettyPrint()` function can access the `Pane()` instance that was used to call the function by simply using the `this` reference. With this knowledge, let's implement the `prettyPrint` extension function.

 Remember to use *Ctrl* + Space bar (*cmd* + Space bar) on all class names for the required import statements, take care to always choose the class name from the `javafx` package.

Here's a list of the fully qualified class names that will be used in the following code, so that you can pick the right class from the correct package (or, if you prefer, to write the `import` statements yourself):

- `javafx.scene.layout.Pane`
- `javafx.scene.text.Text`
- `javafx.scene.text.Font`
- `javafx.scene.text.FontWeight`
- `javafx.scene.paint.Color`

Here's the code of the `prettyPrint` extension function:

```
fun Pane.prettyPrint(y: Double, text: String) {
    val t = Text()
    t.text = text
    t.font = Font.font("Verdana", FontWeight.BOLD, 30.0)
    t.fill = Color.DARKBLUE

    t.x = 0.0
    t.y = y
    this.children.add(t)
}
```

From `src/main/kotlin`, open the `App.kt` file and add the following import statement:

```
import javafxdemo.extensions.prettyPrint
```

Note that the source file, `PaneExtensions`, is not part of the imported function. This is because in Kotlin package names can be completely different than the directory structure organization of the source code files.

If we wanted to add an extension function called `prettyPrint` to other classes in the same file, that would have been fine, and all of them would have been available after the preceding `import` statement.

In the `App.kt` file's `start()` method of the `JavaFXDemo` class, add the following line after the `val scene = Scene(pane, 500.0, 500.0)` line:

```
pane.prettyPrint(100.0, primaryStage.title)
```

The code of the `start()` method should now look like this:

```
override fun start(primaryStage: Stage) {
    primaryStage.title = "Kotlin JavaFX Demo"
    val pane = Pane()
    pane.prettyPrint(50.0, primaryStage.title)

    val scene = Scene(pane, 500.0, 500.0)
    primaryStage.scene = scene
    primaryStage.show()
}
```

Run the program again. It should now print the `Kotlin JavaFX Demo` text in a large font:

As a finishing touch, let's apply an effect to the printed text. Open the `PaneExtensions.kt` file and add the following code above the `this.children.add(t)` line:

```
val shadow = InnerShadow()
shadow.offsetX = 2.0
shadow.offsetY = 2.0
t.effect = shadow
```

To make this effect better visible, also change the line `t.fill = Color.DARKBLUE` to `t.fill = Color.YELLOW`.

Run the program again. It should now look a little bit fancier:

Layout panes

JavaFX has several built-in layout pane classes. You could use the `Pane()` class and place each child control manually by calculating *X* and *Y* positions, as we did in the preceding example. This would be cumbersome though, especially if a window has several controls and the window can be resized.

In most cases, a better solution would be to use the layout pane classes. These classes take care of automatically placing and resizing child controls. The most important built-in layouts are as follows:

Layout class	Description
BorderPane	Provides five subpanes: top, left, center, right, and bottom.
HBox	Places each child control next to the previous one in an horizontal box.
VBox	Places each child control below the previous one in a vertical box.
StackPane	Stacks each control on top of the previous one, so that controls can be mixed.
GridPane	Creates a grid-alike row/column-based form-alike structure.
FlowPane	Based on a maximum wrap length, child nodes are added next to the previous one. When the width exceeds, a new row is created and the node is placed on the first column of the new row. Can also be set to flow vertically instead of horizontally.
TilePane	Similar to `FlowPane`. Each child node has the same size as the others.
AncorPane	Allows to anchor child nodes to a fixed position (top, bottom, left, right or center). When resizing, it makes sure that the child nodes keep their position relative to the anchor points.

Since all layout panes are a subclass of `Pane()`, layout panes can be mixed and matched. We will demonstrate some of the more common layout panes in this chapter.

For full information on the layouts, see the *Work with Layouts* section in the official Oracle JavaFX manual. You can find it at `http://docs.oracle.co m/javase/8/javafx/layout-tutorial/`.

Implementing a BorderPane-based layout

We will add some very simple animation to the window. To get started, let's create a
`BorderPane` that will be the new root pane of the scene. We will assign our current `Pane()`
(which contains the `prettyPrint` output) to the `top` subpane of `BorderPane`. It will act as
a colorful header of our application.

Open the `App.kt` file. Rewrite the start function by replacing the code with the following
code. As always, remember to use *Ctrl* + Space bar (or *cmd* + Space bar) for the class names
that are not imported yet:

```
override fun start(primaryStage: Stage) {
    primaryStage.title = "Kotlin JavaFX Demo"
    val textField = TextField()
    val mainPane = BorderPane()
    mainPane.top = createHeaderPane(primaryStage.title)

    val scene = Scene(mainPane, 500.0, 500.0)
    primaryStage.scene = scene
    primaryStage.show()
}
```

We have refactored the code. The code that creates the `Pane()` instance that represents the
header is now put in its own function, that we will write in a second. A `TextField` class
instance is created that will hold the text entered by the user later. A new `BorderPane`
instance `mainPane` is created, and the `headerPane` is assigned to its top subpane. The
`mainPane` is the new root node of the `Scene`.

Let's write the `createHeaderPane()` function. Add it after the `start()` function in the
same class:

```
fun createHeaderPane(title: String): Pane {
    val pane = Pane()
    pane.prettyPrint(30.0, title)
    return pane
}
```

Run the project. Note that nothing has changed. Thanks to the `BorderPane` instance, we
can now, however, add new panes easily to the left, center, right, and/or bottom of the
window.

We'll create a text input box at the bottom of the window, where the user can enter a text that will move around the screen. Let's start now by creating the function that will create the HBox (horizontal box) that will contain both a label and the text field. Place this new function after the createHeaderPane() function.

Don't forget to use *Ctrl* + Space bar (*cmd* + Space bar) on classes that are not imported yet, and take care to always select classes from the javafx package. To save space, this will not be repeated for the remainder of this chapter.

We'll create and set up the HBox pane in a separate function again. Add the following code below the previous one:

```
fun createInputPane(textField: TextField): Pane {
    val label = Label("Input text:")
    label.minWidth = 65.0

    val inputPane = HBox()
    inputPane.children.add(label)
    inputPane.children.add(textField)

    HBox.setHgrow(textField, Priority.ALWAYS)
    return inputPane
}
```

Let's take a more detailed look at the preceding code:

- A text input field control (called TextField in JavaFX) is passed as input parameter. This is done because we need a reference for this object in different functions. Here we need it to add it the Pane that we are creating.
- We create a a fixed-sized Label (65 pixels wide).
- We then create a HBox layout pane, as we have seen earlier, a HBox panel places its children nodes (controls) next to each other.
- Both the label and textField controls are added to the list of children of our inputPane HBox class instance
- By calling the static setHGrow method of the HBox class, we can let the HBox know that the textField control should take up the remaining space of the HBox.

- Note that the `HBox` class is a subclass of `Pane()`. Therefore, we specified `Pane()` as the return value of the `createInputPane()` function, instead of `HBox`. If we ever decide to change the implementation of this function, the return value of this function can stay the way it was.

Let's add this `HBox` pane to our `BorderPane`, otherwise we won't see our new `createInputPane()` function in action. Scroll up to the `start()` function and add the following below the `mainPane.top = createHeaderPane(primaryStage.title)` line:

```
mainPane.bottom = createInputPane(textField)
```

Now run the application again. You should now see a label and text field at the bottom:

Try to resize the window and note that the label and text field stay at the bottom of the screen (this is because the `LayoutPane` automatically moves the bottom section when changing the window's height) and that the text field's width always takes up the remaining space of the window's width (this is because we called the static `setHGrow` method of the `HBox` class).

Implementing animation

We want a text that is entered by the user to move around the screen. To make animation possible, we'll need to keep track of some values. Therefore, let's create a class that will handle the animation. Unlike Java, Kotlin supports defining multiple classes in one source file, no matter which access modifiers are used for the classes. Add the following code just below the class block that defines the `KotlinJavaFXDemo` class:

```
class AnimatedText {
    val animatedText = Text()
    val animationPane = Pane()
```

```
var directionX = 3.0
var directionY = 3.0

fun getPane(textField: TextField): Pane {
    animatedText.x = 0.0
    animatedText.y = 0.0
    animatedText.font = Font.font("Verdana", FontWeight.BOLD, 15.0)
    animationPane.children.add(animatedText)
    return animationPane
}
}
```

By initializing the x and y properties of the our `javafx.scene.text.Text` object both to `0.0`, we will start the text at the upper-left (0,0) position of the pane represented by the `animationPane` variable. The `directionX` and `directionY` variables will be used when we implement the animation. At each step, we'll use them to move our object 3 pixels horizontally and vertically. Note that we will pass the `TextField` control that will contain the user's input to the `getPane()` function.

Now we need a way to create a function that is called on each frame that calculates the new position of the text and update its direction when necessary. JavaFX offers the `AnimationTimer` class for this. This is an abstract class that has one abstract method called `handle()` that is called for each frame. As input it gets the time of the frame (a long value representing time that has elapsed since the last call, but to keep this example simple, we will ignore it). If you require realistic animation in a real application, you would use this value to calculate the time that has elapsed since the last call and move objects accordingly.

Let's implement the `AnimationTimer` class inside the `AnimatedText` class. Place the cursor after the `var directionY = 3.0` line, add an empty line, and add the following code:

```
val timer = object : AnimationTimer() {
  override fun handle(now: Long) {
    if (animatedText.x < 0.0 || animatedText.x > animationPane
        .width - animatedText.layoutBounds.width)
      directionX = -directionX

    if (animatedText.y < 0.0 || animatedText.y > animationPane
        .height)
      directionY = -directionY
      animatedText.x += directionX
      animatedText.y += directionY
  }
}
```

The `object : AnimationTimer()` syntax may look surprising. As mentioned, the `AnimationTimer` is an abstract class. This means that it cannot be instantiated directly, as classes that will extend this class must provide implementations of its abstract methods. In the mentioned line, we create an anonymous object that extends the `AnimationTimer` abstract class. Note that we did not give the class a name, we only specify that the `timer` reference variable will hold a reference to this object. Since `handle` is the only abstract method of the `AnimationTimer` class, our anonymous class only has to override the `handle` method. Inside the method, we look at the current position of the text and decide whether we need to reverse either the *X* or *Y* direction. We update the *X* and *Y* positions of the `animatedText` object accordingly.

The timer will have to be started. Let's do this in the `getPane()` function of the `AnimatedText` class. After the `animationPane.children.add(animatedText)` line, add the following line:

```
timer.start()
```

We need to load this pane into one of the subpanes of the `BorderPane` layout of the main `Scene`. Scroll back to the `start()` function and add the following line after the `mainPane.bottom = createInputPane(textField)` line:

```
mainPane.center = AnimatedText().getPane(textField)
```

When running the application, you'll note that nothing has changed. Also, nothing happens when you enter text in the text field. Why is this? Well, we did not yet handle the `TextField` input and we did not hard-code any text in the `animatedText` object. It's about time to change this. In many other popular GUI toolkits that are available on the market today, this would mean adding a listener function to the input `TextField` control and then passing its input to the animated `Text` object. JavaFX has a more powerful feature, though.

In JavaFX, a property of a control can be bound to a property of a different control. This can be done in a single direction (meaning that if property A was bound to property B, property A will update B automatically upon changes, but not the other way around) and bi-directional (if property A and B are bound to each other, then they will update each other upon a change). Obviously, bi-directional binding is a rather expensive operation, and in our case we won't need it, as only the `TextField` control can accept changes in our application. To bind the text property of `textField` to the `animatedText` control, add the following line of code to the `getPane()` method of the `AnimatedText` class, above the `return animationPane` line:

```
animatedText.textProperty().bind(textField.textProperty())
```

When the `text` property of `textField` changes, the `text` property of `animatedText` will automatically be updated. But not the other way around. JavaFX protects this by throwing an exception when the `text` property of `animatedText` is changed via code.

Run the application. Once you start typing text in the text box, you'll see your entered text bouncing around the center of the window:

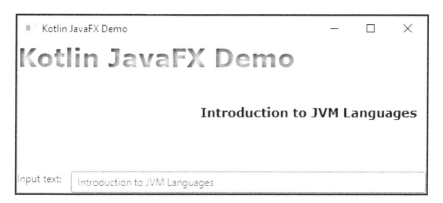

If you experiment by entering long text and/or make the window smaller while the text floats to the right of the window, you'll see that text can get stuck (it will stop moving horizontally), or even get lost (it will remain on the invisible part of the window, when making the window smaller).

Let's try to find the cause of this bug. Stop the program. We are going to use the debugger to find the cause of this bug.

Debugging the program

From Eclipse's **Run** menu, choose **Debug** (or press *F11*). The program now runs in debug mode. Enter some text and try to make it stuck by making the window larger, then when the text floats on the right side of the screen quickly smaller again so that the text either disappears or gets stuck.

When this happens, let's use the debugger to try to understand what is going on:

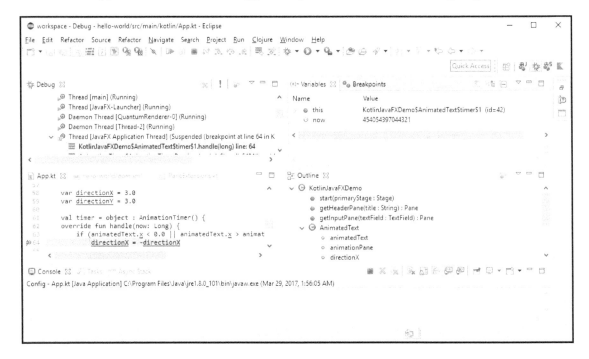

Follow these instructions to open and use the debugger:

1. Keep the program running and return to the Eclipse IDE.
2. Open the `App.kt` file and find the `directionX = -directionX` line. On the left-hand side you'll see the line number. Right-click the line number, and from the menu that appears, choose **Toggle Breakpoint**.
3. Once the program executes the line with the breakpoint, the program will stop executing. Eclipse has a dedicated perspective for debugging. You should see a window asking whether you want to run the Debug perspective. Answer **Yes**, as Eclipse's user interface will then be optimized for debugging.

4. The debugger perspective opens. The top-left window shows all running threads of the current application. The upper-right part shows the variables of the current function and their values. Since the `handler` function does not use local variables, you only see entries for the `this` (the instance variables of `AnimatedText`) and `now` (which is the argument of the handle function) variables.

5. The window containing the code now highlights the line that contains the breakpoint.

6. On the toolbar, find the button with the Resume tooltip. Press it once.

7. You'll find that the program immediately stops on the same breakpoint again. Press the **Resume** button a few times and note that on each call of the `handler` function, it seems it changes the X direction each and every time.

8. To find the cause, in the **Variables** tab, expand the `this` variable. You'll now see the variables of the anonymous `AnimationTimer` instance.

9. Note that it has the `this$0` variable. Expand the `this$0` variable. It contains the variables of the parent of the `AnimationTimer` instance, which is the `AnimatedText` class. Expand its `animatedText` entry. It will show all properties of the `animatedText` object. Find its x property and study its value. It should be larger than 0.

Because `animatedText.x` is larger than the remaining room of the current window, the direction is switched on each call of the handle function and, therefore, the movement stops. On the toolbar, find the button with the Terminate tooltip and press it. Switch back to the Kotlin perspective by finding the Kotlin button on the upper-right of the Eclipse IDE's window.

We can fix the code by resetting the position when changing direction. By doing this, we make sure that the text fits on the window (unless the window itself is too small, but then we are simply out of luck). Let's start by doing this for the X direction first. Find the following two lines:

```
if (animatedText.x < 0.0 || animatedText.x > animationPane.width -
    animatedText.layoutBounds.width)
  directionX = -directionX
```

Replace the preceding code with this:

```
if (animatedText.x < 0.0) {
  animatedText.x = 0.0
  directionX = -directionX
} else if (animatedText.x > animationPane.width - animatedText
          .layoutBounds.width) {
  animatedText.x = animationPane.width - animatedText
                    .layoutBounds.width
  directionX = -directionX
}
```

And do the same for the Y position. Find the following two lines:

```
if (animatedText.y < 0.0 || animatedText.y > animationPane.height)
   directionY = -directionY
```

Replace the preceding code with this:

```
if (animatedText.y < 0.0) {
  animatedText.y = 0.0
  directionY = -directionY
} else if (animatedText.y > animationPane.height) {
  animatedText.y = animationPane.height
  directionY = -directionY
}
```

Run the application again. It should now be much more stable and not get stuck anymore when you resize the window or enter text that does not fit in the remaining space of the window. When the text field does not fit in the window anymore, the text field is moved back, so that it fits (assuming there is enough space).

Summary

In this chapter, we created a small GUI desktop application with a simple animated bouncing text. We started by installing the Kotlin plugin for the Eclipse IDE. We also installed Apache Maven, a very popular build tool for the JVM platform, that uses XML files for its build files. From the Kotlin's team GitHub page, we downloaded a starter kit that contained a Maven build file, that we used as a template for our own project. We imported the project in the Eclipse IDE and because of Eclipse's built-in Maven support, we did not have to configure anything. Eclipse automatically mapped its GUI actions to the correct Maven goals.

Finally, we were ready to write the desktop GUI application. We studied various JavaFX concepts and also learned a new Kotlin feature, extension functions, along the way. When we encountered a bug in the code, we used the debugger to find the cause and fix the problem.

In the next chapter, we will take a good look at Apache Groovy. Groovy, unlike Kotlin, is a dynamically typed language and provides a huge library with additional classes.

11
Groovy

Groovy is one of the earlier alternative JVM-based languages. It was originally built to provide a Python-like experience on the JVM, a marvel and an unheard of idea at the time. At its heart, it is a dynamically typed language, meaning that types do not have to be specified when declaring variables, and method calls are resolved at runtime instead of compile time, which add interesting possibilities that will be hard to implement in static languages, such as Java and Kotlin. Groovy is highly unusual, as the programmer can switch the compiler to a statically typed mode for specific classes. In this mode, the compiler checks the types and method calls at compile time, like the compiler of a statically typed language would have done.

The following topics will be covered in this chapter:

- Installing Groovy
- The GroovyConsole and GroovyShell REPL shells
- Groovy language basics
- Object-oriented programming
- The Groovy Development Kit (GDK)
- Dynamic and static programming
- Quiz

Installing Groovy

Installing Groovy is not much different from the other languages covered so far. Using your favorite browser, visit its home page at `http://groovy-lang.org`:

Here's the installation procedure:

- From the home page, find the **Download** section.
- Click the prominent **Download** button. This will start the download of a ZIP file. At the time of writing, this was `apache-groovy-sdk-2.4.10.zip`.
- Extract the file to a convenient place on your system and add its `bin` directory to your system's path.

Groovy is bundled with two REPL environments: the GUI-based `GroovyConsole` and the text-based `GroovyShell`. Let's validate the installation by launching the GUI application, `GroovyConsole`. After adding the `bin` directory to the PATH of your system, as instructed earlier, launch a new Command Prompt (Windows) or Terminal window (macOS and Linux), and then run the following command:

```
GroovyConsole
```

This will launch the GroovyConsole. This is a convenient program to run small Groovy scripts, and we will use it during this chapter.

GroovyConsole and GroovyShell

As mentioned earlier, Groovy comes with two REPL environments:

- GroovyConsole (desktop GUI application)
- GroovyShell (text-based shell)

Both can be used to try out the snippets in this chapter.

GroovyConsole

GroovyConsole is a user-friendly desktop GUI application that can be used to interactively write and execute Groovy code. We will concentrate on its most commonly used features, but it is worth mentioning that it has some sophisticated features for advanced users as well. To start it, run the `GroovyConsole` launch script on the Command Prompt or Terminal window (macOS and Linux):

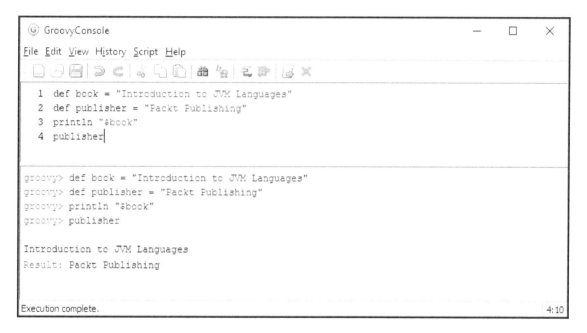

The upper part of the screen is the part where you enter your Groovy code, while the bottom part displays the output and other relevant information.

Since the Groovy language is largely compatible with the Java language syntax, you can also enter the majority of Java statements in both GroovyConsole and GroovyShell. There are some incompatibilities that will be covered in the next chapter, though.

Let's try to enter a snippet of code. In the upper-part of the window, enter the following code:

```
def random = new Random()
random.nextInt(10)
```

Press *Ctrl + R* (*cmd + R* on macOS), or find the button with the Execute Groovy Script tooltip on the toolbar and click it.

In the lower window, you'll see that the executed code is printed and, finally, a number in the **0** to **9** range is printed to the window. GroovyConsole always prints the last value that was evaluated. Run the script a few times. You'll see that each time, the new output is placed below the previous output.

GroovyConsole has quite a lot of customization options. Here's a description of some of the more useful options in the **View** menu:

View submenu item	Description
Clear output	Clears output window (*Ctrl + W* (Windows and Linux) / *cmd + W* (macOS) shortcut)
Auto Clear Output On Run	When enabled, the output window is automatically cleared when running the script. Default is disabled.
Show Script in Output	When enabled (is the default option), the code of the script is printed to the output window.
Show Full Stack Traces	When checked (at default), full stack-traces are printed to the output window when exceptions are thrown. When unchecked, only the bottom entry of the stack-trace is displayed.
Detach output	When enabled (default is disabled), both the input window and output window are placed in separate, independent windows.

Some other notable features are as follows:

- By pressing *Ctrl* + / (*cmd* + / on macOS), you can comment out, or uncomment, the current line or selected lines.
- You can add directories and/or JAR files to its classpath by choosing **Script | Add Jar(s) to the ClassPath** and **Add Directory to the ClassPath**. This is a great feature when you want to dynamically explore an API of an external library or toolkit.
- You can both save and load existing scripts with Groovy code by using the **File | Open** and **File | Save** options.

GroovyShell

GroovyShell is the more traditional text-based REPL shell, which is comparable with the REPL shells that we have seen in Scala, Clojure, and Kotlin. To start it, run the `groovysh` launch script from the `bin` subdirectory:

Most commands are prefixed with a colon `:`; to get a list of commands that are available, enter the `:help` command. There's also the `?` shortcut. You can also use either `:help` or `?` to get more information about a command. For example, for more information about the `:show` command, you can enter `? :show`. To test the `:show` command, enter the following commands one by one:

```
i = 40
j = i + 2
:show variables
```

A list with variables and their values will be shown. The _ entry represents the last evaluated value, which was 42 in our case.

To exit, enter either :exit or :quit (yes, in typical Groovy style, it accepts both commands).

Groovy Language

As the Groovy language is largely compatible with the Java language, it's an easy language to learn for Java developers. Many elements that are required in Java are optional in Groovy. Since Groovy follows the same semantics as Java, we will concentrate mostly on the differences between Java and Groovy in this chapter.

Groovy is all about being compact, comfortable, and flexible. Let's start by looking at a simple class in Java:

```
class Person {
  private String name;
  public String getName() {
    return name;
  }

  public void setName(String name) {
    this.name = name;
  }

  public static void main(String[] args) {
    Person p = new Person();
    p.setName("fooBar");
    System.out.println(p.getName());
  }
}
```

The preceding class will compile and run fine in Groovy; just enter the code in GroovyConsole and execute it. When using Groovy-specific constructs, the same program can be written with much less code, though:

```
class Person {
  String name
  static void main(String[] args) {
    def p = new Person()
    p.name = "fooBar"
    println p.name
  }
}
```

Let's look more closely at the preceding code:

- Groovy does not require semicolons after a line
- Properties can be created by simply specifying the property's type (even this is optional, as we will see soon) and name. Groovy will automatically create a private variable and a public getter/setter method, here called `name`, `getName()`, and `setName()`, respectively.
- Groovy's default access modifier is `public`. Therefore, `static void main()` is the same as Java's `public static void main()`
- When using `def` to declare a variable, no type has to be specified on the left-hand side of the assignment.
- `println` is a built-in function of the Groovy Developers Kit. It's shorter than `System.out.println`.
- Groovy does not even require parenthesis `()` to separate method names with the passed input values. If the compiler is sure that there's no ambiguous situation, it will accept it. In the preceding code, `println p.name` is legal and accepted.
- You can access properties directly by the property name. In the preceding example, Groovy will call the `setName()` and `getName()` methods, respectively.

We will cover many of the previous points in more detail in the coming chapters.

While parentheses are not required by Groovy, this does not automatically mean that it's always a good idea to get rid of them. Many programmers will find code more readable when using parentheses to separate method names and input parameters.

 Groovy's official style guide recommends to omit parentheses in specific situations. This is not covered in this book, but you can consult Groovy's style guide at `http://groovy-lang.org/style-guide.html`.

Object-oriented programming in Groovy

The most important differences between Java and Groovy regarding object-oriented programming, arguably, are as follows:

- Groovy, unlike Java, is a fully object-oriented programming language
- In Groovy, the `public` access modifier is the default access modifier

- Groovy can automatically create getter and setter methods for properties
- Explicitly specifying types for properties, variables, methods, arguments, and return values is optional
- Groovy can automatically create a fully featured POJO
- Immutable classes can be generated automatically

Groovy is fully object oriented

A difference with Java is that Groovy is fully object oriented. It does not create primitive values but always creates objects. Run the following script in `GroovyConsole` (or GroovyShell) to demonstrate this:

```
int i = 555
i.getClass()
```

This will, perhaps surprisingly, print `java.lang.Integer`. While Java would have created a primitive `int` (and therefore, would have refused to compile the preceding code), Groovy always creates an object. Groovy is still fully compatible with Java tools and libraries, however, as it will automatically auto-box primitive values to wrapper classes and vice versa.

Access modifiers

Java applies package-private access when the programmer did not explicitly add an access modifier to a method or a class/instance variable. Groovy, on the other hand, uses `public` as its default access modifier.

 This is an important difference and shows that while most Java code is compatible with Groovy on the syntax level, the resulting behavior may be different and may alter the program in unforeseen ways.

Groovy knows the following access modifiers:

- `public`
- `protected`
- `private`

Since the Groovy team chose `public` as Groovy's default access modifier (when none has been specified explicitly) and Groovy provides no keyword for Java's package-private access level, Groovy does not have built-in support for creating package-private classes or members.

 In rare cases, where it's absolutely necessary to have package-private members, the Groovy Development Kit (GDK) provides the `@PackageScope` annotation, which can be imported from the `groovy.transform` package. This advanced topic is not covered in this book, though.

It has to be noted that Groovy has a long-standing bug regarding the `private` members of a class--it does not respect the `private` access modifier. The following code will not compile in Java (and similar code should not compile or run without errors by any language that respects the `private` access modifier), but runs perfectly fine in the current version of Groovy:

```
public class MainDemoClass {
  public static void main(String[] args) {
    ClassWithSecret secret = new ClassWithSecret();
    System.out.println(secret.privateVariable);
  }
}

class ClassWithSecret {
  private int privateVariable = -1;
}
```

The `privateVariable` instance variable has the `private` access modifier and should not be visible outside its `ClassWithSecret` class. Note that the Groovy compiler correctly marks `privateVariable` as `private` in the generated Java bytecode, so when using the class with a language such as Java, `privateVariable` would not be accessible by the Java code (when not resorting to low-level tricks to access private data, anyway!).

Groovy behaves in a similar manner to a dynamic language, such as Python, in this regard. Python does not really have the notion of public and private members; everything is public. Whether Groovy's lack of support of the private modifier is a bug or a feature has been debated for years.

Adding properties to a class

When not explicitly specifying an access modifier (`public`, `private`, and `protected`) for a property, the Groovy compiler will automatically create a `private` variable with the same name and generate a public getter and setter method for that property:

```
class Person {
    String name
}
```

The preceding code will create the following class:

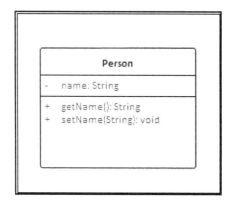

The following will happen when Groovy compiles this code:

- The private variable called `name` will be created
- A public getter method will be created, similar to `public void String getName()`
- A public setter method will be created, similar to `public void setName(String name)`

The compiler only does this when no access modifier has been specified. If you specify one, either `private`, `public`, or `protected`, the compiler assumes that the developer wants to be in full control, and it will just create a variable, leaving it up to you to create the getter and/or setter methods if desired.

Like Kotlin, Groovy does not require calling getters and setters to access properties; you can simply use the property name. Add the following code below the previous example and run it:

```
p = new Person()
p.name = "D. Vader"
println(p.name)
```

The preceding code calls the `getName()` and `setName()` methods that Groovy created automatically. If you want proof that the code does not exploit the `private` access modifier bug that we referred to in the previous section, replace the `Person` class code with the following code:

```
class Person {
  private String personName;
  public void setName(String name) { this.personName = name }
  public String getName() { return this.personName }
}
```

When running the code, you'll see that it runs fine and that it still works, even though the private variable, `name`, does not exist anymore. Groovy really called `setName()` and `getName()`.

Optional types

Groovy fully supports Java's declaration style. In Java, both the variable type and the used instance types are specified, such as the following one:

```
Date date = new Date();
```

In Groovy, it's also possible to declare variables without specifying the variable type. The `def` keyword is used for this:

```
def date = new Date()
```

This is similar to the Java statement, `Object date = new Date()`. The difference is that when declaring it in Groovy using the `def` keyword, all the members of the `java.util.Date` class are still available when using the `date` variable:

```
def date = new Date()
println date.getTime()
```

In Java, the `Object` instance would have to be downcasted back to a `java.util.Date` instance before its members can be used:

```
// Java code, assume java.util.Date was imported
Object date = new Date();
System.out.println(((java.util.Date)date).getTime());
```

As you can see, Groovy's code is much less verbose and more readable, yet again. The main difference between Java and Groovy, in this regard, is that Java checks the available methods at compile time. Java's compiler checks whether the method is available on the variable's reference type. Therefore, it only accepts `getTime()` when the variable is downcasted to the `java.util.Date` class, as the `java.lang.Object` class does not have the `getTime()` method. Groovy, on the other hand, is more relaxed and just tries to call the method at runtime and simply throws an exception if the object does not happen to support the called method and/or its passed parameters. Groovy does not care about the reference variable's type.

It should be noted that a variable that is declared using `def` can hold any type at any time:

```
def d = new Date()
d = new ArrayList()
```

Types are not required for method parameters or their return values, either:

```
def methodWithParameters(parm1, parm2, parm3) {
  // Code...
}
```

The used type for `parm1`, `parm2`, and `parm3` parameter and its return value is `java.lang.Object`.
Also, the use of the `return` statement is optional. The last expression of a function is the return value:

```
int methodWithImplicitReturnValue(int i) {
  i * 10
}
```

Finally, a property can also be defined without explicitly specifying a type:

```
class Sensor {
    def temperature
}
```

In the aforementioned case, a private `java.lang.Object` type variable, `temperature`, is created, along with a `public Object getTemperature()` getter and a `public void setTemperature(Object temperature)` setter.

 It may be a good idea to specify types in most of those cases, anyway, as other developers in your team will be required to read the comments to determine which types are compatible with your methods and properties (you'd always document your code, wouldn't you?).

Automatically creating a fully featured POJO

When prefixing a class name with the `@Canonical` annotation, Groovy generates the following elements if no custom implementations are found in the class itself:

- A parameterless constructor
- A constructor that takes a parameter for each property, in the same order as defined in the code
- A `toString()` implementation that prints all the properties (name and value)
- A `hashCode()` implementation
- An `equals()` implementation

If a class implements either `toString()`, `hashCode()`, and/or `equals()` itself, then it simply skips those methods and continues with the others. So, if you implemented `toString()` in your class yourself, your implementation is the one that will be compiled:

```
import groovy.transform.Canonical
@Canonical
class CanonicalDemo {
    def property1
    def property2
    def property3
}

def demo = new CanonicalDemo("value for property1", "value for
property2")
println("${demo.property1}, ${demo.property2}, ${demo.property3}")
println(demo)
```

We demonstrate a powerful feature of Groovy strings here: they have built-in support for templating. This will be explained in more detail later.

Here's an overview of all the generated properties and methods of the **CanonicalDemo** class:

CanonicalDemo
- property1: Object
- property2: Object
- property3: Object
+ equals(Object): boolean
+ getProperty1(): Object
+ getProperty2(): Object
+ getProperty3(): Object
+ hashCode(): int
+ setProperty1(Object): void
+ setProperty2(Object): void
+ setProperty3(Object): void
+ toString(): String

The preceding code will print `value for property1, value for property2, null` and `CanonicalDemo(value for property1, value for property2, null)`. Note that the generated `toString()` method of the `CanonicalDemo` class only prints the property's values in the order of declaration, but does not print the property names.

As demonstrated, it's not mandatory to provide the values for all the properties. It's also possible to specify values for specific properties only:

```
def demo = new CanonicalDemo(property1:"value 1", property3: "value3")
```

If you only are interested in the `hashCode()` and `equals()` implementations and don't want `toString()` and/or the constructors, you can use the `@EqualsAndHashCode` annotation instead. Likewise, there's the `@ToString` annotation if you only want the `toString()` implementation, and finally, there's the `@TupleConstructor` annotation that can be used when you are only interested in the constructors. Some of those annotations have optional parameters to offer more fine-grained control. This topic is not covered further in this book, but it can be looked up in the documentation.

> All the aforementioned annotations have to be imported from the `groovy.transform` package.

Creating immutable classes

As we have seen in earlier chapters, immutable classes are a cornerstone of functional programming. Groovy offers a lot of features to aid in write code in functional programming style. Mutable classes are a well-known source of bugs, so it could be a good idea to make them immutable even if you don't plan to do much functional programming in Groovy. Use the `@Immutable` annotation from the `groovy.transform` package to make a class immutable:

```
import groovy.transform.Immutable

@Immutable
class Person {
  String name
}
```

Similar to the the `@Canonical` annotation, this annotation tells the compiler to generate the following:

- An argument-less constructor
- A constructor that can take values for each property
- The `hashCode()` implementation
- The `equals()` implementation
- The `toString()` implementation

Unique for @Immutable is that it also:

- Makes the class final, it cannot be inherited by other classes.
- Checks that all types of properties are indeed likely to be immutable. It raises an exception when it thinks that a property is not immutable or does not support immutability at all.
- It will make sure that all setter methods will raise an exception.

If the class contains one or more properties of your own class types, those classes must be annotated with @Immutable as well; otherwise, Groovy will refuse to compile the class. Let's look at an example:

```
import groovy.transform.Immutable

class Person {
  public final String name
  public Person(String name) { this.name = name }
}

@Immutable
class Demo {
  // WILL NOT RUN
  Person person = new Person("test")
}

def d = new Demo()
```

Groovy will refuse to run the preceding code because it does not know whether the Person class is truly immutable:

```
java.lang.RuntimeException: @Immutable processor doesn't know how to handle
field 'person' of type 'Person' while constructing class Demo.
```

To make this code run, replace @Immutable with the following line:

```
@Immutable(knownImmutableClasses=[Person])

class Demo {
  ...
}
```

Groovy will now trust your instincts and believes that it can safely mark this class as immutable. It's also possible to specify a property name instead of a class name:

```
@Immutable(knownImmutables=["person"])
```

This is useful when you want to use `def person = new Person()` instead of `Person person = new Person()`

 Of course, the code would have been easier to understand and maintain if the `@Immutable` annotation were simply added to the `Person` class itself. In such a case, Groovy would have detected this itself and no manual adjustments would have been required in the `Demo` class.

Groovy Development Kit (GDK)

Groovy comes with a large library of classes that can be used to make the life of a developer easier. Some offer new features; the others are wrappers around existing Java Class Library classes to make them easier to use or enhance their functionalities. In this section, we will be looking at some important classes and types of Groovy's runtime library, sometimes called the **Groovy Development Kit** (**GDK**), which is installed as part of your Groovy installation.

Groovy Strings (GStrings)

Groovy offers its own variant of the `java.lang.String` class: `groovy.lang.GString`. Whenever you create a string with double quotes, Groovy looks whether a feature of `GString` is used. If that's the case, then it creates a `GString`; otherwise, it creates an ordinary `java.lang.String` instance:

```
def s = "this is an ordinary java.lang.String instance";
```

The preceding string does not make use of Groovy features, so Groovy creates a normal `java.lang.String`. One of the most useful features of `GStrings` is that it has built-in support for templates:

```
def who = "you"
def msg = "Happy birthday to $who"
```

When running the preceding snippet, `msg` contains `Happy birthday to you`. This creates a `GString`, as we now made use of variables. When you want to use templating variables as part of a whole word, then brackets have to be added:

```
def who2 = "packtpub"
def msg2 = "Please visit ${who2}.com"
```

The preceding example would crash when not using brackets, as `who2` points to a `java.lang.String` instance, which does not have a property called `com`.

If you want to use the dollar sign in the string, one of the possibilities would be to escape the `$` with a backslash: `"US\$ 100"`, this results in the string `US$100`. Another option would be to create a Java string. In Groovy, this is done by using single quotes:

```
def javaString = 'This is a Java string, even though it has ${who}'
```

The preceding code will create a `java.lang.String` and `${variable}` will not have been replaced with any variable. This is different to Java. Java uses single quotes for literal `char` values.

When the declared type is `char` (or its wrapper class, `java.lang.Character`), Groovy still creates a `java.lang.Character` instance (remember that Groovy never creates primitive values):

```
char c = 'C'
c.class
```

The preceding snippet will evaluate to `java.lang.Character`. Note that `char c = "C"` (using double quotes) will also create a `java.lang.Character` instance, while this would result in a compile error on the Java language compiler.

Finally, like many modern languages, Groovy supports multiline strings, both for `GString` and Java strings:

```
def longMsg = """
  Happy birthday
  to ${who}
"""
```

Multiline `GString` instances support variables, just like their single-line version. If you want a multiline Java string, just use three single quotes:

```
def longJavaMsg = '''
  Another long
  message
'''
```

Finally, it should be noted that strings can be compared by using the `==` or `!=` operator in Groovy. Groovy calls the `equals()` method to compare the content:

```
def s1 = "hello"
def s2 = 'hello'
println(s1 == s2)
```

In this case, both strings are `java.lang.String` instances (because no GString features were used in `s1`). When running above's code, `true` is printed to the console. Even if `s1` would have been a GString instance that contained `"hello"`, it would still have printed `true`.

Collections

Regarding collections, Groovy brings a Python-like experience to the JVM. It has built-in support for the most important collections of the Java Class Library, while extending functionality by adding additional features to them. In this topic, we will explore the following:

- Lists
- Maps

 A big difference from Java is that collections in Groovy do not support generics. While the Java syntax for generics is supported by Groovy's parser, Groovy will not enforce generics in any way.

Lists

To create a list, which will be a `java.util.ArrayList` instance, you can simply use brackets:

```
def list = [10, 20, 30, 40, 50]
```

To retrieve one item, you can add the index between brackets:

```
println list[1]
```

This returns `20`. In the preceding example, this is exactly the same as using `list.get(1)`. There's a difference, however: when using brackets, you'll get `null` as the result when the index is out of range, while the `get()` method will throw an `IndexOutOfBoundsException` exception when the index is too small or too large.

When using brackets, you can look at the last items by specifying a negative index. -1 represents the last item, -2 the second last, and so forth. Consider the following example:

```
println list[-4]
```

The preceding code returns 20. Note that the `get()` method does not support negative indexes; it will throw `IndexOutOfBoundsException`.

To slice the list, you can use Groovy's subscript operator `..` (two dots):

```
println list[1..2]
```

Both the specified indexes are inclusive, so this will return `[20, 30]`.
It's also possible to return a selection of indexes:

```
println list[0,3]
```

This returns `[10, 40]`. Both the approaches can even be combined:

```
println list[0..2, 4, 3]
```

This returns `[10, 20, 30, 50, 40]`.

In true dynamic programming style, an empty list evaluates to `false`, while a list with elements evaluates to `true`. This can be used to test whether the list is empty:

```
def emptyList = []
if (!emptyList) {
  println("List is not empty")
}
```

The preceding code will print nothing. Groovy added functional programming features to Java collection classes long before Java 8 appeared. To iterate through collections, a closure can be specified:

```
list.each({
  def bar = "X" * it
  println "${bar} ${it}"
})
```

The closure is called for each item. The `it` variable contains the value of the current element. In the closure, the `bar` variable is created. It contains X, which is repeated for every iterated value. The output is as follows:

```
XXXXXXXXXX 10
XXXXXXXXXXXXXXXXXXXX 20
XXXXXXXXXXXXXXXXXXXXXXXXXXXXXX 30
XXXXXXXXXXXXXXXXXXXXXXXXXXXXXXXXXXXXXXXX 40
XXXXXXXXXXXXXXXXXXXXXXXXXXXXXXXXXXXXXXXXXXXXXXXXXXXX 50
```

Groovy adds some very convenient methods to the `java.util.Collection` interface (or other interfaces that are inherited by the `Collection` interface). The `Collection` interface is inherited by most collection classes, including `java.util.ArrayList`. Here's a table with some of them:

Method name	Description	Example
`any(Closure)`	Returns `true` if the closure returned `true` for at least one item in the list.	`list.any { it > 20 }` Returns: `true`
`every(Closure)`	Returns `true` if closure returned `true` for all the items, otherwise `false`.	`list.every { it < 50 }` Returns: `false`
`find(Closure)`	Closure is called for each entry; when it returns `true`, the iteration stops. Returns found item or `null` when no entry matches.	`list.find { it == 30}` Returns: 30
`findAll(Closure)`	Like `find()`, but does not stop when closure returns `true`.	`list.findAll { it > 30 }` Returns: [40, 50]
`join(String)`	Joins entries in a String with specified character as separator.	`list.join("/")` Returns: 10/20/30/40/50
`min()`	Returns the smallest item.	`list.min()` Returns: 10
`max()`	Returns the largest item.	`list.max()` Returns: 50
`sum()`	Returns the sum of all the items.	`list.sum()` Returns: 150

Maps

Maps are specified by using brackets with key/value pairs:

```
def map = [ key1: "value1", "key2": "value2" ]
```

The default data type for a key is string, so it is not mandatory to use quotes for specifying keys. This can be problematic when you want to add a key that is based on a variable, or a different type than string. In those cases, you'll have to add the key using parentheses `()`:

```
def key1 = "whateverKey"
def otherMap = [ (key1): "whateverValue"]
```

To create an empty map, you'll have to use the following notation:

```
def emptyMap = [:]
```

You can read from and write to a map using brackets:

```
map["key1"] = "anotherValue1"
println map["key1"]
```

Groovy treats maps like a POJO. So, to retrieve a key-value pair, you can use the dot notation to read from and write to a map:

```
map.key1 = "yetAnotherValue1"
println(map.key1)
```

This only works when the key is a String, which is a valid Java identifier. If either one is not the case, you'll have to use the brackets or the `get` method:

```
map[30] = "thirty"
println(map.get(30))
```

Since `30` is not a string, it cannot be a valid Java identifier and either the map's `get()` method or the bracket notation has to be used to access it.

Since the `Map` interface inherits the `Collection` interface, the same methods as described by the list are available to a map. The difference is that closures get a `MapEntry` object that contains the `key` and `value` properties to obtain either the key or value of each entry.

Let's look at some examples to iterate through key-value pairs:

```
map.each({
  println("$it.key --> $it.value")
})
```

It's also possible to use key-value pairs in a closure. You'll have to add two parameters to the closure:

```
map.find({ k, v -> k =="key2" && v == "value2" })
```

In the preceding example, the `k` and `v` parameters represent the key and value of each entry of the map.

Dynamic and static programming

A major difference between statically typed and dynamically typed programming languages is that for the former, the compiler resolves method calls and compiles references in the compiled program (in the case of a JVM language in the generated Java byecode), while in a dynamic programming language such as Groovy, Clojure, and Python, these decisions are taken while running the program.

As always in life, both the approaches have their own advantages and disadvantages:

Programming Style	Advantages	Disadvantages
Static	• Applications run fast • Many trivial errors are caught in the compile phase • Top-notch IDE support, offering excellent refactoring tools that increase productivity a lot	• Compilation phase generally takes up considerable time • Often requires writing of more code to satisfy the compiler
Dynamic	• Typically requires less code to be written • Compilation phase is generally very fast • Offers meta-programming tricks	• Applications often perform less well. • Most errors are detected at runtime only. Trivial errors could be hidden for a long time, until they occur one day. • Requires writing of code to validate whether valid parameter types were passed to a function. • IDE support is not among the best, as it is much harder to implement well.

When calling a method in a dynamic language such as Groovy and Clojure, but also non-JVM languages such as JavaScript, Python, and Ruby, at runtime it is determined whether the object instance has that method, and if it has it, whether the passed arguments are valid. Whereas, in a static programming language such as Java, Scala, and Kotlin, but also languages such as C, C#, C++, and modern Visual Basic, this is done once by the compiler, and at runtime, the compiled instructions are simply executed directly.

You may wonder what might be the advantage of resolving method calls and the accessing of properties at runtime, as it will be rather obvious that this takes up at least some processing power while running the application. The answer is, it makes meta-programming possible and very convenient to implement. We will cover meta-programming in the next section.

Meta programming

To understand the meta programming concept, let's create a small class:

```
class MetaProgrammingDemo {
}

def demo = new MetaProgrammingDemo()
// Next line throws an exception!
demo.nonExistingProperty = "some value"
println(demo.nonExistingProperty)
```

As expected, when running this code, an exception is thrown when the last line is executed by the JVM:

```
groovy.lang.MissingPropertyException: No such property: nonExistingProperty
for class: MetaProgrammingDemo
```

Now add the following methods inside the MetaProgrammingDemo class:

```
def propertyMissing(String name) {
  println("Non-existent property '$name' was read")
  return -1
}

def propertyMissing(String name, args) {
  println("Non-existent property '$name' was written to: '$args'")
}
```

When you now run the code, the JVM no longer throws an exception! It prints the following to the console, instead:

```
Non-existent property 'nonExistingProperty' was written to: 'some value'
Non-existent property 'nonExistingProperty' was read
-1
```

Note that the value that was read, is completely different than the value that the code thought it was writing to the property. This is because the `-1` return value was hard-coded. The first `propertyMissing(String name)` method is called when a non-existent property is read, while the `propertyMissing(String name, args)` method is called when code tries to set a value to a non-existent property.

When accessing any property in Groovy code, either for reading and writing, Groovy does the following at runtime:

1. If the corresponding property getter/setter method exists, it is called.
2. If no getter/setter exists, it looks for a instance or class variable and accesses it when found.
3. If the variable does not exist, it looks for the `propertyMissing` method; if found, it is called.
4. If all else fails, it throws the `groovy.lang.MissingPropertyException` exception.

> In reality, the flow is more complex than depicted, as Groovy offers more ways to work with meta-programming than discussed in this chapter.

Dynamically tricking code to let it think that a property exists is something that would be next to impossible to implement in a statically typed language. It may not be obvious right now why and when this technique would be useful. In the next chapter, we will be using Groovy's XML builder that was implemented heavily using metaprogramming, and this will probably give you some ideas on how to use this powerful technique in your own classes.

We only covered properties, for methods a similar technique is available. Add the following method to the `MetaProgrammingDemo` class:

```
def methodMissing(String name, args) {
  println("Non-existent method '$name' was called with '$args'
          parameters")
}
```

Finally, add the following code to the existing test code:

```
demo.methodThatDoesNotExist(1000, "demo")
```

The following additional output is written to the console when running the code:

Non-existent method 'methodThatDoesNotExist' was called with '[1000, demo]'
parameters

 This is a trick that is specific to Groovy. When using this class with a different JVM language, the JVM will not automatically redirect unknown property read/write statements to the `missingProperty()` methods or unknown method calls to `missingMethod()`.

Static programming in Groovy

To turn the compiler in static programming mode for a specific class or method, you can add the `@TypeChecked` annotation, after importing it from the `groovy.transform` package:

```
import groovy.transform.TypeChecked

@TypeChecked
class TypeCheckedClass {
}
```

When applied on a class, the compiler does a lot of checks that a compiler of a normal statically typed language would do and compile direct references to methods and properties, instead of letting the code determine at runtime which method must be called. This code in the application will run a bit faster, although in reality this will probably only be really noticeable when it is called many times in a tight loop, or by many threads simultaneously.

When a class uses the `@TypeChecked` annotation, it can no longer rely on dynamic programming tricks such as, metaprogramming. The following code will fail to compile:

```
import groovy.transform.TypeChecked

@TypeChecked
class Demo {
  static void main(String[] args) {
    def d = new Demo()
    // WILL FAIL TO COMPILE
    d.thisMethodDoesNotExist()
  }
```

```
    def methodMissing(String name, args) {
      println("Method '$name' was called")
    }
  }
```

When running this code in `GroovyConsole` (which still compiles the code under the hood, before running it), it produces the following compile-time error:

```
[Static type checking] - Cannot find matching method
Demo#thisMethodDoesNotExist(). Please check if the declared type is right
and if the method exists.
```

Since the compiler cannot predict whether or not the `methodMissing()` will support the `thisMethodDoesNotExist()` call (it could throw an exception, or only handle specific method names), the compiler refuses to compile this code. To solve this problem, you could remove the `@TypeChecked` annotation from the `Demo` class completely. Luckily, there's also a different option, you can tell the compiler's type checker to skip certain methods. Add the following annotation above the `static void main(String[] args)` line:

```
@TypeChecked(groovy.transform.TypeCheckingMode.SKIP)
static void main(String[] args) {
   ...
}
```

The type checker now understands that it should not check the `main()` method. Of course, if you have to put this above many methods in a class, you probably don't need `@TypeChecked` for this whole class. It's also possible to use the `@TypeChecked` annotation on certain methods only:

```
class Demo2 {
  def static void main(String[] args) {
    def d = new Demo()
    d.typeCheckedDemoMethod()
  }

  @TypeChecked
  def typeCheckedDemoMethod() {
    // Statically typed implementation code here...
  }
}
```

Quiz

1. Groovy is largely compatible with the Java language. Does this mean that Groovy compiles compatible Java code in exactly the same way as the Java compiler, without any side effects?

   a) Yes, the Java compiler and Groovy compiler produce exactly the same Java bytecode. The resulting class will always behave exactly the same.

   b) No, Java and Groovy are not compatible at the syntax level at all.

   c) No, Groovy crashes when encountering Java's primitive data types.

   d) No, Groovy is mostly compatible with the Java language syntax, but due to different design choices by the Groovy team, the class may not behave exactly the same as the same class that was compiled by a Java compiler.

2. What will be the content of the `msg1` variable?

   ```
   def name1 = 'reader'
   def msg1 = "hello, $name1"
   ```

   a) `"hello, reader"`

   b) `"hello, $name"`

   c) This program will throw an exception

   d) None of the above

3. What will be the content of the `msg2` variable?

   ```
   def name2 = "reader"
   def msg2 = 'hello, $name2'
   ```

   a) `"hello, reader"`

   b) `"hello, $name"`

   c) This program will throw an exception

   d) None of the above

4. What will be the data type of `longValue`?

    ```
    long longValue = 999
    ```

    a) Primitive long
    b) `groovy.lang.Long`
    c) `java.lang.Long`
    d) Other

5. Is the following true: An advantage of a dynamic language is that the generated code always runs faster than similar code compiled in a static language.

    a) Yes

    b) No

Summary

In this chapter, you were introduced to Groovy, a popular dynamic language on the JVM. We downloaded and installed it and explored its two REPL shells, GroovyConsole (desktop GUI application) and GroovyShell (text-based shell). We discovered that while Java and Groovy syntax are (for the most part) compatible, Groovy code can be much more compact, as many elements that are required in Java are optional in Groovy. We tried various annotations that generate code automatically on the fly, including annotations that generate valid implementations for the `toString()`, `equals()` and `hashCode()` methods, but also generate complete constructors. We briefly explored the **Groovy Development Kit (GDK)** and looked at the differences between dynamic programming and static programming and discovered that Groovy supports both methods.

In the next chapter, we will create a simple web service that generates XML and consumes data from a database by using the **Java Database Connectivity (JDBC)** interface. We will use our new Groovy knowledge, but also explore more classes from the GDK.

12
Groovy Programming

We are going to build a simple web service in Groovy using the popular Vert.x microservice framework. Our program will make use of the H2 **Database Management System** (**DBMS**), a database system that is fully written in Java. We will use the **Java Database Connectivity** (**JDBC**) standard to interact with H2. XML will be generated using Groovy's MarkupBuilder, a class that is offered in the **Groovy Development Kit** (**GDK**), Groovy's runtime library.

This time, we will not use an external build tool responsible for building the project; instead, we'll let the Eclipse IDE handle this job for us. We will be needing some external dependencies (to use the mentioned H2 and Vert.x open source projects) and will use Apache Ivy for this. The Eclipse IDE does not come with Groovy support out of the box, so we need to install a plugin for this language as well. The following topics will be covered in this chapter:

- Installing the Groovy Eclipse plugin
- Apache Ivy and IvyDE plugin for Eclipse
- Creating and configuring the Groovy project
- Java Database Connectivity (JDBC)
- Generating XML using MarkupBuilder
- The Vert.x microservice platform

Installing the Groovy Eclipse plugin

Groovy Eclipse, the plugin that adds Groovy support to Eclipse IDE, is on the Eclipse Marketplace, but at the time of writing this book, that version was really out of date. We will therefore install the plugin manually from the Groovy Eclipse team's own server. Visit the project's GitHub page to find the correct download link: `https://github.com/groovy /groovy-eclipse/wiki`

Find the version of Eclipse IDE that you are running by choosing Help | About from its menu bar. Then, in the GitHub page, scroll down to the Releases section and look for a released version. If there's no stable release for your version of Eclipse IDE, then find the Snapshot Builds section and look there for your installed Eclipse IDE version. At the time of writing this book, no stable release was available for my installed release of Eclipse Neon (4.6), so I had to resort to a snapshot build:

 If there's no stable release available for your Eclipse IDE (yet), or the development version is not stable enough, you can download an older version of Eclipse and use that for your Groovy development until a stable version is released for your version of Eclipse.

To install your chosen version in Eclipse IDE:

1. Copy the **Release Update Site URL** of the corresponding version from the GitHub page to the clipboard.
2. In Eclipse IDE, choose **Help | Install New Software....**

3. On the **Available Software** dialog, click the **Add** button next to the **Work with** text field.

4. Enter `Groovy Eclipse` as the name and paste the URL in the **Location** field. Click on **OK**:

5. The **Available Software** dialog now displays the found packages. Check the **Groovy-Eclipse (required)** option and click the **Next** button.

6. You may see a dialog warning that the selection was modified; it added Groovy compilers to the selection. Acknowledge that this is OK by pressing **Next**. Also, accept the license if you agree with its terms. Click **Finish** to install the plugin.

7. When the Eclipse IDE asks to restart, choose **Yes**.

Switching to Java perspective

The Groovy Eclipse plugin does not add a dedicated Groovy perspective to Eclipse IDE's user interface. Instead, like Clojure's Counterclockwise plugin, it uses the normal Java perspective. On the toolbar on the upper right-hand side of the screen, click the Java perspective button:

Alternatively, find the button with the **Open Perspective** tool tip and choose the **Java (default)** option:

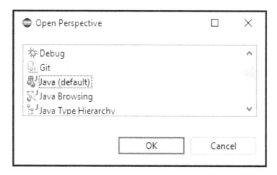

Apache Ivy and IvyDE

Unlike the other languages we have covered so far, we are not going to use a separate build tool to build the project. We'll be using Eclipse IDE's built-in build capabilities, which internally are based on Apache Ant. Ant was the first popular build tool that was dedicated to the JVM. During the course of the project, we will let Eclipse IDE take care of the build process.

 Groovy is well-supported by many popular (and even some other, less popular) JVM-based build tools. If you need more control than the build process of your IDE provides, Gradle and Maven are both very good choices for building your Groovy-based projects.

To build the web-service example that accesses a database, we need several external dependencies:

- The Vert.x framework to build microservices
- A local Database management system (DBMS), including the JDBC driver

We could download the needed files from various sites, install them in the correct directory, and manually adjust the JVM class path, but this would be a lot of work, as the dependencies may themselves depend on other external libraries. Groovy has a built-in dependency manager called Grape, but it has issues when using it within Groovy Eclipse.

Therefore, we will be using Apache Ivy for our dependency management in this chapter. Ivy is a dependency manager (not a build tool), which is compatible with Maven repositories and knows the most popular servers that host repositories. Although we will not be needing this in our example, if you need dependencies from a custom server that Ivy does not support out of the box, you can easily add the definition of the server yourself. Ivy is often used with the Apache Ant build tool, which does not have dependency management features of its own but Ivy is a fully standalone, independent product.

We will need to install a plugin in Eclipse IDE to add Ivy support.

Installing Apache IvyDE plugin for Eclipse IDE

To install the Apache IvyDE plugin, follow these instructions:

1. From the menu bar, choose **Help** | **Eclipse Marketplace...**.
2. Search for `Ivy`. Look for the **Apache IvyDE** entry, which credits the **Apache Software Foundation**. Click its **Install** button:

Apache IvyDE™

Apache IvyDE™ is the Eclipse plugin which integrates Apache Ivy's dependency management into Eclipse. It lets you manage your dependencies declared in an ivy.xml... **more info**

by Apache Software Foundation, Apache 2.0

apache ivy ivyde

3. Follow the prompts. You'll get a warning that the code was not signed; accept this if you want to use the plugin. Finally, Eclipse asks for a restart. Click **Yes** to restart.

The Apache IvyDE plugin is now installed and ready for action.

Creating and configuring the project

Now that we have installed all required plugins in Eclipse IDE, we can create the project. We will also define and fetch the first external dependency of the project. The following subjects will be covered:

- Creating a new Groovy Eclipse project
- Creating an `ivy.xml` file for Ivy

Creating a new Groovy Eclipse project

To create a Groovy-based project in Eclipse:

1. Right-click an empty spot in the Package Explorer and choose **New | Other....**
2. In the **Select a wizard** dialog, select **Groovy | Groovy Project** and click **Next**.
3. Enter GroovyWebservice as the project name.
4. Click **Finish** to generate the project.

Groovy Eclipse generates a bare-bones project. It does not contain any example file, so let's create one to validate the installation:

1. Right-click the **(default package)** entry from the project's src directory and choose **New | Other....**
2. In the **Select a wizard** dialog, select **Groovy | Groovy Class** and click **Next**.
3. Enter webservice as the package name and Main as the class name.
4. Click **Finish** to generate the class.

Again, Groovy Eclipse generates a rather minimalistic class:

```
package webservice

class Main {
}
```

Let's add a simple main() method to verify that Groovy Eclipse is properly configured to compile and run the project. Add the following method to the Main class:

```
static void main(String[] args) {
  println("Project is running fine!")
}
```

Press *Ctrl + F11* (*cmd + F11* on macOS), or find the **Run** icon on the toolbar and click it.

It is possible that you'll get an error stating that a non-existent project was referenced, or that a previous project runs instead of the expected project. This is caused because Groovy Eclipse currently does not create a **Run Configuration** automatically when initializing the project. If you have this issue, you can fix it by choosing **Run | Run Configurations...** from Eclipse IDE's menu bar. In the list with configurations, find the Groovy Script entry and right-click it and select **New**. A configuration is generated. Close the window by selecting the **Run** button. Eclipse IDE will now associate this configuration with the project and you should now see the message in the console.

Creating an ivy.xml file for Ivy

We'll need to create a simple XML file that will contain the dependency information. The IvyDE plugin will fetch the dependencies using Apache Ivy and add them to the correct ClassPaths. To create the ivy.xml file:

1. Right-click the project name and choose **New | Other**....
2. Choose **IvyDE | Ivy File** and click **Next**.
3. Press the **Browse** button next to **Container** and select the **Webservice** project.
4. Click **Finish** to generate the file.

An ivy.xml file is now created. It will not contain dependencies, so let's add the first one.

We'll be using the popular H2 file-based database system in this example. For now, we will concentrate on fetching the required dependencies for the H2 database system. In the next section, we'll explain more about H2 and database connectivity using the JVM in general.

Let's search for the H2 database on Maven's **The Central Repository** website, a widely used repository. In your favorite web browser, visit the URL: http://search.maven.org

In the search bar, enter `h2` and press *Enter*:

A list with the found dependencies should appear. Look for the `com.h2database` entry, which should usually be one of the first entries, and click its version number under the **Latest Version** column. In my case, it was 1.4.195.

You should now see a page with various build tools. Those of you who have read the previous chapters will see familiar names such as Gradle, Scala SBT, Leiningen, and Maven. To retrieve the required Ivy code, do the following:

1. Click the **Apache Ivy** entry; it should expand and reveal the required Ivy XML entry.
2. Copy and paste the XML entry to the clipboard.
3. In Eclipse, open the `ivy.xml` file that we generated earlier.
4. Paste the line as the last element within the `<ivy-module>` and `</ivy-module>` tags.

In my case, the `ivy.xml` file now looks like this (I have cut the huge license terms comments for brevity):

```
<ivy-module version="2.0"
  xmlns:xsi="http://www.w3.org/2001/XMLSchema-instance"
  xsi:noNamespaceSchemaLocation="http://ant.apache.org/ivy/
                          schemas/ivy.xsd">
  <info
    organisation=""
```

```
        module=""
        status="integration">
    </info>
    <dependency org="com.h2database" name="h2" rev="1.4.194" />
</ivy-module>
```

Your version number may be different than the one listed here.

To fetch the dependencies and add them to the **ClassPath**, perform the following steps:

1. Right-click on the `ivy.xml` file and choose **Add Ivy Library...**:

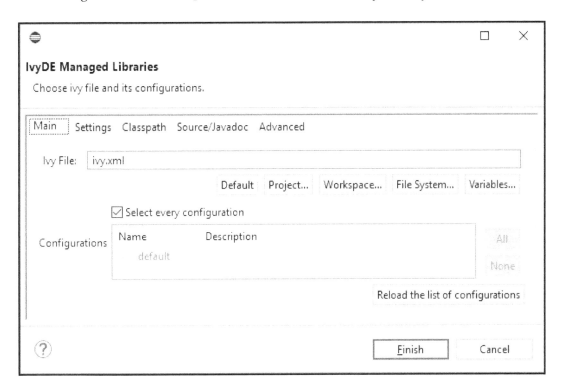

2. In the **IvyDE Managed Libraries** dialog, simply click **Finish**.

Apache Ivy will fetch the required H2 DBMS files from the correct repositories and add all the files to the project's **ClassPath**.

Java Database Connectivity (JDBC)

The **Java Database Connectivity** (**JDBC**) standard is a standard that makes it possible to access **Database management system** (**DBMS**) servers in JVM applications. Popular examples of popular, enterprise-ready DBMS servers are:

- Oracle Database
- Oracle MySQL
- MariaDB
- Microsoft SQL Server
- IBM DB2
- PostgreSQL

To connect a JVM application to a DBMS server using JDBC, a custom JDBC driver for that database system is required. The application will load the JDBC driver and provide a connection string that usually contains the server's hostname, port, and credentials. The JDBC system will ensure that the proper driver is initialized correctly and that the driver will connect to the database and return a `Connection` object that the application will use to communicate with the database.

 Those of you who are familiar with Microsoft development environments can compare JDBC with the ADO.NET or the ODBC standards.

The JDBC standard does not require the DBMS server itself to be implemented in Java or JVM, although the JDBC driver itself will usually have been written in Java (or possibly any other JVM language). The JDBC standard allows the JDBC driver to make use of native (platform-specific) drivers or libraries. JDBC drivers that make use of native software may require more complicated installation procedures and may not be compatible with all JVM-compatible platforms.

There are four types of JDBC drivers:

Type	Description
Type 1: JDBC-ODBC bridge	JDBC driver that uses an ODBC-based driver under the hood to communicate with a database server.
Type 2: Native API driver	JDBC driver that uses locally installed native drivers to communicate with the database server.
Type 3: Network-Protocol	JDBC driver that connects to a middle tier (middleware) that manages the database connection. The middleware often runs on a separate server. The logic that communicates with the database is implemented in the middle tier; therefore, no database-specific drivers are required on the client.
Type 4: Database-Protocol driver	A JDBC driver that is fully implemented in Java (or an other JVM language) and is therefore platform independent. Drivers of this type connect directly to the database server.

A JDBC driver can often be installed as part of the JVM application by simply placing the files on the JVM's application class path. In some situations, the drivers have to be installed separately from the JVM application. This will often be the case when the driver requires platform-specific software to be installed along with the driver, or when it's simply dictated by its license terms. Database vendors, or open source teams, are expected to create and maintain JDBC drivers for their products themselves. Because of Java's huge market influence, JDBC drivers are available for most popular DBMS systems. Even Microsoft offers a free JDBC driver for their Microsoft SQL Server product line.

The popular SQL query language is used to create, update, and delete records (also known as CRUD actions). Most database systems support creating new databases and/or creating new, or updating existing, tables, indexes, views, and so forth via SQL as well. The SQL query language is standardized to a large degree, so if you are careful, you can write applications that work with a variety of different database servers. Since each database offers its own proprietary extensions to the SQL language (including custom function names, special data types, and custom syntax for queries), this is actually hard to accomplish in practice. A database system is free to decide which SQL statements and features it will support; this is not dictated by the JDBC standard.

H2 database

In this chapter, we will be using the H2 database. H2 is a relatively small, self-contained, and open source DBMS system that is fully written in Java. It is a database system that writes files to the local filesystem or even keeps full databases in memory only. It does not require a full installation procedure, unlike products such as MySQL and PostgreSQL, and similarly, databases created by H2 do not require a lot of maintenance. Just by adding some JAR files to the ClassPath, the JVM application has full access to both the H2 database system and its type 4 JDBC driver.

 H2 can be compared, in a way, to the popular public domain SQLite database. While open source wrappers and even JDBC drivers are available for SQLite, H2 is more convenient to use in JVM languages such as Groovy, as H2 was fully written with the JVM in mind.

A self-contained database system such as H2 is suited especially well for single-user applications. It is probably not the best choice for multithreaded applications that need to serve hundreds of users that read and write to the database simultaneously, require storing gigabytes of data, or require other enterprise-grade reliability and/or features. Do not underestimate the power of a database system like H2, however; it provides an option to run a database server, for instance, which can be handy if multiple applications need access to the same database, and even advanced clustering options are available. Also, a command-line driven tool is available to query, analyze, and backup or restore the database from the convenience of the operating system's command-line interface.

It is advisable to keep the H2 database project's homepage handy for reference while reading this chapter: `http://www.h2database.com`

Creating an in-memory database

In this project, we will create a memory-only database that is destroyed immediately after the application ends. This is convenient in the prototype stage, as we don't have the hassle with manually upgrading data in the database when we change the database structure. Another advantage is that we don't need to keep track of the path where we will store the database permanently.

To connect to a database with JDBC, a connection string has to be provided. The connection string tells JDBC which driver to use, the location of the database, and (often) the required credentials to use when accessing the database. It can also contain DBMS-specific configuration options.

 In the older versions of JDBC, it was required to manually register the JDBC driver with code. Nowadays, modern JDBC drivers register themselves automatically, and placing the JAR files of the driver in the application's class path is usually enough to make them available for the application.

In this example, we will be using H2's embedded mode, which means that we embed the complete H2 database system in our application and do not require an external server application to be running at the same time. We will create an in-memory database that is alive until the application is closed. The H2 connection string that must be supplied to JDBC for this type of H2 database looks as follows:

```
String connectionString = "jdbc:h2:mem:blogs;DB_CLOSE_DELAY=-1"
```

The connection string is a colon-separated list. Let's look at all the items on the connection string:

- The first entry of a JDBC connection string is always `jdbc`.
- The second entry is the name that identifies the database system. The JDBC drivers register their names during the JDBC driver loading process. Since Ivy added the H2 JDBC driver to the project's ClassPath, the `h2` name will be recognized by the JDBC system.
- The third entry is the name of the database. H2 does not always require in-memory databases to have a name but, as we will see in the next entry, in our use case, this is actually required.
- The fourth entry is an option that tells H2 to keep the database in memory even when there are no active connections. Usually, H2 deletes in-memory databases that have no active connections, but we want to have access to the database as long as the application runs. We do this by specifying the `DB_CLOSE_DELAY=-1` option.

Only the first two elements in the connection strings are standard. Other elements in a connection string are usually different for different JDBC drivers.

Time to write some code. In the Eclipse IDE, open the `Main.groovy` file. We will create a method to open a new database connection. Place the method inside the body of the `Main` class:

```
def createDatabaseConnection() {
  def connection = DriverManager.getConnection("jdbc:h2:mem:test;
                                   DB_CLOSE_DELAY=-1")

  return connection
}
```

 Use the Eclipse IDE's *Ctrl* + Space bar feature when typing the `DriverManager` class name so that the required import statement for `java.sql.DriverManager` is automatically written for you.

The `connection` variable holds the object that points to the created database connection and can be used to issue commands to the database system. It's fully qualified type name will be `java.sql.Connection`, which is a Java interface, but since we are writing Groovy code, we don't need to specify its type. `DriverManager` is a class provided by the JDBC system and knows how to access the registered JDBC drivers.

In our case, we use an embedded database system, and H2 will create a new temporary in-memory database when H2's JDBC driver passes the connection string to the embedded H2 database engine. The database will automatically be destroyed once the application is closed because we specified the `DB_CLOSE_DELAY=-1` option in the connection string.

We started the chapter by creating a console-based application; we will change the implementation to a web-service later. So, let's rewrite the existing `main()` method and let it call the `createDatabaseConnection()` method that we just created:

```
static void main(String[] args) {
  def app = new Main()
  def connection = app.createDatabaseConnection()
  connection.close()
}
```

The `main()` method is `static`, so it cannot access the instance variable and instance methods of the `Main` class directly. Therefore, we create an instance of the `Main()` class and use that instance to call its instance methods.

We should point out one common problem right away. A JDBC object that can be opened must always be closed to prevent the leaking of valuable system resources. When an exception is thrown after opening the database connection, but before closing the connection, the database connection will remain open. This can lead to unforeseen problems and crashes, since database resources are finite resources. It is always recommended to work with try...catch blocks when working with JDBC objects. You can close the connection in a finally block, as explained back in Chapter 4, *Java Programming*. This will ensure that the connection is always closed properly, even when exceptions were thrown.

We can now create a database, but an empty database is not particularly interesting. We need to create some tables that will hold data, called records in a relational database. We will first use the JVM's JDBC classes directly and will later switch to Groovy's built-in JDBC wrapper classes, so you can see for yourself that Groovy makes it easier to communicate with relational database systems.

We are going to create a mini blog application. First, we create a table that will hold the users of the application. Add the following new method to the Main class:

```
def createDatabaseStructure(connection) {
    def statement = connection.createStatement()
    def sqlUsers = """
        CREATE TABLE user (
            id INT AUTO_INCREMENT NOT NULL,
            name VARCHAR(255),
            PRIMARY KEY (id)
        )
    """
    statement.executeUpdate(sqlUsers)
}
```

The createStatement() method returns an object that implements the java.sql.Statement interface. A Statement object is used to execute SQL statements.

SQL statements are ordinary strings that contain the SQL statement. In our case, we execute a CREATE TABLE SQL query that creates a new table. The table has two fields: id and name. Its id field is the primary key, a value that must be unique and can be used to quickly identify a record. By specifying the AUTO_INCREMENT option, we tell the H2 database that it should generate its id value itself. For each created record, it will increment the id automatically. The name field is a simple text field that can be up to 255 characters long.

Even when using the JDBC classes directly, Groovy saves a lot of time. Since the methods of JDBC classes usually throw checked exceptions, in Java, you'd have to either handle those inside `try...catch` blocks every time or add the `throws` clause to all of your methods. Groovy does not care whether methods throw checked or unchecked exceptions.

We now need to create a table that will hold the blog posts themselves. Add the following code to the end of the `createDatabaseStructure()` method:

```
def sqlBlog = """
    CREATE TABLE blog (
        id INT AUTO_INCREMENT NOT NULL,
        title VARCHAR(255) NOT NULL,
        user INT NOT NULL,
        post CLOB,
        PRIMARY KEY (id),
        FOREIGN KEY(user) REFERENCES user(id))
"""
statement.executeUpdate(sqlBlog)
statement.close()
```

In the blog table, we have the `user` field, which points to a record in the `user` table. The `user` field is called a foreign key. A foreign key points to a record in a (usually different) table of the database. Here, it uses the id record field of `user` to identify the user that created the blog post.

Let's not forget to call the `createDatabaseStructure()` method inside the `main()` method. Add it below the `createDatabaseConnection()` call:

```
static void main(String[] args) {
  def app = new Main()
  def connection = app.createDatabaseConnection()
  app.createDatabaseStructure(connection)
  connection.close()
}
```

You can run the application. If everything's OK, then you should see no output, as we did not add `print()` statements to the code yet. If you see a stack trace, double-check the code and SQL statements.

Let's add some hardcoded example records. This time, we will use Groovy's `Sql` class instance to communicate with the database. Add the following new method to the `Main` class:

```
def addDemoRecords(connection) {
  def sql = new Sql(connection)
  def createdUsers = sql.executeInsert("INSERT INTO user (name)
                                       VALUES (?)", ["Admin"])
  def userId = createdUsers[0][0]
  sql.execute("""
      INSERT INTO blog (title, user, post)
      VALUES (?, ?, ?)""",
      ["Test post", userId, "This is a test post"])
  sql.close()
}
```

Remember to use the *Ctrl* + Space bar (or *cmd* + Space bar on macOS) key combination when entering the `Sql` class name, you should select the entry from the `groovy.sql` package.

Groovy's `executeInsert` method of the `groovy.sql.Sql` class returns the values that were generated for the primary key fields. Because an `INSERT` query can potentially create more than one record, and each record can have multiple primary key fields, it returns a nested list with columns inside a list of records. In our case, we added only one record. Since our table blog only has one primary key field, called `id`, we can retrieve the generated user id by reading `createdUsers[0][0]`. The first index specifies the row (record), the second index represents its column (field) that we want to read.

Sql objects, like database connection objects, take up valuable and finite database-related resources. Strange problems can occur when not closing them when they are no longer required. So, in a real application, always use a `try...catch` block to ensure that the object is closed properly, even when exceptions are thrown.

Add the `addDemoRecords()` call to the `main()` method, by placing it below the `createDatabaseStructure()` call:

```
....
def app = new Main()
def connection = app.createDatabaseConnection()
app.createDatabaseStructure(connection)
app.addDemoRecords(connection)
connection.close()
...
```

Run the application; it should again exit without printing any messages. Let's change this by printing an XML representation of a blog post.

Generating XML using MarkupBuilder

Groovy's XML `MarkupBuilder` class is an example of a class that has been created using Groovy's dynamic programming features. We looked at dynamically intercepting method calls in the previous chapter, something that would be impossible to implement in such a seamless way in a static language, such as Java or Kotlin.

For illustration, here's an example code using the Groovy's XML `MarkupBuilder` class. There's no need to enter this code in the Eclipse IDE yet, but you could enter this code in GroovyConsole and run it there:

```groovy
def xmlContent = new StringWriter()
def xmlWriter = new groovy.xml.MarkupBuilder(xmlContent)
xmlWriter.items {
  item(id: 1) {
    name("Item one")
  }
  item(id: 2) {
    name("Item two")
  }
}
println(xmlContent)
```

A lot is happening in the preceding code. However, before we take a detailed look at it, let's look at the result. The preceding code will print the following output to the console:

```xml
<items>
  <item id='1'>
    <name>Item one</name>
  </item>
  <item id='2'>
    <name>Item two</name>
  </item>
</items>
```

The `MarkupBuilder` class takes an object that implements Java's Writer interface as parameter; this is the object where the generated data is written to. We could have used a `FileWriter` instance to store the output in a text file, but in this case, we want a String, so we passed a `StringWriter` instance.

Remember that the parentheses for functional calls are optional in Groovy. The `xmlWriter.items { ... }` line could have been written as follows:

```
xmlWriter.items({
  ...
})
```

In the preceding example, it is clear that the code simply calls the `items()` method, which takes a closure as its input parameter. The `MarkupBuilder` class does not have an `items()` method. Instead, it intercepts unknown method calls and property access calls and builds XML elements based on the used method names and its arguments.

Generating XML based on SQL

With the knowledge of how to work with a `MarkupBuilder`, we can write a method that generates XML for our blog posts records. This will be a somewhat complicated method, so we will write it in smaller steps. We start by defining the `generateXML()` method and adding the variables that will generate the XML. Add the following method to the `Main` class:

```
def generateXML() {
  def xmlContent = new StringWriter()
  def xmlWriter = new groovy.xml.MarkupBuilder(xmlContent)
}
```

We will now define the SQL query that retrieves both the post data and the user name with one query. Add the following code to the last line in the body of the `generateXML()` method:

```
def connection = createDatabaseConnection()
def sql = new Sql(connection)
def sqlQuery = """
  SELECT B.id, B.title, B.post, U.name AS user_name
  FROM blog B
  INNER JOIN user U ON B.user = U.id"""
sql.eachRow(sqlQuery) { record ->
}
```

It's always a good idea to retrieve as much information in a single query as you can. This is always faster than executing two or more SQL queries after each other. In this case, we use an INNER JOIN clause to link the user table to the blog table. The query returns the following columns:

- blog.id
- blog.title
- blog.post
- user.name

In our query, we specified an alias for the user.name column. By doing this, we can refer to the user name using its user_name alias in the code.

We use the Sql class's eachRow() method to iterate through the returned records. This method is inspired by the functional programming paradigm. Instead of manually writing a loop to iterate through the records, we just specify a closure function that is called for each returned record. The closure code can use the record parameter to read the values of each record. Inside the closure, we will create an XML entry for each record. Inside the closure's body, add the following code:

```
xmlWriter.posts {
  post(id: record.id) {
    title(record.title)
    user(record.user_name)
    def p = record.post
    post(p.getSubString(1, p.length().intValue()))
  }
}
```

This code should look fairly familiar. We create an XML with the <posts> root node. A record can be read by simply treating the SQL query's column names (or aliases, in the case of user_name) as property names. The only exception is the post field. The post field was defined as a CLOB field type, back when creating the table. This was done because we didn't know how many lines of text a post will take. A CLOB field is of an undetermined size, and to read it, we have to specify how many characters we want to read at once. As we expect that our posts will fit easily in memory, we read the whole string at once, by calling the post CLOB field's length() function.

In a production grade application, it would be a good idea to limit the number of characters that is read at once, to make sure that the field will not consume too much memory of the server. One possible way to do this would be to read and process data from the field in smaller batches.

Finally, we need to close the database connection and let the function return the generated XML as an ordinary Java String. Add the code to the end of the `generateXML()` function's body:

```
def generateXML() {
    def xmlContent = new StringWriter()
    def xmlWriter = new groovy.xml.MarkupBuilder(xmlContent)
    ...
    sql.close()
    return xmlContent.toString()
}
```

Add a call to the `generateXML()` method to the `main()` method by adding it after the `closeDatabaseConnection()` line:

```
...
app.openDatabaseConnection()
app.createDatabaseStructure()
app.addDemoRecords()
connection.close()
println(app.generateXML())
...
```

You may wonder why we created a new database connection and don't reuse the `connection` variable for the `generateXML()` method. This is explained later, when we change the implementation to a web service.

When you now run the program, you should see the following output:

```
<posts>
  <post id='1'>
    <title>Test post</title>
    <user>Admin</user>
    <post>This is a test post</post>
  </post>
</posts>
```

The Vert.x microservice platform

Vert.x is a modern micro web service framework for the JVM platform. It was initially developed by VMWare, but nowadays, it is an Eclipse Foundation project. Vert.x is truly a polyglot framework; its official documentation is available for multiple JVM languages, including Java and Groovy, but also Scala, Kotlin, Nashorn (JavaScript), JRuby, and Ceylon.

Vert.x is all about high performance and scalability, and to achieve this, it uses a model similar to the popular Node.js model, called the asynchronous programming model. In simplified terms, Vert.x has one main event loop that looks for events and, when something happens, it calls the registered event handler in your code that should handle the event. The event handler in your application is expected to return as soon as possible. While your code executes, Vert.x's main event loop will not be able to retrieve new events and handle them.

If all the event handlers in the system can handle events quickly, a single instance of the Vert.x application can serve hundreds, or even thousands, of requests on its own. In Node.js and Python, this is the end of the story. When more power is needed, you'll need to run multiple standalone instances of the application because these languages cannot take full advantage of multicore CPUs. This wastes precious memory and resources. Since Vert.x runs on the JVM, it can run multiple event loops on different CPU cores from one single instance, making full advantage of today's powerful CPUs. To keep it simple for the developer, a specific event handler is usually available in one event loop only. Therefore, in general, the developer never has to worry about complex concurrency and multithreading issues.

The possibilities do not end here. It's possible to cluster multiple instances of your Vert.x-based application. Instances in a cluster can run either on the same machine, on different servers, or even on a combination of both.

Sometimes, some actions may take a long time. For example, when querying and computing complex data structures returned from a busy database server, we cannot guarantee that the event handler will return quickly. In such cases, Vert.x offers a simple solution. It can delegate long-running tasks to separate worker threads. The event loop delegates the task to the worker threads and continues handling other events itself. Every once in a while, it will check whether the task has finished and, if so, will handle the event with the computed result. Since the amount of available threads can be configured, the available server resources (available memory, threads, and so forth) can be managed well in a Vert.x-based application.

Adding Vert.x dependency to Ivy

To discover the required dependency information of Vert.x, we will use the same technique as we used for the H2 database system. We will use Maven's online search engine: `http://search.maven.org`

To find and add the correct dependency information to Ivy's `ivy.xml` file, do the following:

- Visit the aforementioned URL and search for `vertx-core`.
- Find the entry with **Groupid io.vertx** and **ArtifactId vertx-core**. Click its version number. At the time of writing this book, it was **3.4.1**.
- On the artifact details page, click the Apache Ivy name. Copy the XML entry to the clipboard:

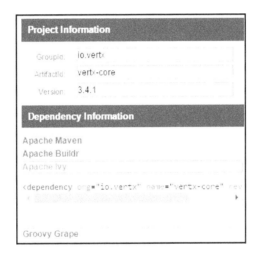

In my case, it was `<dependency org="io.vertx" name="vertx-core" rev="3.4.1" />`.

- In Eclipse, open the `ivy.xml` file. Paste the line after the `<dependency>` entry used for the H2 database.

To let Ivy fetch the required dependencies and add them to the project's class, perform the following steps:

1. Right-click on the `ivy.xml` file and choose the **Add Ivy Library...** option.
2. Click **Finish.** Ivy will now fetch the required dependencies.

Creating the web service

Let's start by adding the required `import` statements to the top of the `Main.groovy` file after the `package` statement:

```groovy
package webservice

import java.sql.DriverManager
import groovy.sql.Sql
import io.vertx.core.AbstractVerticle
import io.vertx.core.Future
import io.vertx.core.Vertx
import io.vertx.core.http.HttpMethod
```

A class that can handle Vert.x events is called a `Verticle`. By extending the abstract class, `AbstractVerticle`, provided by the Vert.x framework, we can easily change our class into a `Verticle`. Take the following line:

```groovy
class Main {
  ...
}
```

Change the preceding line to the following:

```groovy
class Main extends AbstractVerticle {
  ...
}
```

The most important method of the `AbstractVerticle` abstract class is called `start()`. This method is called when Vert.x is initializing our `Verticle` and should be used to start Vert.x's built-in HTTP server and register the event handlers. We are going to create this method in smaller steps again. Let's start by defining the `start()` method itself:

```groovy
public void start(Future<Void> fut) {
}
```

The passed `Future` object is used to tell Vert.x whether the `Verticle` could successfully initialize and start itself. Since we are dealing with setting up an HTTP server in our example, it could take some time to set up and configure everything. Vert.x does not wait for the `start()` method of our class; instead, it continues executing other tasks while our `Verticle` is initializing. It requires us to call the `Future` object's `complete()` method when we started, or `fail()`, if we could not start for any reason.

The `AbstractVerticle` class provides a variable called `vertx` that we can use to communicate with the Vert.x framework. Let's first write the code that sets up the built-in HTTP server. Add the following code to the `start()` method's body:

```
vertx
  .createHttpServer()
  .requestHandler() { request ->
}
.listen(8080) { result ->
  if (result.succeeded()) {
    fut.complete()
  } else {
    fut.fail(result.cause())
  }
}
```

The `vertx` variable that the `AbstractVerticle` abstract class makes available points to an instance of a class that implements the `io.vertx.core.Vertx` interface. Each method of this class returns the same object that the `vertx` variable points to. This trick makes it possible to chain method calls from this object. If that is the case, we would have to prefix all the three method calls with `vertx`.

We let the HTTP server listen to port **8080**. The closure passed to the `listen()` method is called when the HTTP server has finished initializing. Its `succeeded()` method returns `true` when the server could successfully start. In such a case, the `complete()` method is called on the `future` object that was passed to the `start()` method. The Vert.x system then knows that our `Verticle` is ready for action. If the HTTP server could not start for any reason (for example, because port 8080 was in use by a different application), the `fail()` method on the `future` object is called, which will halt the application.

The `requestHandler()` method sets up a HTTP request handler. The closure that is passed as a parameter will be called when the Vert.x main event loop encounters an HTTP request. There are extensions for Vert.x available that add sophisticated router features so that the URLs can be registered beforehand, and that can be compared to popular web application frameworks, such as Express (Node.js) and Flask (Python). We will not be using these extensions here, as we have no need for them in this simple example project.

Let's write the HTTP request handler. Place the following code inside the
`.requestHandler() { request -> }` block:

```
if (request.path() == "/blogs/" && request.method() == HttpMethod.GET){
  request
    .response()
    .putHeader("content-type", "application/xml")
    .end( generateXML().toString() )
} else {
  request
    .response()
    .setStatusCode(404)
    .end("Error 404");
}
```

All methods of the request object return the same request object, so method calls on the
`request` object can be chained as well. The code is rather straightforward when a GET
HTTP request for the `/blogs/` URL is encountered; the `generateXML()` function is called
that will return the XML data. Otherwise, a 404 (page not found) HTTP code is returned.

One more detail about the `generateXML()` method. It creates a new database connection,
generates the XML, and to closes the database connection. It is recommended to not share
JDBC database connections in a large application, especially multithreaded ones. We have
chosen here to create a new connection for each request and close it when we are finished.
This is fine for a small example like this, but more sophisticated web applications should
use a connection pooling system. The creation of a new database connection is a very
expensive process and a pooling system makes sure that unused connections are placed
inside a pool and can be reused. There are a lot of different pooling systems available for the
JVM platform.

The only thing that is left to do is to make sure that our `Verticle` is started. One of the
options is to simply do this in the JVM's `static main()` method. Rewrite the `main()`
method so that it looks as follows, by removing the `println(app.generateXML())` line
and adding the highlighted lines of code:

```
static public void main(String[] args) {
  def app = new Main()
  def connection = app.createDatabaseConnection()
  app.createDatabaseStructure(connection)
  app.addDemoRecords(connection)
  connection.close()
  Vertx vertx = Vertx.vertx()
  vertx.deployVerticle(new Main())
}
```

We keep the code that generates the database structure and creates demo records. We then create a `Vertx` instance and deploy it using its `deployVerticle` method. This starts the Vert.x system, which in turn will call the `start()` method of our `Verticle`.

You should now be able to run the code. Press *Ctrl + F11 (cmd + F11)*. If everything goes well, you should see the following output on the console window:

```
SLF4J: Failed to load class "org.slf4j.impl.StaticLoggerBinder".
SLF4J: Defaulting to no-operation (NOP) logger implementation
SLF4J: See http://www.slf4j.org/codes.html#StaticLoggerBinder for further
details.
```

Since we didn't add the Simple Logging Facade For Java (SLF4J) dependency to our project, the Vert.x system doesn't know how to log. We can safely ignore this warning. The application will keep running without any further output. If you see a stack trace here, double-check the code. Now, launch your favorite browser and visit the following URL: `http://localhost:8080/blogs/`

You should see the XML of the example blog post in your browser:

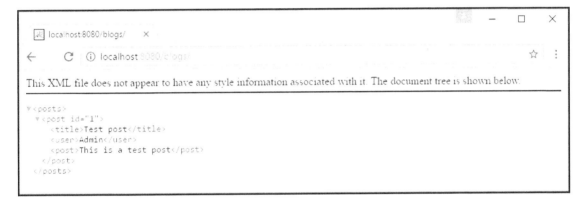

You'll see that if you change the URL, the web service will return a 404 error page:

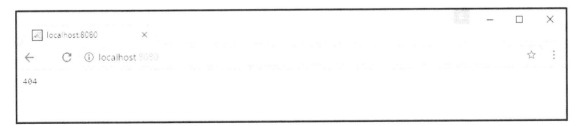

To stop the application, press the button with the Terminate tool tip text on the console tab's toolbar:

Summary

In this chapter, we implemented a simple web service with Groovy, using various technologies. We started by installing the Groovy Eclipse plugin for Eclipse IDE and the Apache IvyDE plugin for Eclipse for dependency management. We embedded the H2 DBMS in our application and communicated with it using the JDBC industry standard. We created two tables and populated both the tables with an example record. We generated an XML based on the database content by using Groovy's `MarkupBuilder` class, a class that is made possible because Groovy is a dynamic programming language. We initially created a simple console program, but after exploring the Vert.x framework, we changed it into a web service.

By now, we have covered all the five main languages that are covered in this book: Java, Scala, Clojure, Kotlin, and Groovy. We hope that this book helped you find your favorite JVM language. There are even more JVM languages available, though. The appendix will discuss some dialects of mainstream languages that have implementations on the JVM and will also look at some other up-and-coming languages as well.

A
Other JVM languages

There are way more languages that run on the JVM than the ones that were discussed in the previous chapters. In this appendix, we will take a quick look at some of the other languages. Most of these are custom JVM implementations of popular mainstream programming languages, such as JavaScript, Python, Ruby, and Haskell. The following are the implementations of languages that we will discuss here:

- Oracle Nashorn (JavaScript)
- Jython (Python)
- JRuby (Ruby)
- Frege (Haskell)
- Ceylon

Oracle Nashorn

Nashorn is Oracle's open source server-side JavaScript dialect. It has been supplied as part of the Java Runtime Environment (JRE) since version 8, meaning that everyone who installed Java 8 (or later) on a mainstream platform (Windows, macOS, and Linux, including Raspberry Pi) has a copy. It replaces Mozilla's Rhino, a JVM JavaScript dialect that was supplied with Oracle's implementation of **Java Development Kit** (**JDK**) versions 6 and 7.

Nashorn can be compared with Node.js, the popular server-side JavaScript platform that is powered by Google's V8 JavaScript engine. Both run JavaScript scripts on the server, in contrast to a client-side JavaScript engine that runs inside an internet browser. It's important to realize that Node.js and Nashorn scripts are not compatible with each other. This is because both Node.js and Nashorn add their own unique and incompatible extensions to the ECMAScript language. A big difference between Node.js and Nashorn is that Node.js's built-in asynchronous event system is not implemented in Nashorn.

 Oracle sponsored an open source project, which aimed to add Node.js compatibility to Nashorn, but it has been canceled and abandoned since.

Since Nashorn is fully implemented on the JVM, Nashorn is compatible with JVM libraries and frameworks. It can interact with Java objects and pass JavaScript objects to Java libraries and frameworks. When running JavaScript code, Nashorn internally compiles the JavaScript code to Java bytecode and runs the dynamically generated bytecode from memory. We have seen the same behavior when we used the interactive shells of Scala, Clojure, Kotlin, and Groovy in the previous chapters to run text files with source code. Like these languages, Nashorn also offers an interactive REPL shell, which can be used to enter JavaScript interactively from the console.

The official documentation for the Java 8 version of Nashorn can be found at the following URL:

```
https://docs.oracle.com/javase/8/docs/technotes/guides/scripting/nashorn/
```

A Nashorn-compatible version of the Nodeclipse plugin (a plugin that adds Node.js support to Eclipse) is available on the Eclipse Marketplace to add Nashorn compatibility to the Eclipse IDE:

Nodeclipse Java 8 Nashorn JJS 0.12+

 `jjs` is util inside Java 8 JDK to work with Nashorn JavaScript engine (https://blogs.oracle.com/nashorn/). Nodeclipse JJS feature lets you create new Nashorn... **more info**

by Nodeclipse/Enide, Other Open Source
nodeclipse enide javascript jjs nashorn ...

Embedding Nashorn in JVM-based projects

One cool feature of Nashorn is that its engine can easily be embedded in projects that are written in any Java-compatible JVM language. If you need to support custom business logic validations in a Java project that is only applicable to one particular customer, you can let customers or your trained business consultants enter custom scripts in the JavaScript language that are executed at runtime by Nashorn. These scripts do not have to be distributed with an application; they could reside in different directories or even a central database.

> This can lead to serious security issues, however, since Nashorn scripts have full access to the JVM and application internals, unless additional steps are taken. A proper knowledge of security practices is required when opening up a project to the outside world.

As explained in the `Chapter 1`, *Java Virtual Machine*, being able to mix code from different JVM languages in a single JVM-based project is one of the nicer features of the JVM platform. Mixing Java and JavaScript code on the backend of a web application can lead to interesting possibilities. Many mainstream JavaScript frameworks that are normally used on the JavaScript engine of the web browser cannot run directly on server-side JavaScript engines, such as Nashorn, as-is. This is because Nashorn, like Node.js, does not provide a **domain object model** (**DOM**) to JavaScript scripts, unlike the JavaScript engine of an internet browser. Still, a small but growing number of JavaScript libraries, or even careful hand-designed JavaScript code, do not require the presence of a DOM and can therefore be run both on server-side engines such as Nashorn and an internet browser's client-side JavaScript engine. This makes it possible to run frontend JavaScript code on the server and feed its server-side rendered output to the generated HTML. Search engines can then see the JavaScript-generated HTML output that was previously only available for AJAX-enabled web browsers.

> The DOM is a feature provided by the web browser to its JavaScript engine, not a feature of the JavaScript language itself.

The JavaScript language is a language that is not really suited to concurrent programming. JavaScript code relies heavily on mutable global variables, which means that both functions and data can easily change in one thread, which can lead to obscure bugs in other threads that are running simultaneously. Most server-side JavaScript engines do not allow running code in multiple threads at the same time. Since Nashorn can make use of the JVM threading classes, in Nashorn this is actually possible. It requires careful planning, however.

Running Nashorn

Since Nashorn is installed as part of Java 8 and higher, both in the **Java Development Kit** (**JDK**) and **Java Runtime Environment** (**JRE**), running Nashorn is easy. You simply run a command that is installed in the JDK's or JRE's `bin` directory. See Chapter 2, Developing on the Java Virtual Machine, for more information about running commands from this directory.

From the JRE or JDK `bin` directory, run the following command:

```
jjs
```

The `jjs` command stands for **Java JavaScript**. When not specifying command-line options, it will start its interactive REPL shell. This command can be used to run a specific JavaScript script file; simply pass the path to the script. The command has many command-line options; pass the `-help` command-line option to see all the available command-line options.

Jython (Python)

Python is a dynamic language and is, generally, both easy to learn and very powerful. It has a rich runtime library and, thanks to its rising popularity, a very lively ecosystem. It supports object-oriented programming but does not enforce it. Likewise, it supports a lot of constructs required for functional programming. Jython, a JVM implementation of Python, is currently based on the Python 2.7 version of the language. At the time of writing this book, it was announced that the development of a Python 3-based version of Jython will be started.

 Python 3 fixed a lot of issues with the earlier Python versions, but to do so, it had to break compatibility in many places. The result was that for years, many developers stayed on Python 2 for their projects. The tide is turning and the Python team is expected to abandon Python 2 development in the year 2020.

Jython is an open source implementation of the Python language that runs solely on the JVM. Predating Groovy, it was one of the first alternative languages that was introduced for the JVM. Sun Microsystems, the company behind Java at the time, was enthusiastic about the project and even hired some of its developers to work on Jython. The Python Software Foundation, the foundation responsible for the core Python distribution, also contributed to the project.

Jython can be downloaded from its homepage:

```
http://www.jython.org
```

To add Jython support to the Eclipse IDE, the PyDev plugin, available from the Eclipse Marketplace, is a very good choice:

```
http://www.pydev.org
```

PyDev - Python IDE for Eclipse 5.7.0

PyDev is a plugin that enables Eclipse to be used as a Python IDE (supporting also Jython and IronPython). It uses advanced type inference techniques which... **more info**

by Brainwy Software EPL

IDE Python Aptana Pydev Django ...

Differences between CPython and Jython

Python's reference implementation is called CPython. The CPython name indicates that it was written in the C language. While CPython supports multithreading programming by default, it cannot run threads on multiple cores of a multicore CPU. A single CPU core will be used to run all the threads, and CPython will quickly switch between threads instead of running threads on multiple cores simultaneously. Since Jython is based on JVM's powerful threading implementation, Jython does not have this limitation. Also, CPython is known for being relatively slow compared with other modern programming languages, while the JVM is generally praised for providing good and predictable performance.

 The execution of Jython code can still be slower than similar Java code because Jython is a dynamic language. A lot of things are decided at runtime, while, in a static language such as Java, such decisions are made at compile time. This is explained in more detail in `Chapter 11`, *Groovy*.

Jython, on its part, cannot run Python code that relies on native C (or other platform-specific) libraries. This means that many popular Python frameworks and libraries cannot be used with Jython, as many frameworks depend on C libraries to improve performance. This problem is not unique to Jython; other alternative Python implementations, such as the PyPy project, have the same issue. Since Jython is a JVM-based language, Jython code can make use of most JVM-based frameworks and toolkits, instead.

Running Jython

After downloading and installing Jython, add its `bin` subdirectory to your system's path. Run the following command to start Jython's REPL:

```
jython
```

Execute the `exit()` function to quit the REPL application.

Add the `--help` parameter to the jython command to see a list with the available command-line options.

JRuby (Ruby)

Ruby is a popular dynamic object-oriented programming language that powers a lot of web applications, thanks to the popularity of the Ruby-on-Rails framework. Like Python, Ruby's reference implementation is interpreter-based and is written using the C language. Ruby is much more object-oriented than Python, though, and the syntax of both the languages differs a lot. While (almost) everything is public in Python, Ruby supports access modifiers such as private and protected, similar to Java.

JRuby is the JVM-based implementation of Ruby. While Ruby's main implementation, called MRI (Maz's Ruby Interpreter, named after Ruby designer Yukihiro Matsumoto), is actively developed, most alternative Ruby implementations have been abandoned at this point. JRuby is one of the few alternative Ruby implementations that is still actively developed. JRuby takes full advantage of newer features of the JVM. At the time of writing this book, JRuby was compatible with the latest reference implementation of Ruby.

JRuby can be downloaded from the following website:

```
http://jruby.org
```

Eclipse support for JRuby can be added by installing the Eclipse Dynamic Languages Toolkit; search for Ruby (DLTK) on the Eclipse Marketplace:

Ruby (DLTK) 5.7.1

If you ever wondered, Eclipse has project for Ruby (along with PHP & Python) inside DLTK (Dynamic Languages Toolkit) project. You can install it any time from... **more info**

by Eclipse.org. EPL
Ruby dltk fileExtension_rb

Ruby on Rails and JRuby

Ruby on Rails is a web development framework that is very popular, and many of its original ideas have been adopted by other frameworks for other languages. It is based on the standard **Model-View-Controller (MVC)** paradigm and advocates *convention over configuration*, meaning, as we have seen earlier, that less code has to be written when adhering to Ruby on Rail's rules.

JRuby is not compatible with Ruby's C language extensions, so a lot of common Ruby dependencies cannot be used with JRuby. The good news is that the Ruby on Rails framework works fine with JRuby. This brings a lot of new possibilities to Ruby on Rails-based applications, as JVM frameworks or even **Java Enterprise Edition (Java EE)** features can now be used with Ruby on Rails-based web applications.

Like Python's CPython, Ruby's standard MRI implementation does not support running multiple threads on different CPU cores, while JRuby can take full advantage of all cores of a modern CPU. This can be a huge advantage for Ruby on Rails applications, although programmers must take care that their application is written with concurrency in mind.

Running JRuby

After downloading and extracting JRuby, add its bin subdirectory to your system's path. Run the following command to start JRuby's interactive console:

```
jirb
```

Simply type `exit` to exit the console.

Run the `jirb --help` command to see a list of all the available command-line options.

Frege (Haskell)

Frege, a dialect of the Haskell language, is arguably the first pure functional programming language for the JVM. In Frege, functions are first-class citizens and can be passed to other functions; variables are always immutable (the language simply does not supply any assignment statements) and methods created in the language have no side-effects.

Another difference from Clojure is that Frege is a statically typed language while Clojure is dynamically typed. Variables in Frege have a fixed type and the type must be known at compile time. Frege can infer the types, most of the time, from code, though.

 Interestingly, the Frege compiler translates the Frege source code to Java and calls the standard JDK `javac` compiler to translate the generated Java code to Java bytecode.

The Frege website can be found here (at the time of writing this book, it simply redirected to its GitHub page):

`http://frege-lang.org`

To download the compiler, visit its GitHub releases page at `http://github.com/Frege/fre ge/releases`.

Frege is a relatively new language, and currently, its available tooling set leaves something to be desired. While a plugin is available for the Eclipse IDE, when the book went to press, it was not compatible with the latest Eclipse version. According to Frege's wiki page (available directly from its GitHub page), JetBrains' IntelliJ IDEA IDE is a good choice for Frege development. This should work both with the free Community Edition and the paid edition of IntelliJ IDEA.

Calling Java code from Frege

The JVM itself does not adhere to pure functional programming's rules. Many of the built-in classes of the Java Class Library are mutable, just like most classes provided by popular frameworks and libraries. Frege designers, therefore, had to come up with workarounds to allow Frege code to call impure JVM methods.

Since there is no reliable way to auto-detect whether a method is free from side-effects (it could alter instance variables directly or call methods that alter variables in their turn), the programmer has to tell Frege whether a method can be considered *pure* (side-effect-free) or not. When a JVM method is declared as pure, it can be called like any other Frege function. Otherwise, when a method that keeps state is declared, the method is called using a built-in monad. The monad will return an immutable value computed by the method. The mutable data is kept inside the monad, so the program cannot access it directly.

Running Frege

Frege is distributed in a single, executable JAR file. An REPL is currently not bundled with the standard distribution but can be downloaded separately from `http://github.com/Frege/frege-repl/releases`.

Download the latest release and extract the ZIP file to a directory on your system. You can choose the same directory as the Frege compiler's JAR file. Then, from its `bin` subdirectory, run the following command to run the program:

```
frege-repl
```

Enter `quit` to exit the shell.

Alternatively, for very simple programs, the online REPL can be used:

`http://try.frege-lang.org`

Ceylon

Ceylon is another object-oriented and statically typed language. It is developed by Red Hat, a company that has a lot of expertise with Java and its ecosystem. Like some of the other languages covered in this book, Ceylon can compile code to other targets than the JVM as well. Ceylon code can be compiled to both client-side JavaScript (to be run inside an internet browser) and server-side JavaScript (using Node.js).

Ceylon's feature set looks remarkably familiar to Kotlin's. Both are statically typed languages, are object-oriented, while offering functional programming features, and have a type system that enforces null safety. One of the unique features of Ceylon is that it has built-in support for modular applications. While Java 9 introduced a new module system called Jigsaw, Ceylon supports the JBoss module system.

 JBoss is a company that is owned by Red Hat, so the choice for this particular modular system is not really surprising. JBoss modules are used extensively in Red Hat's WildFly Java EE application server and related products.

Ceylon's website can be found at `http://ceylon-lang.org`.

For Ceylon support in Eclipse, the Ceylon IDE plugin is available on the Eclipse Marketplace:

Ceylon IDE 1.3.1

 Ceylon IDE provides eclipse support for Ceylon (http://ceylon-lang.org). This is a full-featured development environment for Ceylon, including interactive error... **more info**

by Red Hat, Other Open Source
ceylon fileExtension ceylon

Ceylon's module system

While Java and the JVM, until version 9, did not feature a built-in module system, they supported JAR files. JAR files, as we saw in `Chapter 2`, *Developing on the Java Virtual Machine*, can bundle multiple class files in a single file, so what would a module system add to a language? One of the more important features that JAR files lack is support for defining version information and dependencies.

The Apache Maven build tool improved this situation by defining an XML object model where libraries, which are often distributed via JAR files, can specify its dependencies. When a library specifies a dependency in Maven's `build.xml` file, then Maven (or other build tools that feature dependency managers, such as Gradle) download those dependencies, including dependencies of its dependencies, and put them all on the project's classpath.

Still, there's more to a mature modular system than this. In a good modular system, it should be possible to specify what code should be exposed to the consumers of a module. Code that is meant for internal use only should not be made available to the outside world. While Java supports private members of a class, it is not possible to hide public classes (classes that should be available to classes that are not in the same package), even if those classes are meant for internal use by the module only.

Ceylon's built-in modular system supports storing version information, specifying dependencies, and offers much more control over the visibility of classes inside the module to the outside world. Also, the Ceylon team maintains a free online repository called Ceylon Herd, where Ceylon modules can be downloaded and shared. Ceylon's module system is fully integrated inside the compiler and its tools. In fact, Ceylon's JVM compiler will not compile code to separate class files but will always create a module for the project.

Running Ceylon

At this time, no REPL is available for Ceylon. An alternative could be the online REPL from the Ceylon website (`http://try.ceylon-lang.org`):

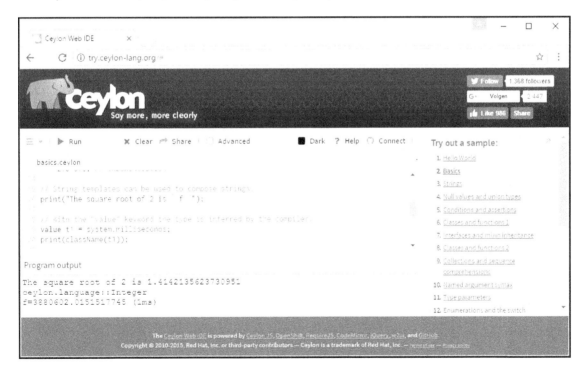

Summary

In this appendix, we discussed yet another selection of JVM languages: Oracle's Nashorn (JavaScript), Jython (Python), JRuby (Ruby), Frege (Haskell), and Ceylon (a unique language). For each language, we discussed the main language and looked at a particularly interesting or unique feature or library. We also mentioned the name of the required Eclipse IDE plugin (if available for the language) and gave instructions on how to run the language using the interactive REPL shell, if the language provided one.

This concludes our book. We hope it helped provide you a better overview of both the JVM itself and some of the more important languages that target this powerful and stable virtual machine--a virtual machine that powers a lot of the popular mainstream online services and websites that millions of people use around the globe, and is expected to take full advantage of new technologies and trends as they emerge.

B
Quiz Answers

Chapter 3: Java

Questions	Answers
1	c
2	b
3	a
4	b
5	d

Chapter 5: Scala

Questions	Answers
1	b
2	a
3	c
4	c
5	b

Chapter 7: Clojure

Questions	Answers
1	b
2	c
3	a
4	b
5	a

Chapter 9: Kotlin

Questions	Answers
1	b
2	b
3	d
4	b
5	c

Chapter 11: Groovy

Questions	Answers
1	d
2	a
3	b
4	c
5	b

Index

www.ingramcontent.com/pod-product-compliance
Lightning Source LLC
LaVergne TN
LVHW081328050326
832903LV00024B/1067